Shoulder-a-Coffin Kuro by Satoko Kiyuduki

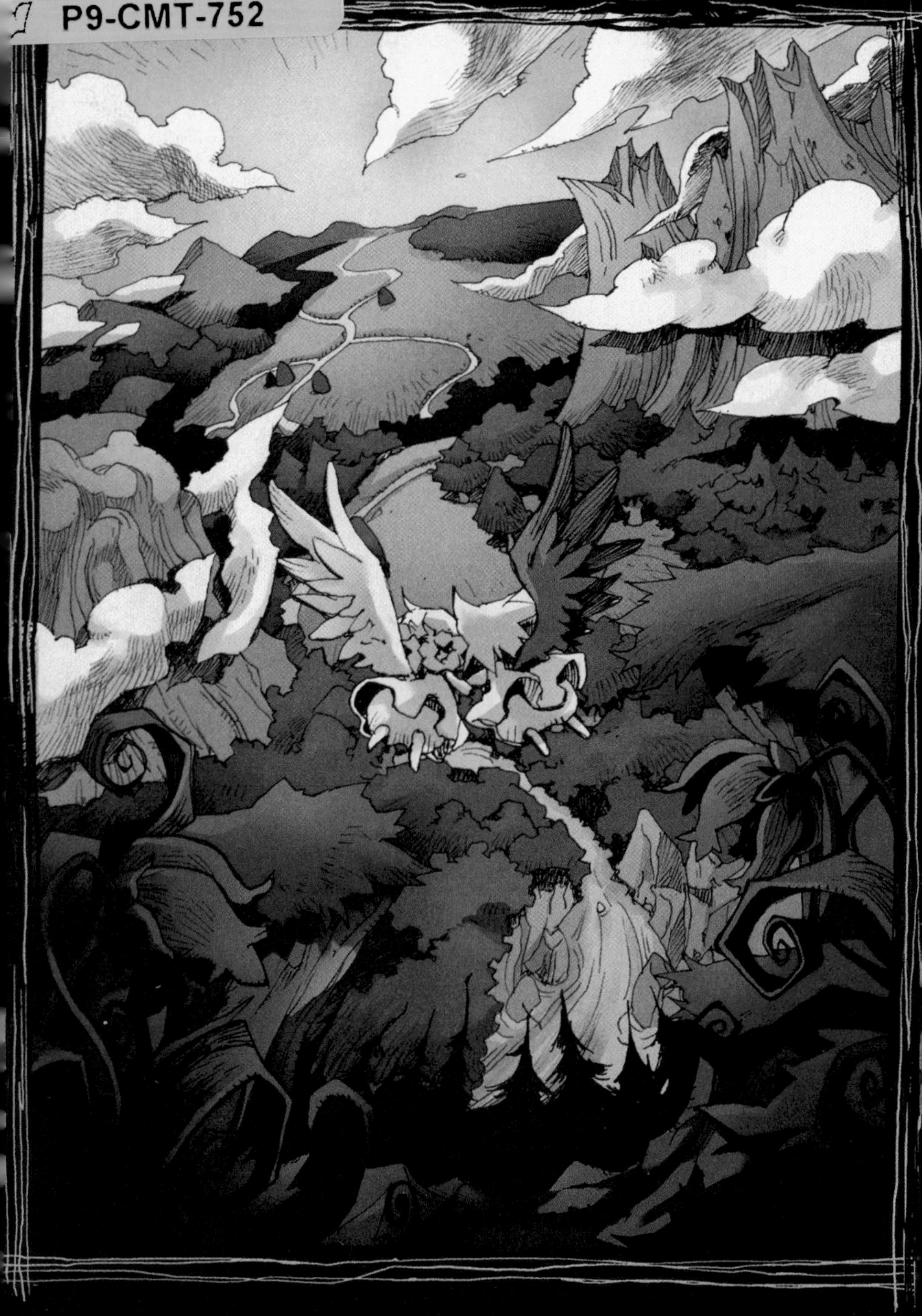

"Wow. The 'outside world' is amazing."

The sight was the grandest thing the children had witnessed on their journey so far.

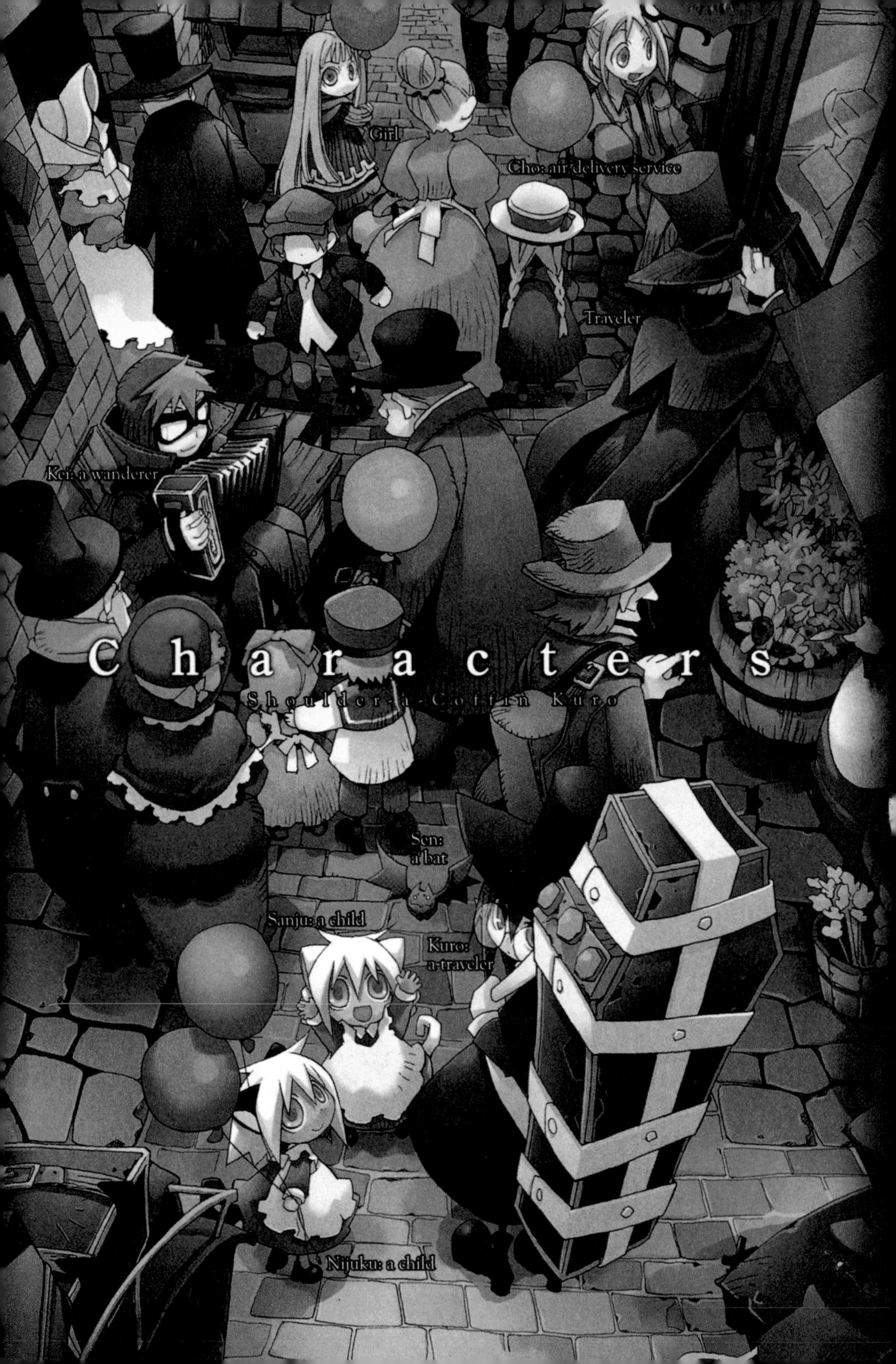
Characters
Shoulder-a-Coffin Kuro
Girl
Cho: air delivery service
Traveler
Kei: a wanderer
Sen: a bat
Sanju: a child
Kuro: a traveler
Nijuku: a child

I KEEP WALKING AND WALKING.

I KEEP WALKING THE ENDLESS STREETS.

"...IT WOULD'VE BEEN EASIER TO TRAVEL."

"IF THE WORLD WAS ONLY AS BIG AS THE PALM OF A HAND...

...BUT I THINK THIS IS WHAT I THOUGHT WHEN I WAS ON THE ROAD:

THERE ARE SOME WHO SEEK PHILOSOPHY, ADVENTURE, OR MEANING IN LIFE BY TRAVELING...

SHOULDER-A-COFFIN KURO

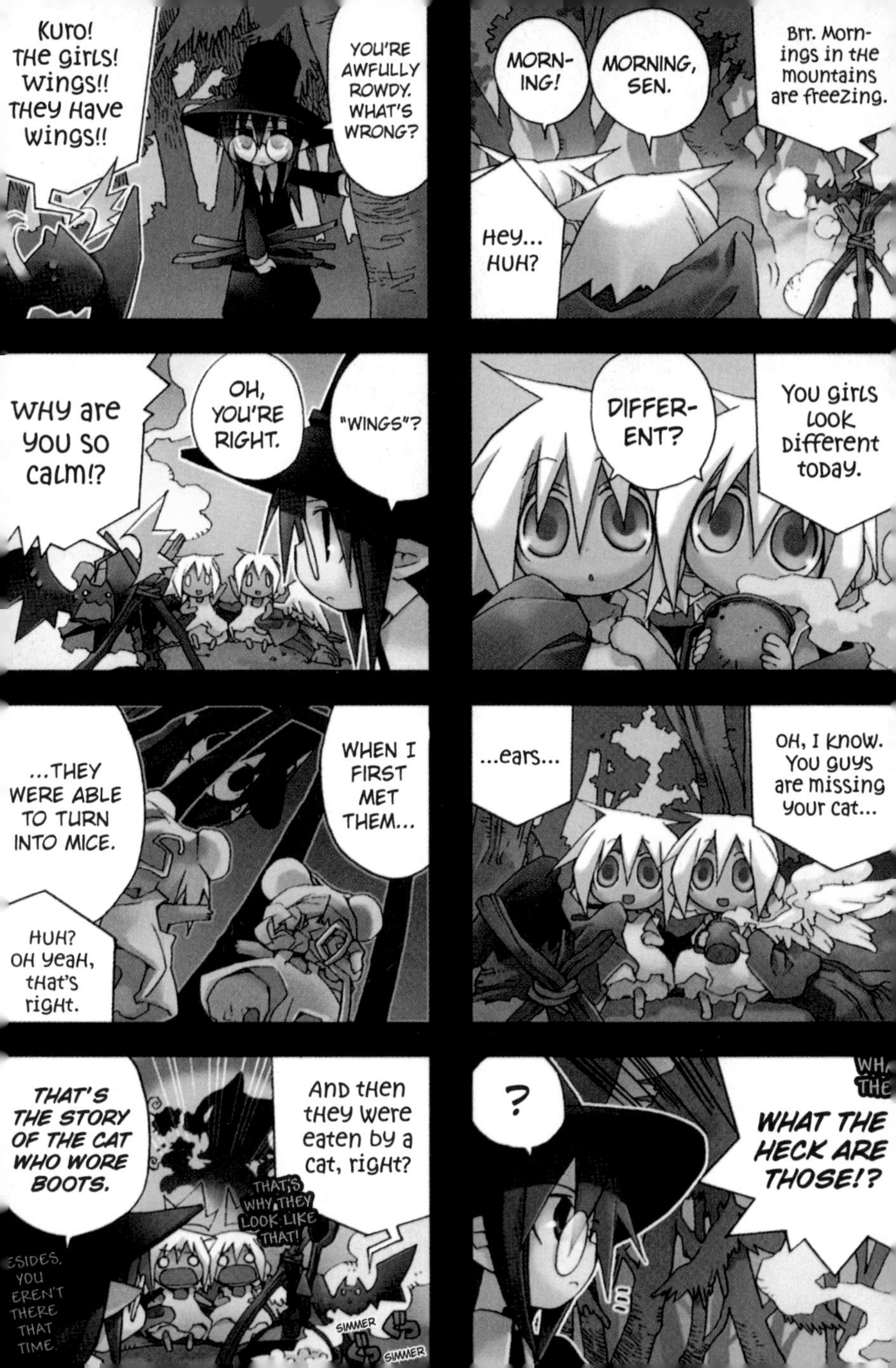

Brr. Mornings in the mountains are freezing.
MORNING, SEN.
MORNING!
Hey... HUH?
YOU'RE AWFULLY ROWDY. WHAT'S WRONG?
Kuro! The girls! Wings!! They have wings!!
You girls look different today.
DIFFERENT?
"WINGS"?
OH, YOU'RE RIGHT.
WHY are you so calm!?
OH, I know. You guys are missing your cat...
...ears...
WHEN I FIRST MET THEM...
...THEY WERE ABLE TO TURN INTO MICE.
HUH? OH yeah, that's right.
WH, THE
WHAT THE HECK ARE THOSE!?
?
And then they were eaten by a cat, right?
THAT'S THE STORY OF THE CAT WHO WORE BOOTS.
THAT'S WHY THEY LOOK LIKE THAT!
SIMMER
SIMMER
ESIDES. YOU EREN'T THERE THAT TIME.

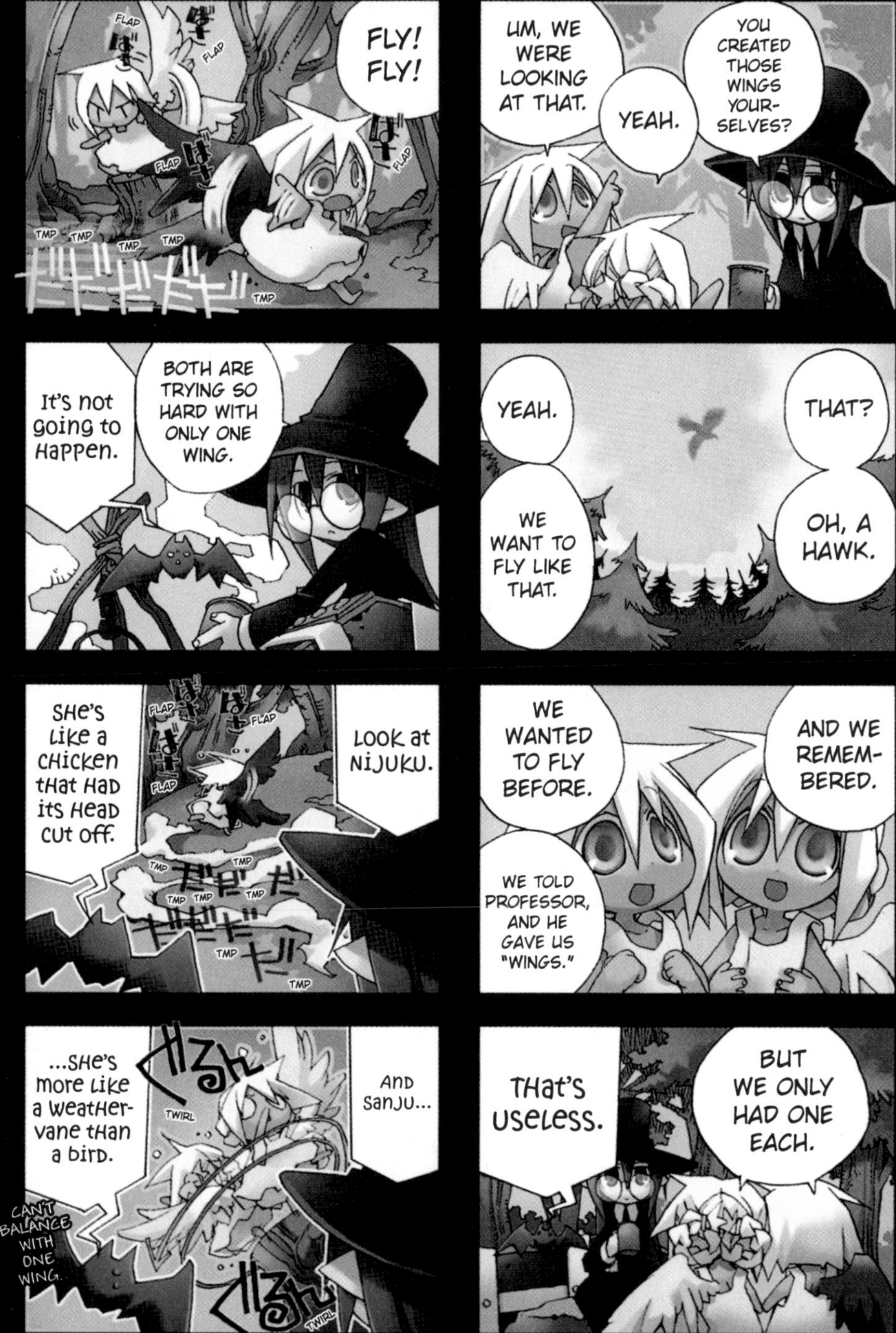
YOU CREATED THOSE WINGS YOURSELVES?
YEAH.
UM, WE WERE LOOKING AT THAT.
THAT?
OH, A HAWK.
YEAH.
WE WANT TO FLY LIKE THAT.
AND WE REMEMBERED.
WE WANTED TO FLY BEFORE.
WE TOLD PROFESSOR, AND HE GAVE US "WINGS."
BUT WE ONLY HAD ONE EACH.
That's useless.
FLAP
FLAP
FLY! FLY!
FLAP
FLAP
TMP TMP TMP TMP
TMP
BOTH ARE TRYING SO HARD WITH ONLY ONE WING.
It's not going to happen.
Look at NIJUKU.
SHE's Like a CHicken tHat Had its Head cut off.
FLAP
FLAP
FLAP
TMP TMP TMP TMP TMP
TMP
TMP
And sanju...
...SHE's more Like a WeatHer-vane tHan a bird.
TWIRL
CAN'T BALANCE WITH ONE WING.
TWIRL

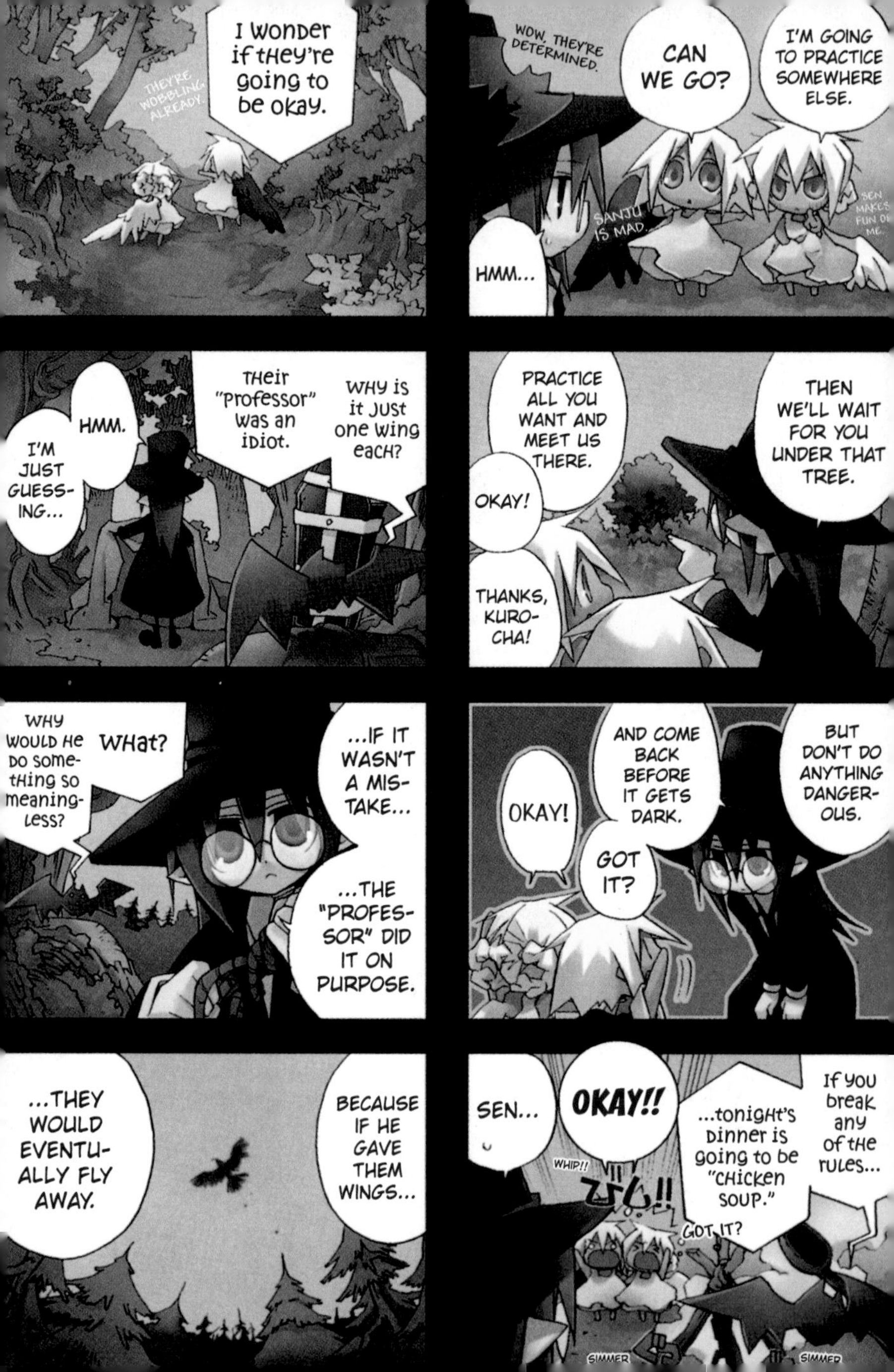
I'M GOING TO PRACTICE SOMEWHERE ELSE.
CAN WE GO?
WOW, THEY'RE DETERMINED.
SEN MAKES FUN OF ME.
SANJU IS MAD.
HMM...
I wonder if they're going to be okay.
THEY'RE WOBBLING ALREADY.
THEN WE'LL WAIT FOR YOU UNDER THAT TREE.
PRACTICE ALL YOU WANT AND MEET US THERE.
OKAY!
THANKS, KURO-CHA!
WHY is it JUST one wing each?
Their "professor" was an idiot.
HMM.
I'M JUST GUESSING...
BUT DON'T DO ANYTHING DANGEROUS.
AND COME BACK BEFORE IT GETS DARK.
OKAY!
GOT IT?
...IF IT WASN'T A MISTAKE...
...THE "PROFESSOR" DID IT ON PURPOSE.
WHAT?
WHY WOULD HE DO SOMETHING SO MEANINGLESS?
If you break any of the rules...
...tonight's dinner is going to be "Chicken soup."
OKAY!!
SEN...
WHIP!!
GOT IT?
SIMMER
SIMMER
BECAUSE IF HE GAVE THEM WINGS...
...THEY WOULD EVENTUALLY FLY AWAY.

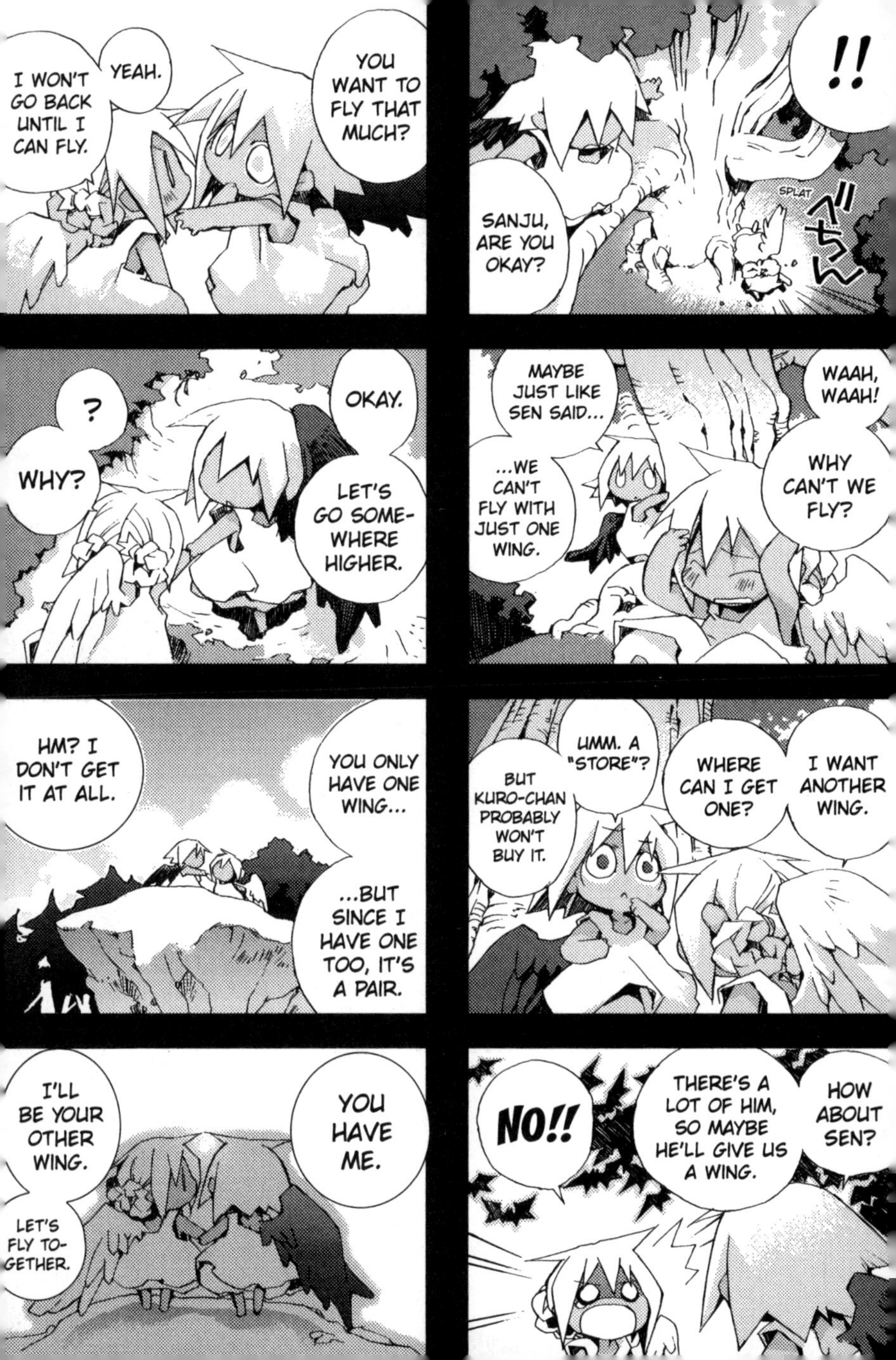
!!
SANJU, ARE YOU OKAY?
SPLAT
YOU WANT TO FLY THAT MUCH?
YEAH.
I WON'T GO BACK UNTIL I CAN FLY.
WAAH, WAAH!
WHY CAN'T WE FLY?
MAYBE JUST LIKE SEN SAID...
...WE CAN'T FLY WITH JUST ONE WING.
OKAY.
LET'S GO SOME-WHERE HIGHER.
?
WHY?
I WANT ANOTHER WING.
WHERE CAN I GET ONE?
UMM. A "STORE"?
BUT KURO-CHAN PROBABLY WON'T BUY IT.
YOU ONLY HAVE ONE WING...
...BUT SINCE I HAVE ONE TOO, IT'S A PAIR.
HM? I DON'T GET IT AT ALL.
HOW ABOUT SEN?
THERE'S A LOT OF HIM, SO MAYBE HE'LL GIVE US A WING.
NO!!
YOU HAVE ME.
I'LL BE YOUR OTHER WING.
LET'S FLY TO-GETHER.

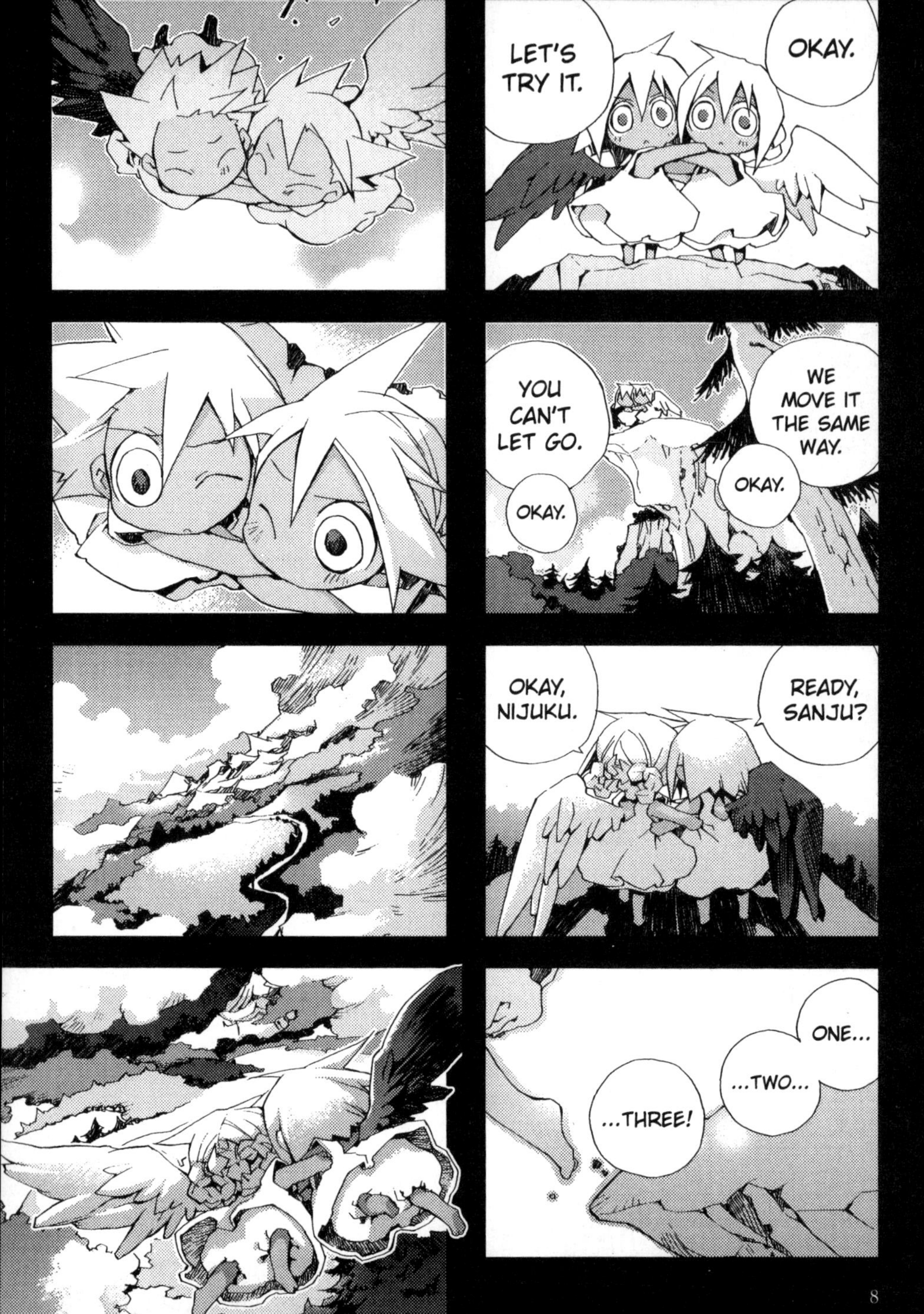
OKAY.
LET'S TRY IT.
WE MOVE IT THE SAME WAY.
YOU CAN'T LET GO.
OKAY.
OKAY.
READY, SANJU?
OKAY, NIJUKU.
ONE...
...TWO...
...THREE!

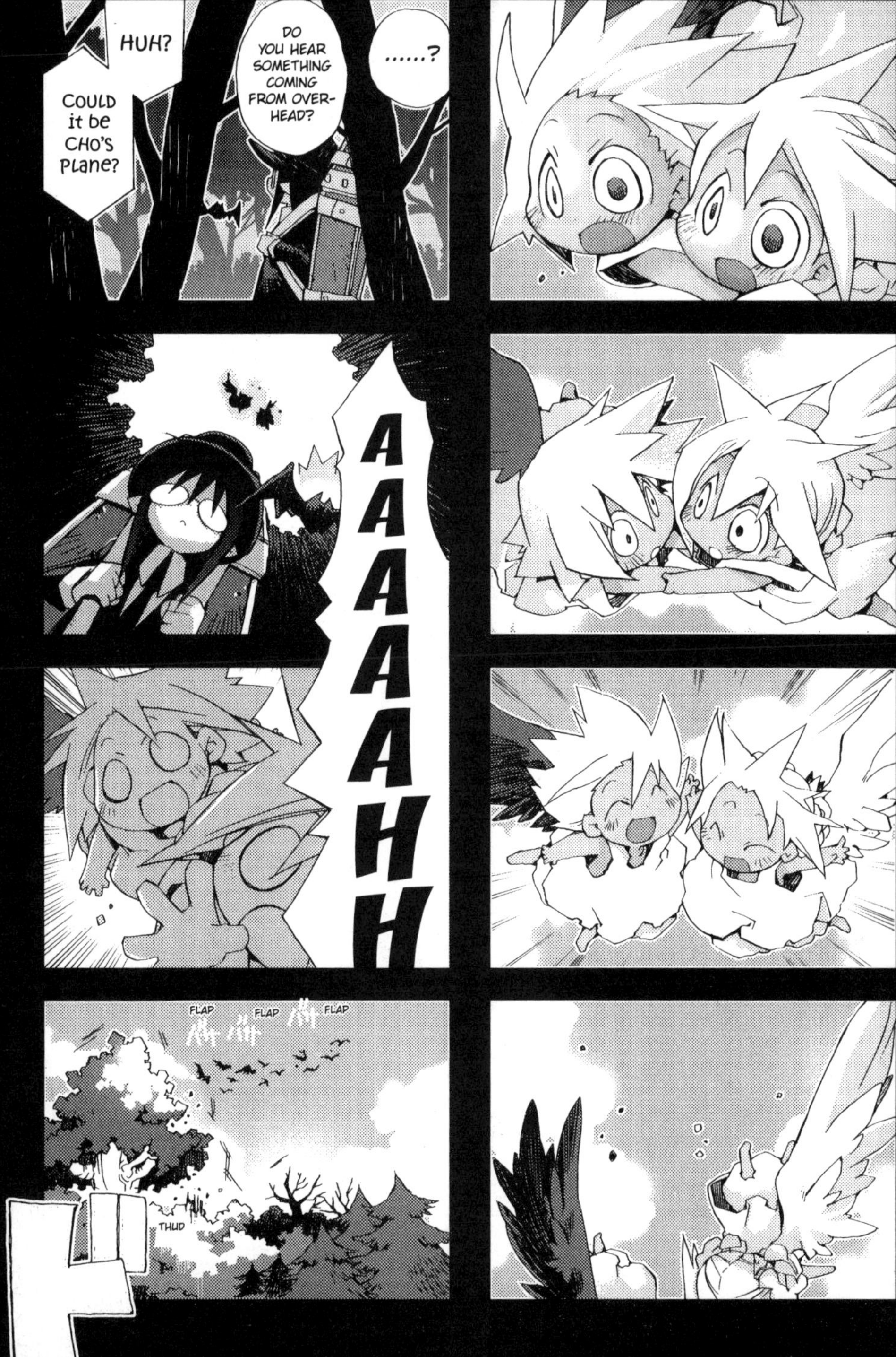
......?
DO YOU HEAR SOMETHING COMING FROM OVER-HEAD?
HUH?
COULD it be CHO'S PLane?
AAAAAAAHH
FLAP
FLAP
FLAP
THUD

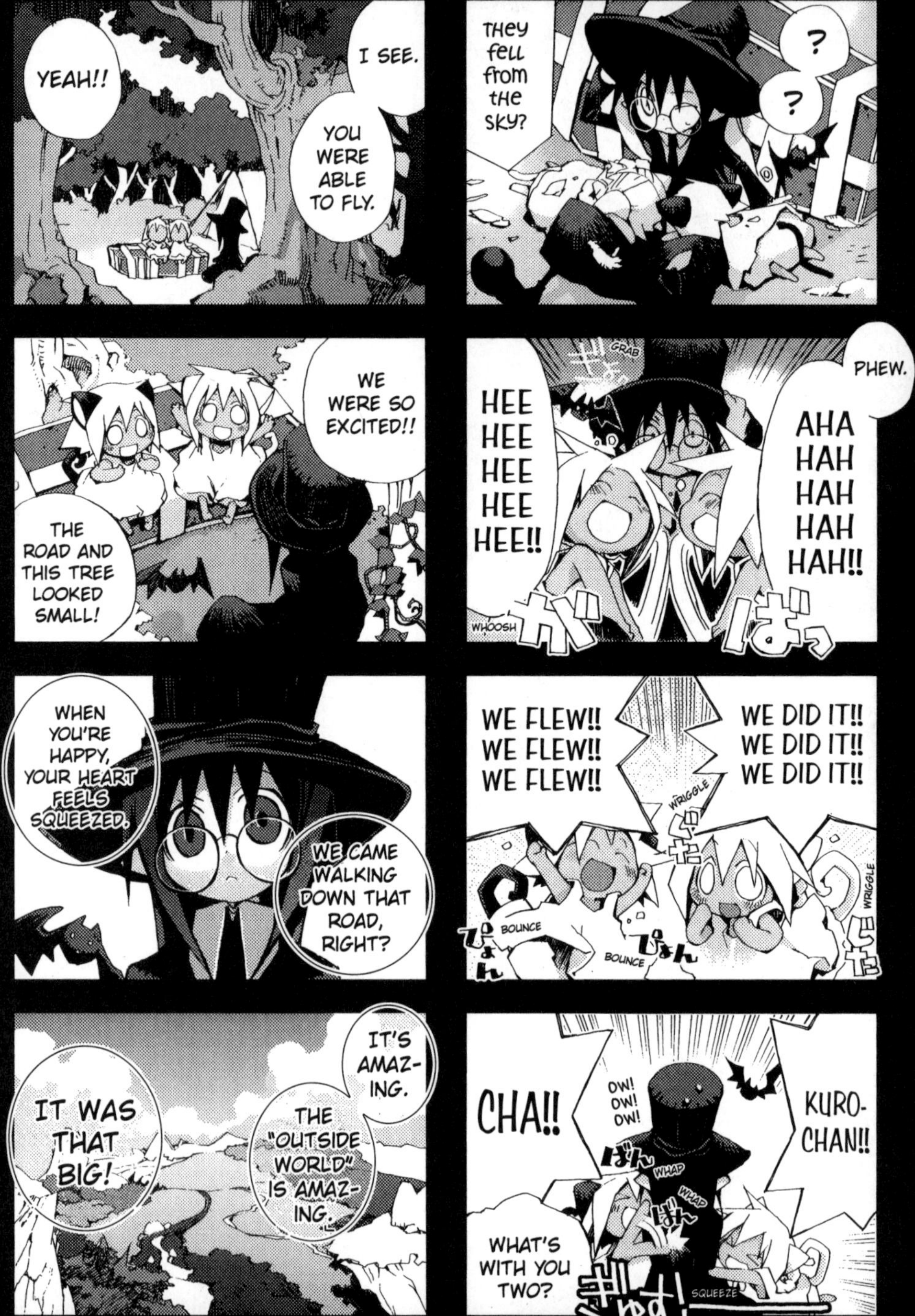
They fell from the sky?
?
?
I SEE.
YOU WERE ABLE TO FLY.
YEAH!!
GRAB
PHEW.
AHA HAH HAH HAH HAH!!
HEE HEE HEE HEE HEE!!
WHOOSH
WE WERE SO EXCITED!!
THE ROAD AND THIS TREE LOOKED SMALL!
WE DID IT!! WE DID IT!! WE DID IT!!
WE FLEW!! WE FLEW!! WE FLEW!!
WRIGGLE
WRIGGLE
BOUNCE
BOUNCE
WE CAME WALKING DOWN THAT ROAD, RIGHT?
WHEN YOU'RE HAPPY, YOUR HEART FEELS SQUEEZED.
KURO-CHAN!!
OW! OW! OW!
CHA!!
WHAP
WHAP
WHAT'S WITH YOU TWO?
SQUEEZE
IT'S AMAZ-ING.
THE "OUTSIDE WORLD" IS AMAZ-ING.
IT WAS THAT BIG!

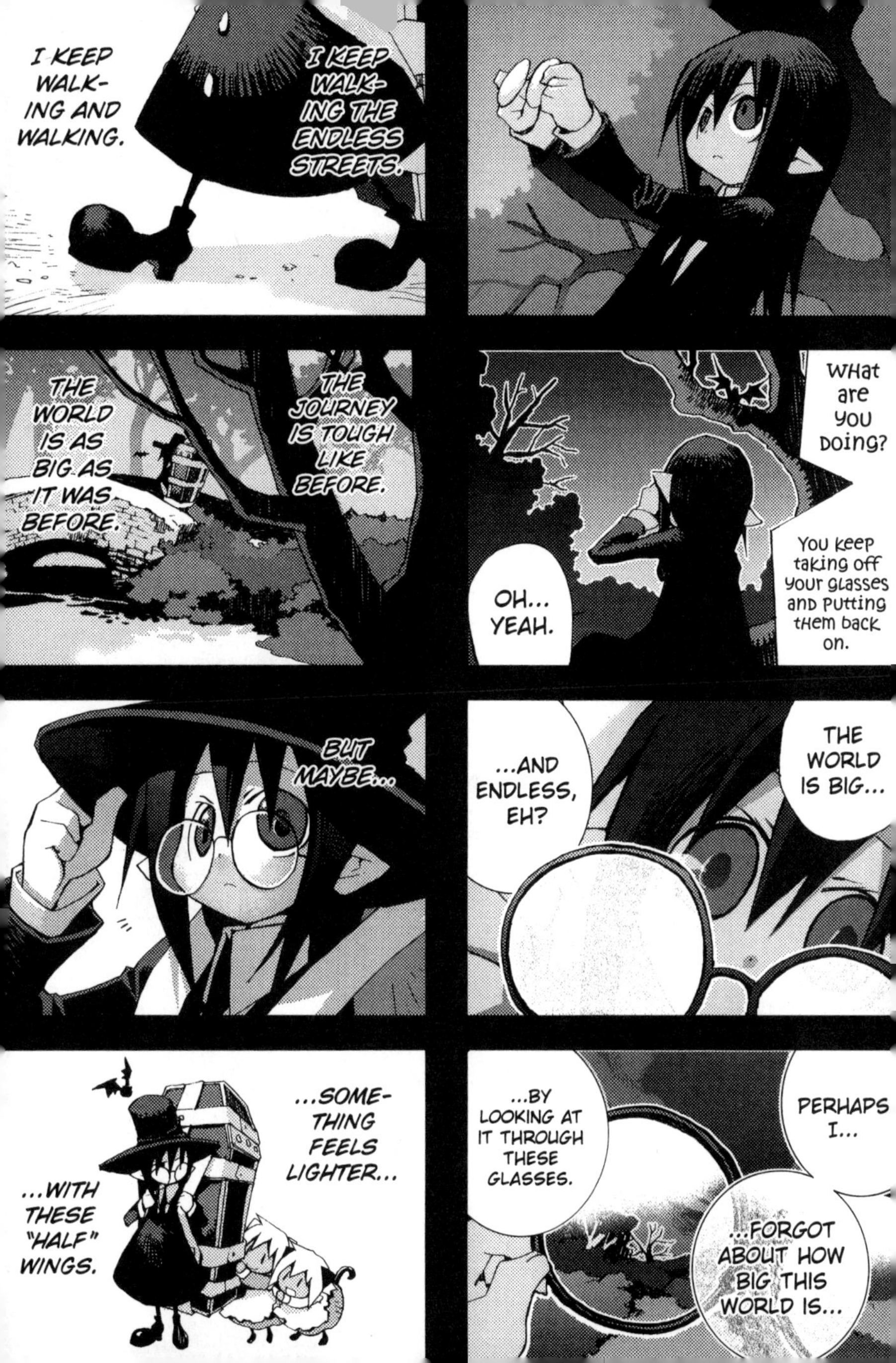
I KEEP WALKING THE ENDLESS STREETS.
I KEEP WALKING AND WALKING.
WHAT ARE YOU DOING?
YOU KEEP TAKING OFF YOUR GLASSES AND PUTTING THEM BACK ON.
OH... YEAH.
THE JOURNEY IS TOUGH LIKE BEFORE.
THE WORLD IS AS BIG AS IT WAS BEFORE.
THE WORLD IS BIG...
...AND ENDLESS, EH?
BUT MAYBE...
PERHAPS I...
...BY LOOKING AT IT THROUGH THESE GLASSES.
...FORGOT ABOUT HOW BIG THIS WORLD IS...
...SOMETHING FEELS LIGHTER...
...WITH THESE "HALF" WINGS.

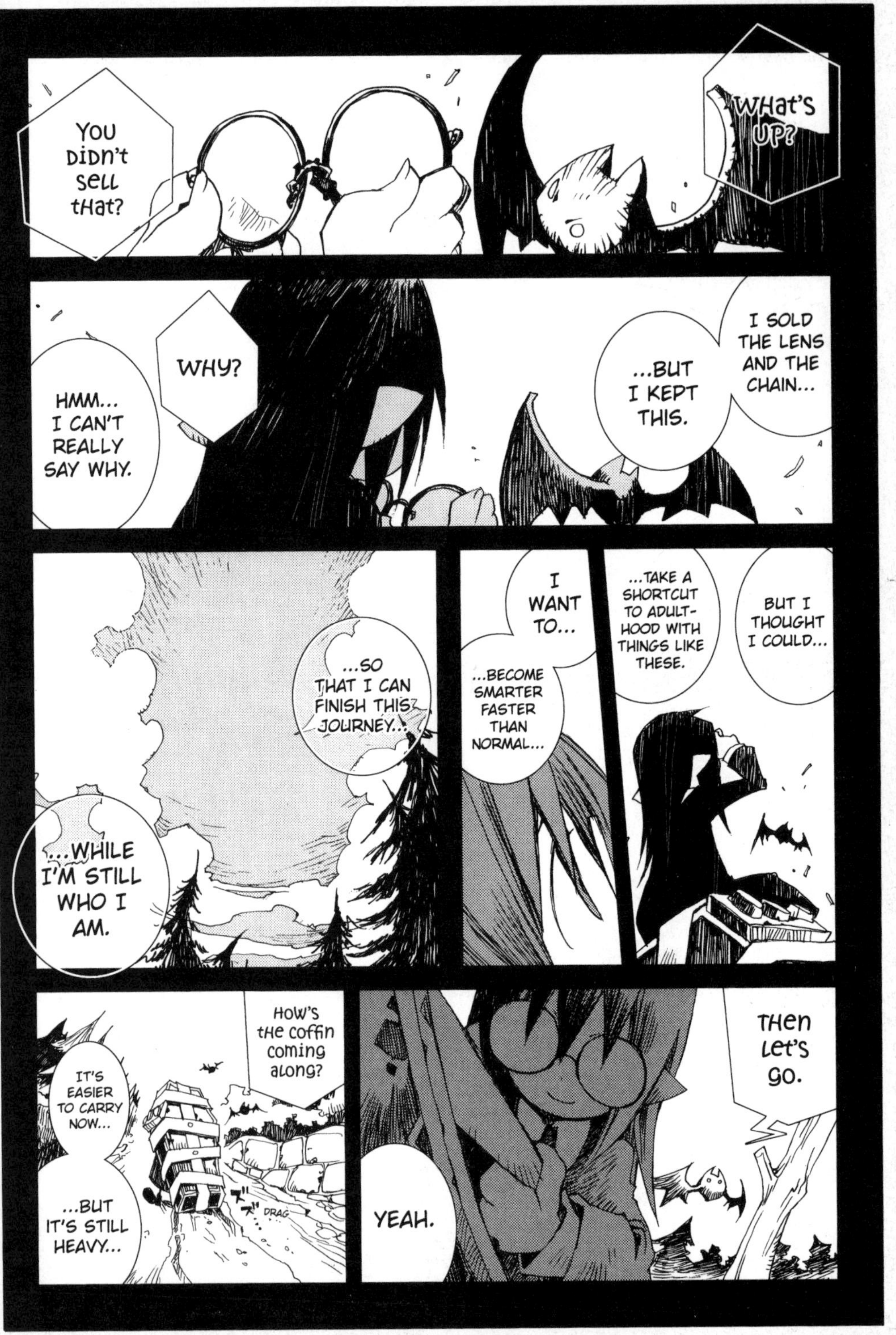
WHAT'S UP?
YOU DIDN'T SELL THAT?
I SOLD THE LENS AND THE CHAIN...
...BUT I KEPT THIS.
WHY?
HMM... I CAN'T REALLY SAY WHY.
BUT I THOUGHT I COULD...
...TAKE A SHORTCUT TO ADULT-HOOD WITH THINGS LIKE THESE.
I WANT TO...
...BECOME SMARTER FASTER THAN NORMAL...
...SO THAT I CAN FINISH THIS JOURNEY...
...WHILE I'M STILL WHO I AM.
THEN LET'S GO.
YEAH.
HOW'S THE COFFIN COMING ALONG?
IT'S EASIER TO CARRY NOW...
...BUT IT'S STILL HEAVY...
DRAG

HEY, NIJUKU AND SANJU.

You can smell the ocean, right?

NIJUKU! LOOK AT THIS!

I SEE A TALL "CASTLE"!

IT'S THE "OCEAN"!

Ever since that incident with the old man, their imagination's gotten wild.

TREA-SURE!?

WE FOUND A "TREA-SURE MAP"!

"pirit"? You mean "pirate"?

THAT'S JUST A FISHER-MAN'S BOAT.

IS THAT A "PIRIT" SHIP!?

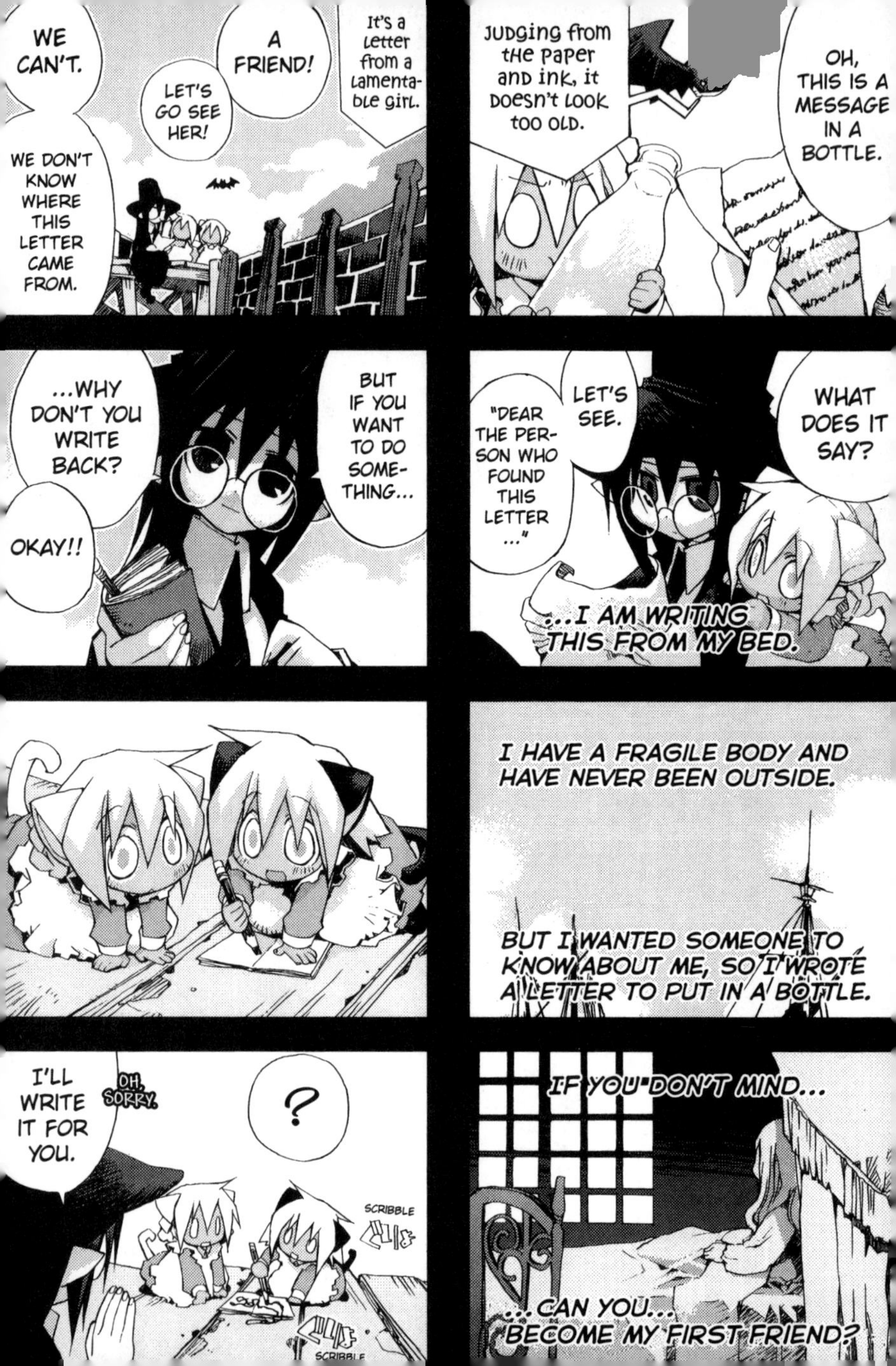
OH, THIS IS A MESSAGE IN A BOTTLE.
JUDGING FROM THE PAPER AND INK, IT DOESN'T LOOK TOO OLD.
IT'S A LETTER FROM A LAMENTABLE GIRL.
A FRIEND!
LET'S GO SEE HER!
WE CAN'T.
WE DON'T KNOW WHERE THIS LETTER CAME FROM.
WHAT DOES IT SAY?
LET'S SEE.
"DEAR THE PERSON WHO FOUND THIS LETTER..."
...I AM WRITING THIS FROM MY BED.
BUT IF YOU WANT TO DO SOMETHING...
...WHY DON'T YOU WRITE BACK?
OKAY!!
I HAVE A FRAGILE BODY AND HAVE NEVER BEEN OUTSIDE.
BUT I WANTED SOMEONE TO KNOW ABOUT ME, SO I WROTE A LETTER TO PUT IN A BOTTLE.
IF YOU DON'T MIND...
...CAN YOU... BECOME MY FIRST FRIEND?
?
OH, SORRY.
I'LL WRITE IT FOR YOU.
SCRIBBLE
SCRIBBLE

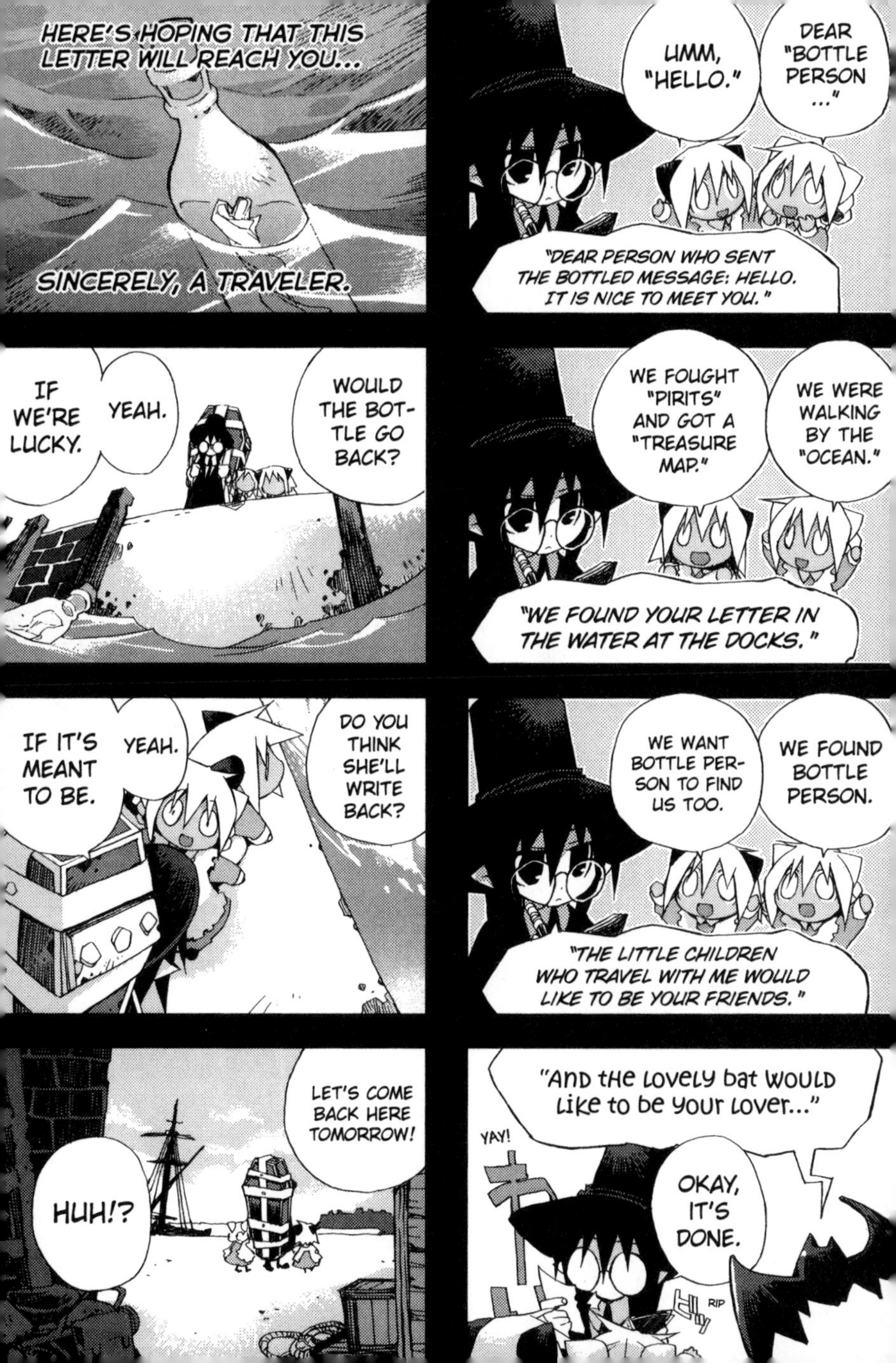
DEAR "BOTTLE PERSON ..."
UMM, "HELLO."
"DEAR PERSON WHO SENT THE BOTTLED MESSAGE: HELLO. IT IS NICE TO MEET YOU."
WE WERE WALKING BY THE "OCEAN."
WE FOUGHT "PIRITS" AND GOT A "TREASURE MAP."
"WE FOUND YOUR LETTER IN THE WATER AT THE DOCKS."
WE FOUND BOTTLE PERSON.
WE WANT BOTTLE PERSON TO FIND US TOO.
"THE LITTLE CHILDREN WHO TRAVEL WITH ME WOULD LIKE TO BE YOUR FRIENDS."
"And the lovely bat would like to be your lover..."
YAY!
OKAY, IT'S DONE.
RIP
HERE'S HOPING THAT THIS LETTER WILL REACH YOU...
SINCERELY, A TRAVELER.
WOULD THE BOT-TLE GO BACK?
YEAH.
IF WE'RE LUCKY.
DO YOU THINK SHE'LL WRITE BACK?
YEAH.
IF IT'S MEANT TO BE.
LET'S COME BACK HERE TOMORROW!
HUH!?

THE BOTTLE PERSON!?

IT LOOKS LIKE A RESPONSE TO OUR LETTER.

"DEAR TRAVEL-ERS..."

THANK YOU FOR THE LETTER. I'M REALLY HAPPY.

THOSE TWO DIDN'T WANT TO LEAVE THE DOCKS BECAUSE OF THE LETTER.

SIGH. WE WERE SET BACK.

WHEN I OPENED THE BOTTLE, IT HAD A MYSTERIOUS SCENT, AND I WAS EXCITED.

She's prob-ably talking about the smell of the ocean.

I'M SURE THAT YOU GET TO SEE DIFFERENT PARTS OF THE WORLD BECAUSE YOU'RE A TRAVELER!

HEY, TRY TO STAY CLOSE, GIRLS.

WHERE?

SANJU, LOOK. THERE'S A BUNCH OF FLOWERS HERE.

RUSTLE

WHEN I THINK ABOUT IT, I ONLY KNOW WHAT MY ROOM...

...AND THE VIEW FROM MY ROOM LOOK LIKE.

DEAR TRAVELER, CAN I ASK FOR A FAVOR?

I WOULD LIKE TO KNOW ANY ONE THING ABOUT THE OUTSIDE WORLD.

Are you serious!?

THE "TREASURE MAP"!!

WE FOUND IT AGAIN!!

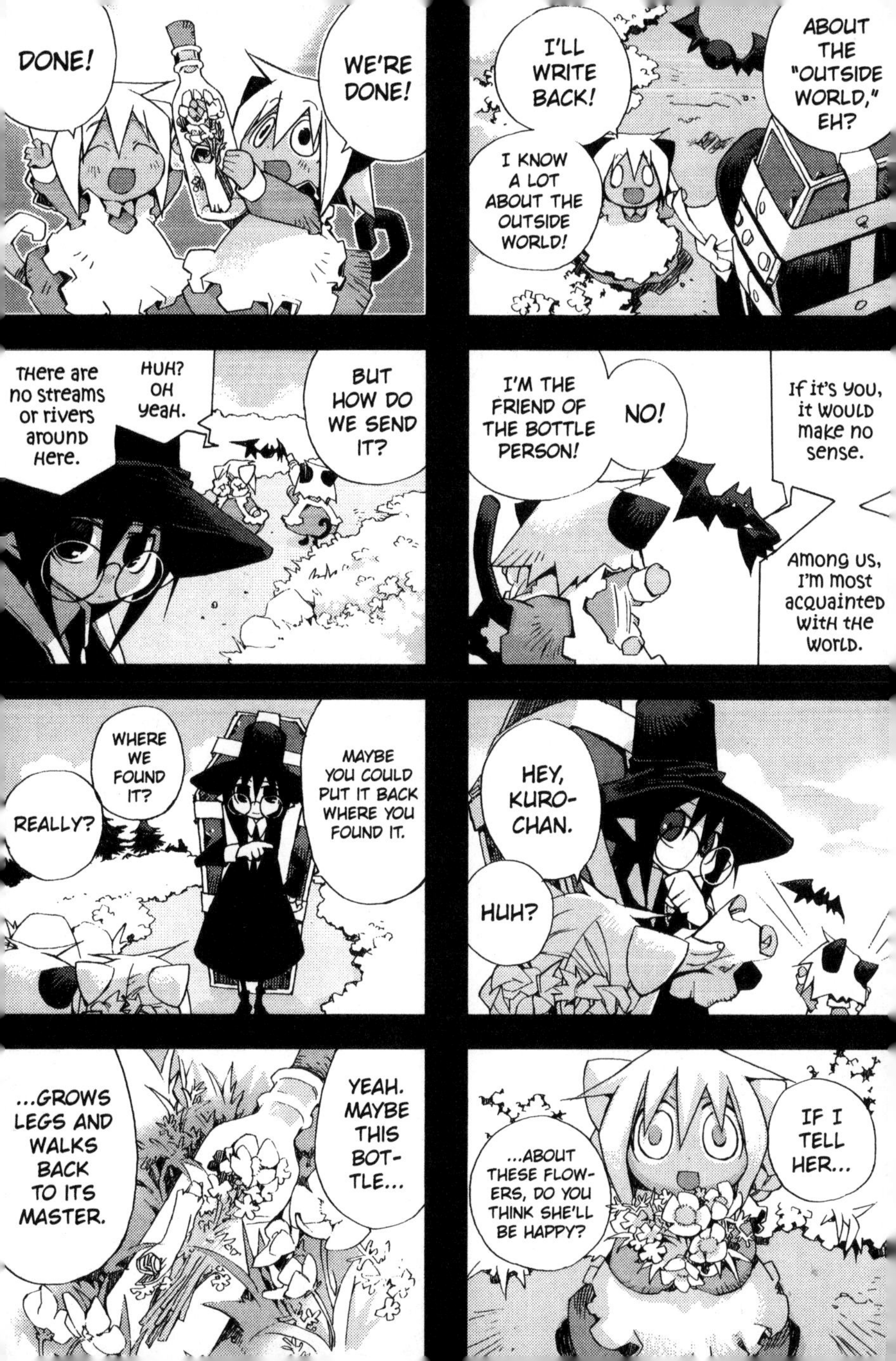
ABOUT THE "OUTSIDE WORLD," EH?
I'LL WRITE BACK!
I KNOW A LOT ABOUT THE OUTSIDE WORLD!
If it's you, it would make no sense.
NO!
I'M THE FRIEND OF THE BOTTLE PERSON!
Among us, I'm most acquainted with the world.
HEY, KURO-CHAN.
HUH?
IF I TELL HER...
...ABOUT THESE FLOWERS, DO YOU THINK SHE'LL BE HAPPY?
WE'RE DONE!
DONE!
BUT HOW DO WE SEND IT?
HUH? OH yeah.
There are no streams or rivers around here.
MAYBE YOU COULD PUT IT BACK WHERE YOU FOUND IT.
WHERE WE FOUND IT?
REALLY?
YEAH. MAYBE THIS BOTTLE...
...GROWS LEGS AND WALKS BACK TO ITS MASTER.

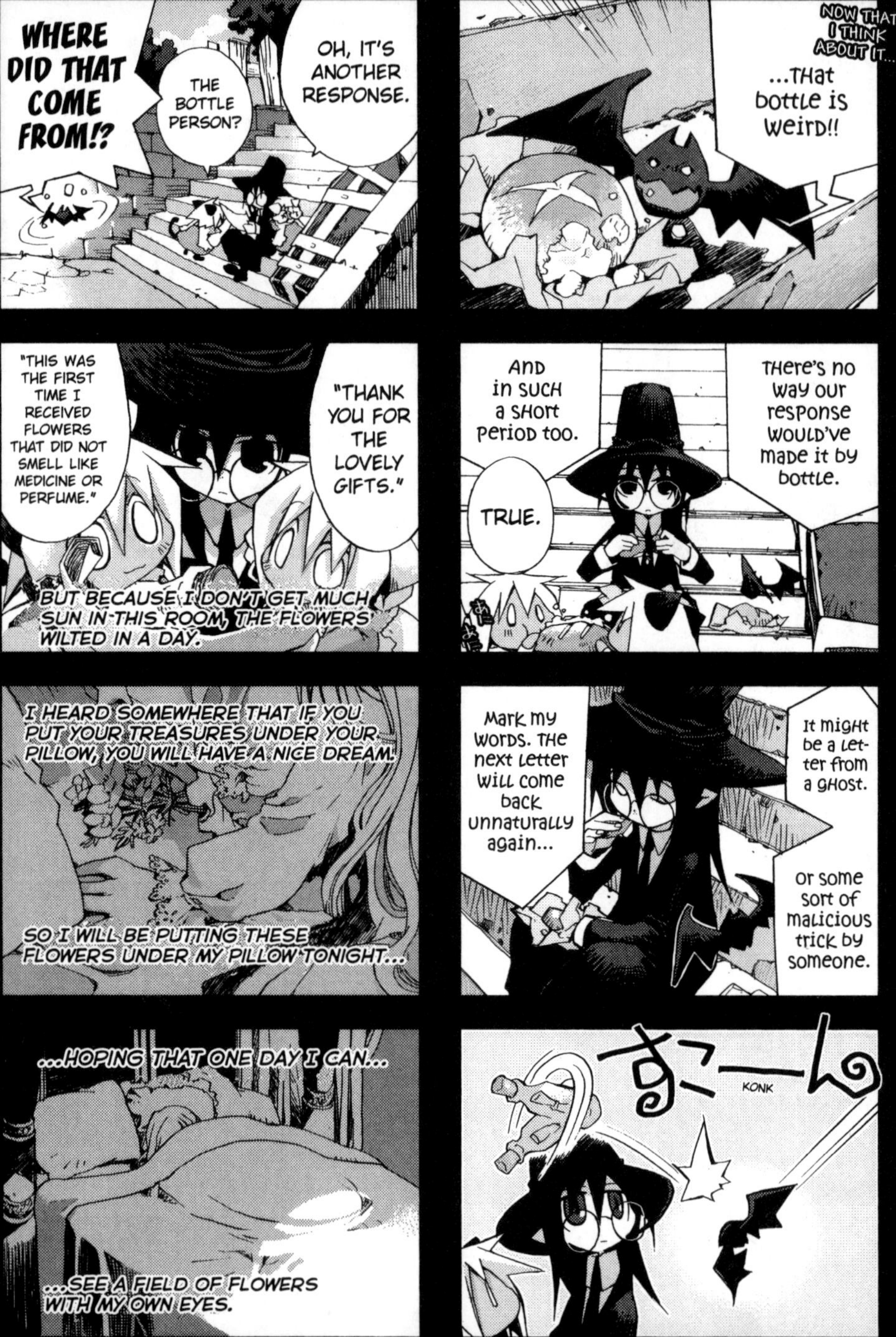
NOW THAT I THINK ABOUT IT...
...That bottle is weird!!
WHERE DID THAT COME FROM!?
OH, IT'S ANOTHER RESPONSE.
THE BOTTLE PERSON?
There's no way our response would've made it by bottle.
And in such a short period too.
TRUE.
"THANK YOU FOR THE LOVELY GIFTS."
"THIS WAS THE FIRST TIME I RECEIVED FLOWERS THAT DID NOT SMELL LIKE MEDICINE OR PERFUME."
BUT BECAUSE I DON'T GET MUCH SUN IN THIS ROOM, THE FLOWERS WILTED IN A DAY.
It might be a letter from a ghost.
Mark my words. The next letter will come back unnaturally again...
Or some sort of malicious trick by someone.
I HEARD SOMEWHERE THAT IF YOU PUT YOUR TREASURES UNDER YOUR PILLOW, YOU WILL HAVE A NICE DREAM.
SO I WILL BE PUTTING THESE FLOWERS UNDER MY PILLOW TONIGHT...
すこーん
KONK
...HOPING THAT ONE DAY I CAN...
...SEE A FIELD OF FLOWERS WITH MY OWN EYES.

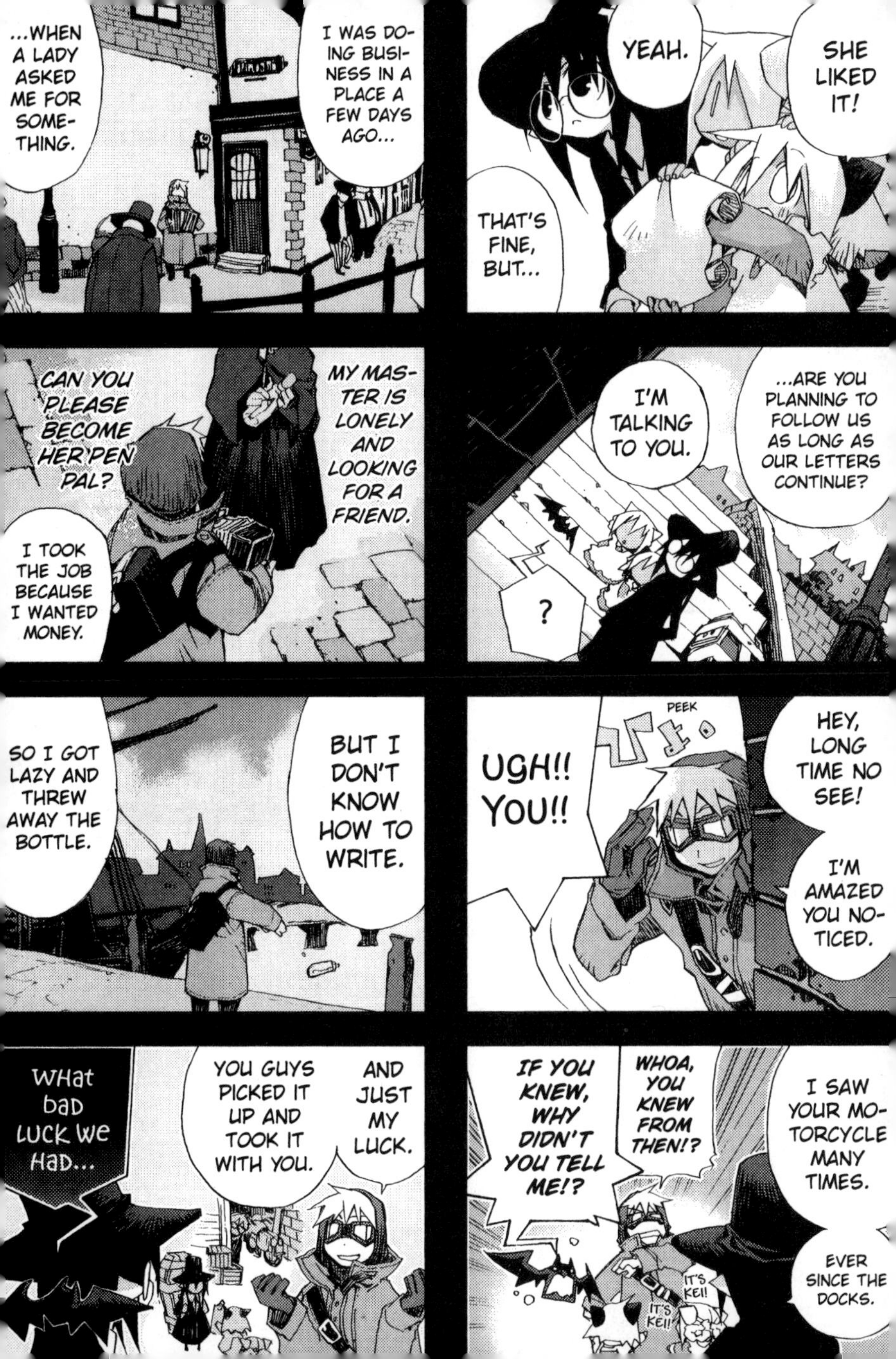
SHE LIKED IT!
YEAH.
THAT'S FINE, BUT...
I WAS DOING BUSINESS IN A PLACE A FEW DAYS AGO...
...WHEN A LADY ASKED ME FOR SOMETHING.
...ARE YOU PLANNING TO FOLLOW US AS LONG AS OUR LETTERS CONTINUE?
I'M TALKING TO YOU.
?
MY MASTER IS LONELY AND LOOKING FOR A FRIEND.
CAN YOU PLEASE BECOME HER PEN PAL?
I TOOK THE JOB BECAUSE I WANTED MONEY.
HEY, LONG TIME NO SEE!
PEEK
UGH!! YOU!!
I'M AMAZED YOU NOTICED.
BUT I DON'T KNOW HOW TO WRITE.
SO I GOT LAZY AND THREW AWAY THE BOTTLE.
I SAW YOUR MOTORCYCLE MANY TIMES.
WHOA, YOU KNEW FROM THEN!?
IF YOU KNEW, WHY DIDN'T YOU TELL ME!?
EVER SINCE THE DOCKS.
IT'S KEI!!
IT'S KEI!!
AND JUST MY LUCK.
YOU GUYS PICKED IT UP AND TOOK IT WITH YOU.
What bad luck we had...

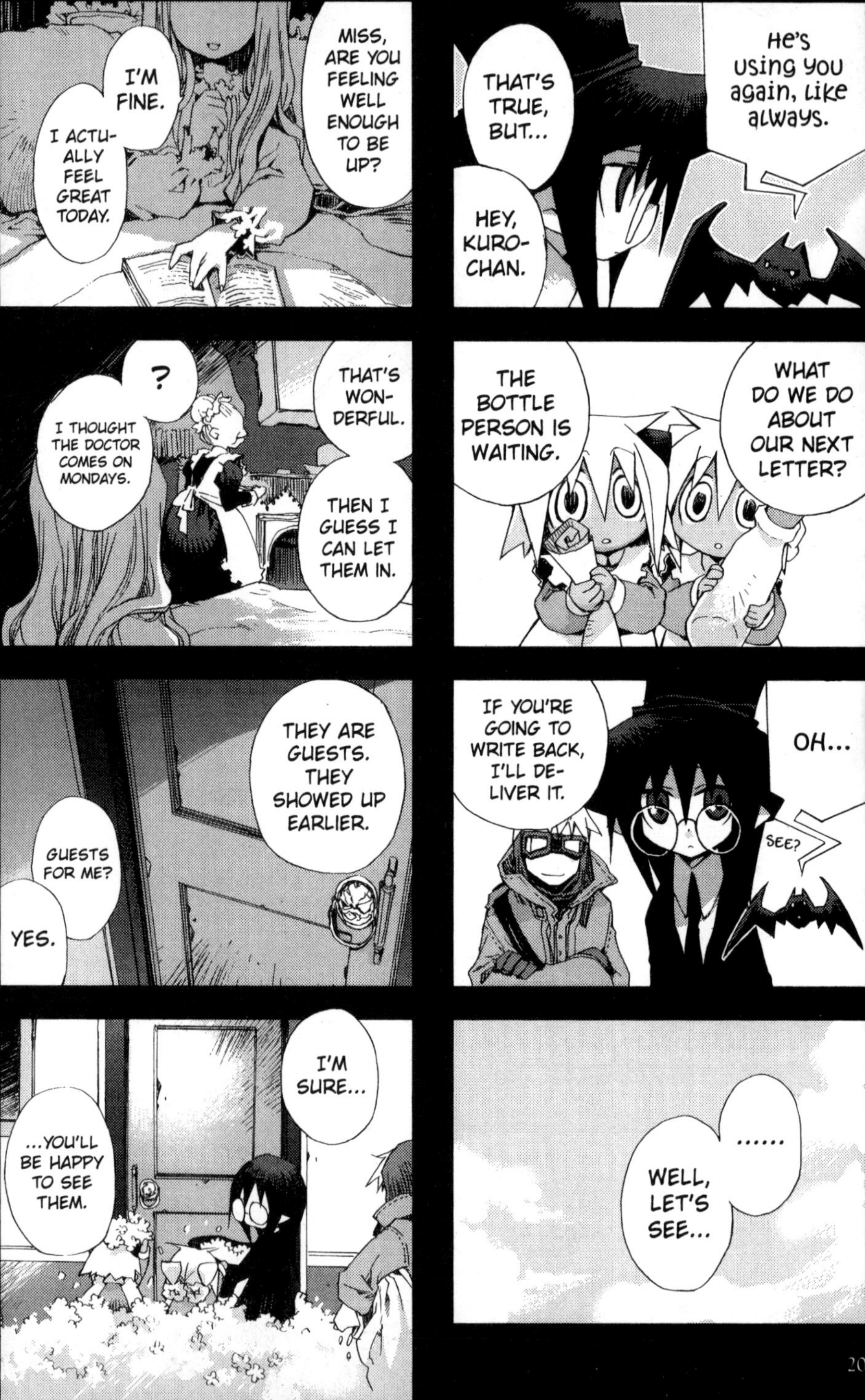
He's using you again, like always.
THAT'S TRUE, BUT...
HEY, KURO-CHAN.
MISS, ARE YOU FEELING WELL ENOUGH TO BE UP?
I'M FINE.
I ACTUALLY FEEL GREAT TODAY.
WHAT DO WE DO ABOUT OUR NEXT LETTER?
THE BOTTLE PERSON IS WAITING.
THAT'S WONDERFUL.
THEN I GUESS I CAN LET THEM IN.
?
I THOUGHT THE DOCTOR COMES ON MONDAYS.
OH...
SEE?
IF YOU'RE GOING TO WRITE BACK, I'LL DELIVER IT.
THEY ARE GUESTS. THEY SHOWED UP EARLIER.
GUESTS FOR ME?
YES.
......
WELL, LET'S SEE...
I'M SURE...
...YOU'LL BE HAPPY TO SEE THEM.

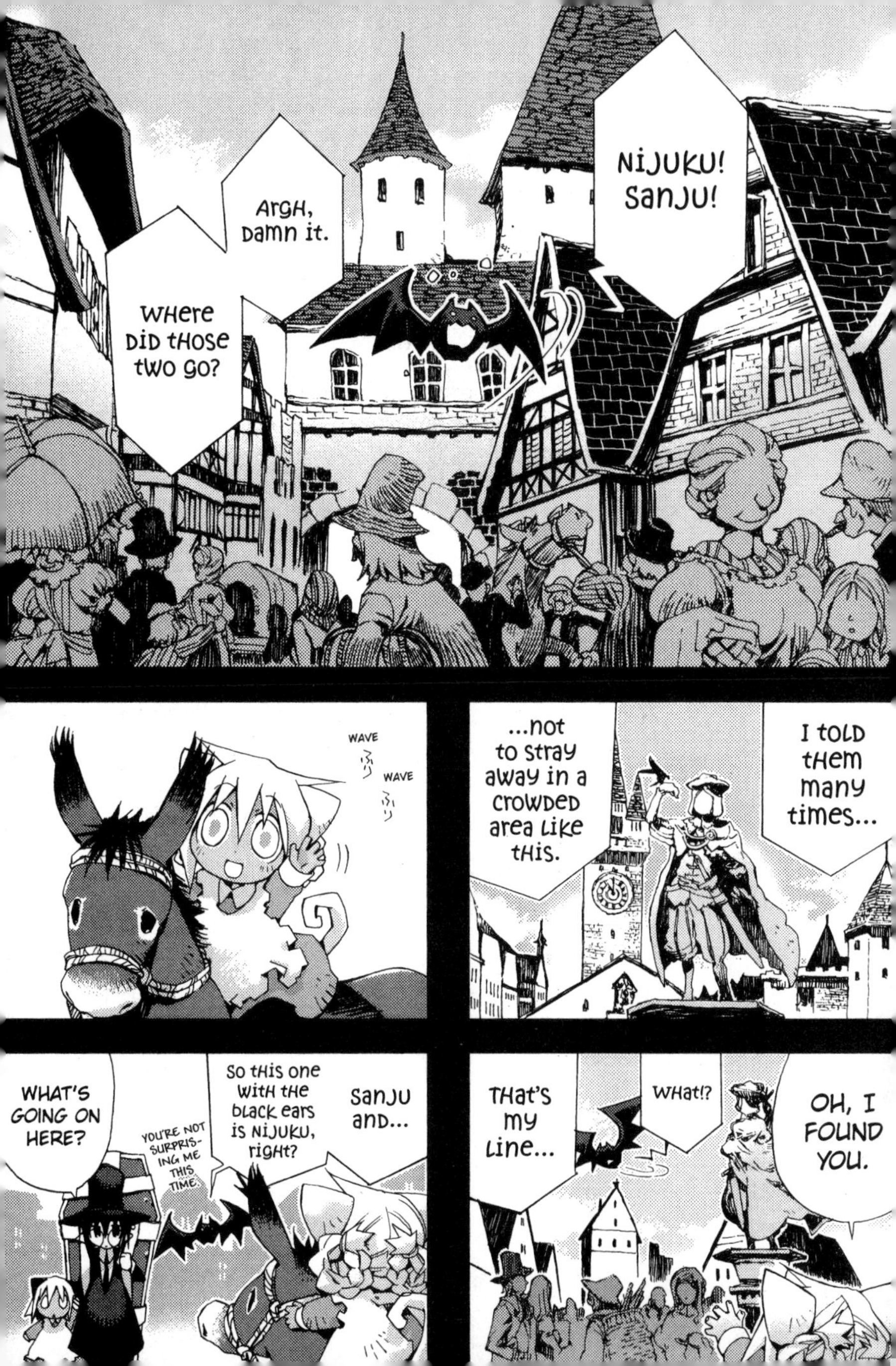
NIJUKU! SANJU!
ARGH, DAMN IT.
WHERE DID THOSE TWO GO?
I TOLD THEM MANY TIMES...
...NOT TO STRAY AWAY IN A CROWDED AREA LIKE THIS.
WAVE
WAVE
OH, I FOUND YOU.
WHAT!?
THAT'S MY LINE...
SANJU AND...
SO THIS ONE WITH THE BLACK EARS IS NIJUKU, RIGHT?
YOU'RE NOT SURPRIS-ING ME THIS TIME.
WHAT'S GOING ON HERE?

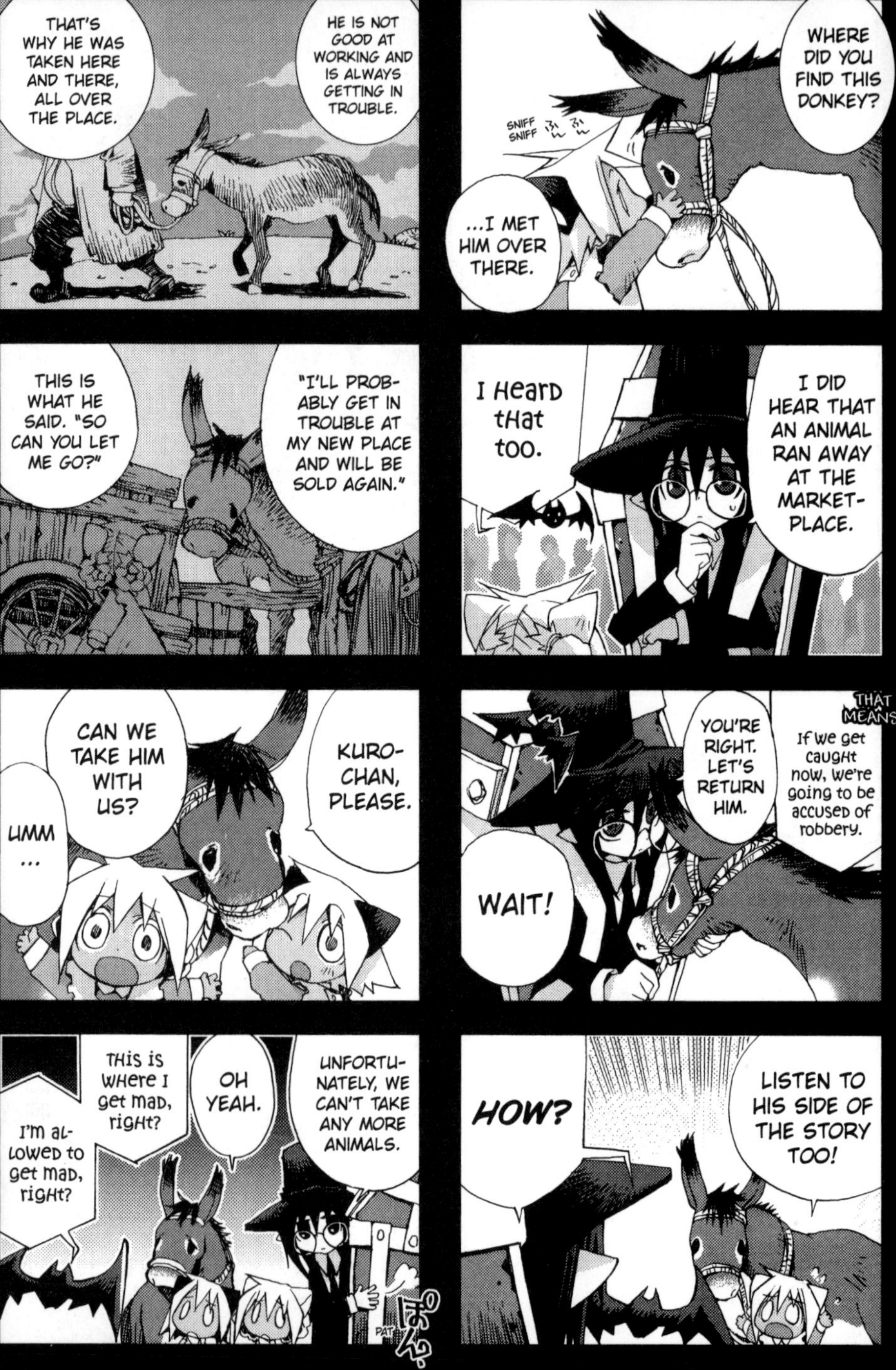
WHERE DID YOU FIND THIS DONKEY?
SNIFF SNIFF ふんふん
...I MET HIM OVER THERE.
HE IS NOT GOOD AT WORKING AND IS ALWAYS GETTING IN TROUBLE.
THAT'S WHY HE WAS TAKEN HERE AND THERE, ALL OVER THE PLACE.
I DID HEAR THAT AN ANIMAL RAN AWAY AT THE MARKETPLACE.
I Heard tHat too.
"I'LL PROBABLY GET IN TROUBLE AT MY NEW PLACE AND WILL BE SOLD AGAIN."
THIS IS WHAT HE SAID. "SO CAN YOU LET ME GO?"
THAT MEANS
If we get caught now, we're going to be accused of robbery.
YOU'RE RIGHT. LET'S RETURN HIM.
WAIT!
KURO-CHAN, PLEASE.
CAN WE TAKE HIM WITH US?
UMM ...
LISTEN TO HIS SIDE OF THE STORY TOO!
HOW?
UNFORTUNATELY, WE CAN'T TAKE ANY MORE ANIMALS.
OH YEAH.
THIS is where I get mad, right?
I'm allowed to get mad, right?
PAT
ぽん

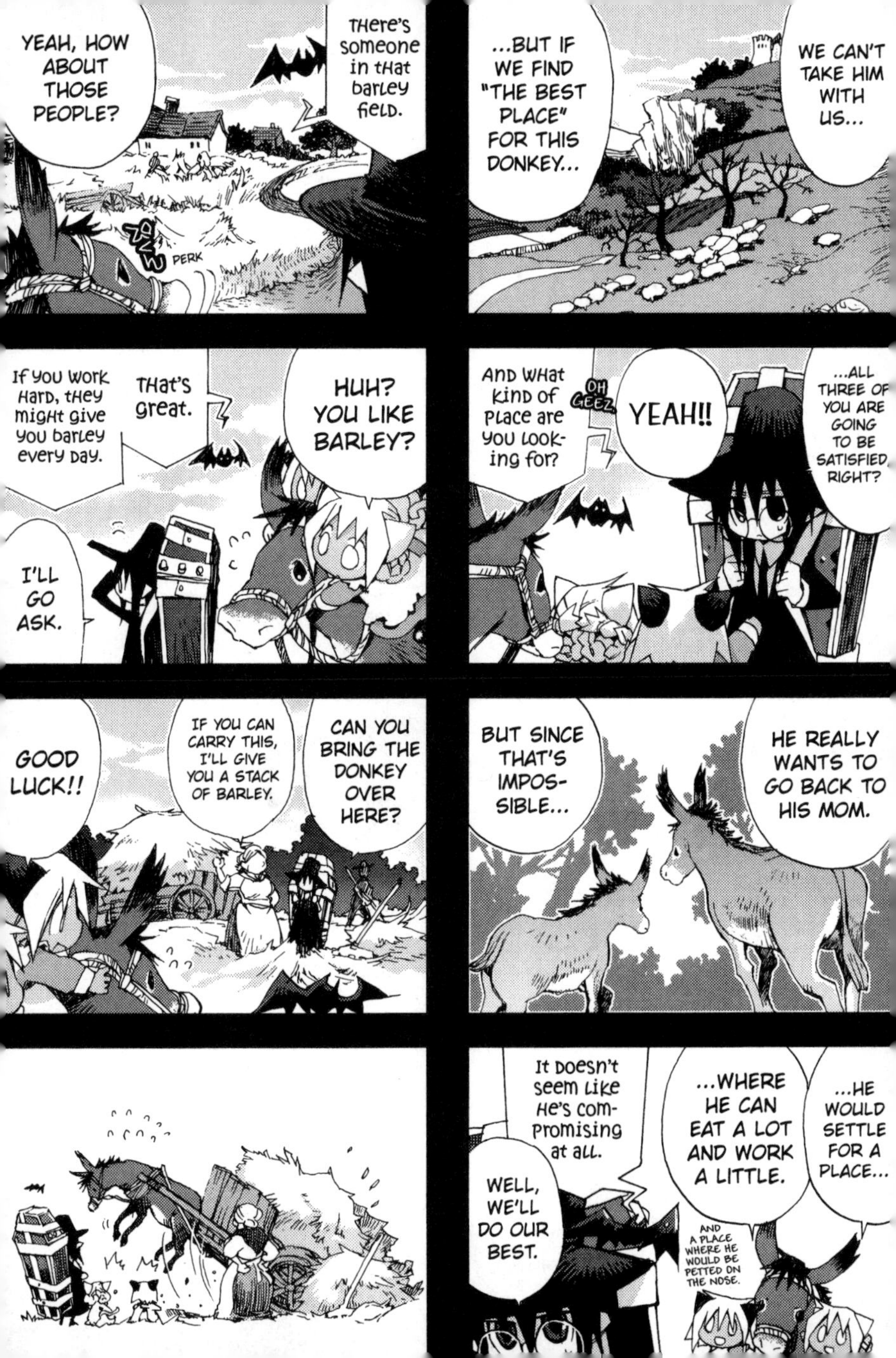

WE CAN'T TAKE HIM WITH US...
...BUT IF WE FIND "THE BEST PLACE" FOR THIS DONKEY...
...ALL THREE OF YOU ARE GOING TO BE SATISFIED, RIGHT?
YEAH!!
OH GEEZ
And what kind of place are you look-ing for?
HE REALLY WANTS TO GO BACK TO HIS MOM.
BUT SINCE THAT'S IMPOS-SIBLE...
...HE WOULD SETTLE FOR A PLACE...
...WHERE HE CAN EAT A LOT AND WORK A LITTLE.
AND A PLACE WHERE HE WOULD BE PETTED ON THE NOSE.
It doesn't seem like he's com-promising at all.
WELL, WE'LL DO OUR BEST.
There's someone in that barley field.
YEAH, HOW ABOUT THOSE PEOPLE?
PERK
HUH? YOU LIKE BARLEY?
That's great.
If you work hard, they might give you barley every day.
I'LL GO ASK.
CAN YOU BRING THE DONKEY OVER HERE?
IF YOU CAN CARRY THIS, I'LL GIVE YOU A STACK OF BARLEY.
GOOD LUCK!!

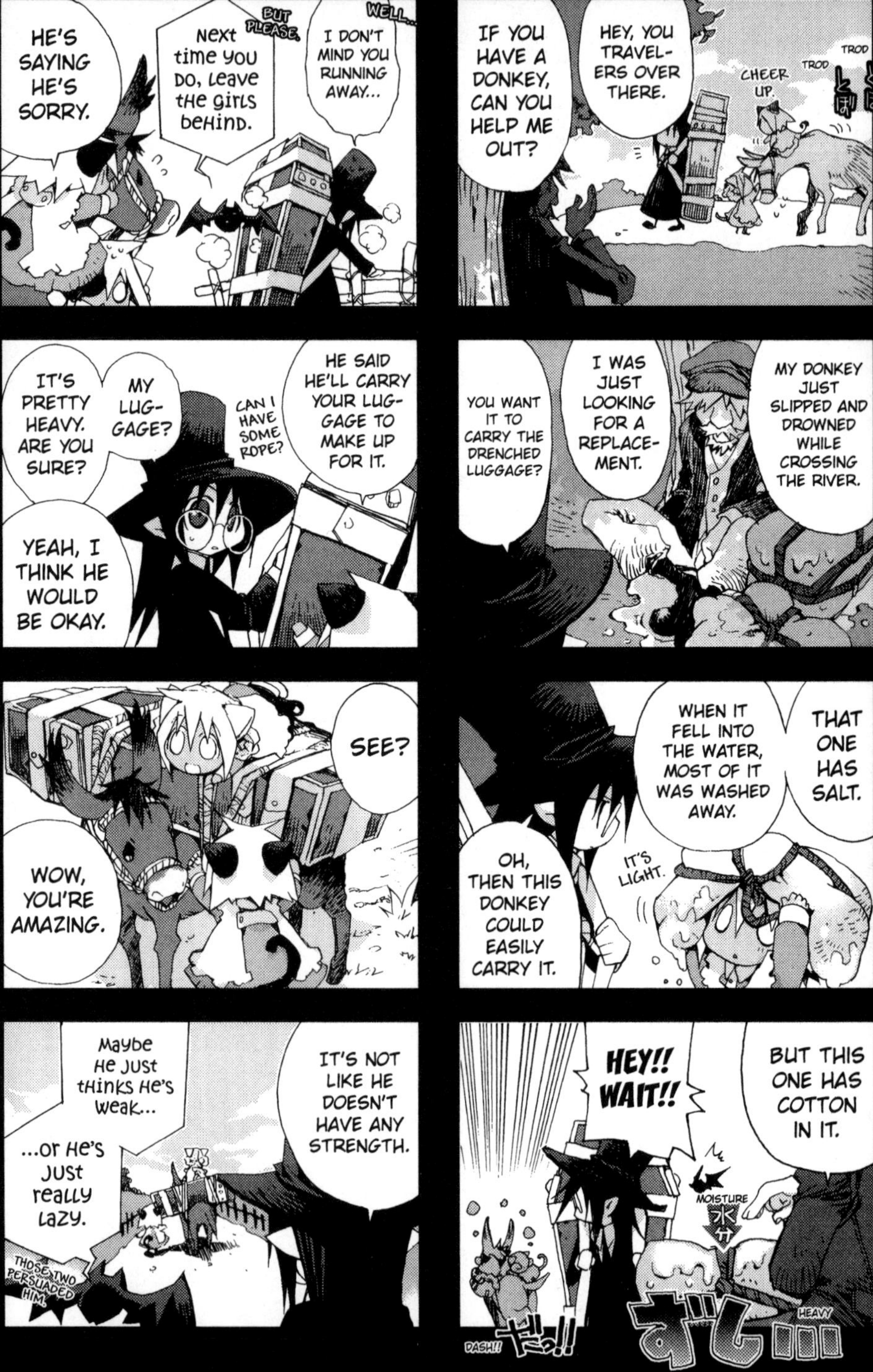
TROD
TROD
CHEER UP.
HEY, YOU TRAVELERS OVER THERE.
IF YOU HAVE A DONKEY, CAN YOU HELP ME OUT?
WELL...
I DON'T MIND YOU RUNNING AWAY...
BUT PLEASE.
Next time you do, leave the girls behind.
HE'S SAYING HE'S SORRY.
MY DONKEY JUST SLIPPED AND DROWNED WHILE CROSSING THE RIVER.
I WAS JUST LOOKING FOR A REPLACEMENT.
YOU WANT IT TO CARRY THE DRENCHED LUGGAGE?
HE SAID HE'LL CARRY YOUR LUGGAGE TO MAKE UP FOR IT.
CAN I HAVE SOME ROPE?
MY LUGGAGE?
IT'S PRETTY HEAVY. ARE YOU SURE?
YEAH, I THINK HE WOULD BE OKAY.
THAT ONE HAS SALT.
WHEN IT FELL INTO THE WATER, MOST OF IT WAS WASHED AWAY.
IT'S LIGHT.
OH, THEN THIS DONKEY COULD EASILY CARRY IT.
SEE?
WOW, YOU'RE AMAZING.
BUT THIS ONE HAS COTTON IN IT.
HEY!! WAIT!!
MOISTURE 水分
HEAVY ずし...
DASH!! だっ!!
IT'S NOT LIKE HE DOESN'T HAVE ANY STRENGTH.
Maybe he just thinks he's weak...
...or he's just really lazy.
THOSE TWO PERSUADED HIM.

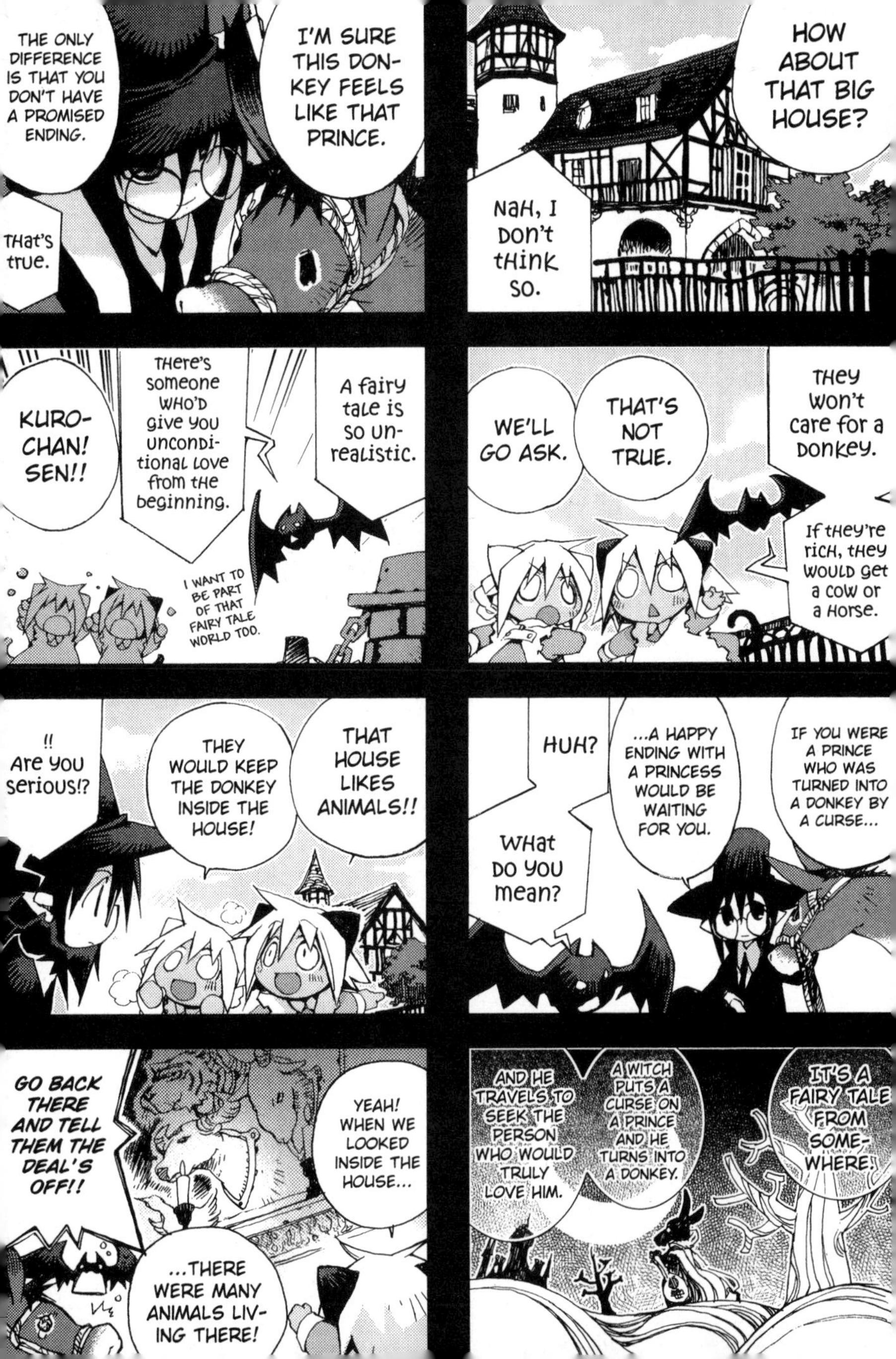
HOW ABOUT THAT BIG HOUSE?
NaH, I Don't tHink so.
I'M SURE THIS DONKEY FEELS LIKE THAT PRINCE.
THE ONLY DIFFERENCE IS THAT YOU DON'T HAVE A PROMISED ENDING.
THat's true.
THey won't care for a Donkey.
If tHey're ricH, tHey would get a cow or a Horse.
THAT'S NOT TRUE.
WE'LL GO ASK.
A fairy tale is so unrealistic.
THere's someone wHo'd give you unconditional Love from tHe beginning.
KURO-CHAN! SEN!!
I WANT TO BE PART OF THAT FAIRY TALE WORLD TOO.
IF YOU WERE A PRINCE WHO WAS TURNED INTO A DONKEY BY A CURSE...
...A HAPPY ENDING WITH A PRINCESS WOULD BE WAITING FOR YOU.
HUH?
WHat DO YOU mean?
THAT HOUSE LIKES ANIMALS!!
THEY WOULD KEEP THE DONKEY INSIDE THE HOUSE!
!! Are you serious!?
IT'S A FAIRY TALE FROM SOMEWHERE.
A WITCH PUTS A CURSE ON A PRINCE AND HE TURNS INTO A DONKEY.
AND HE TRAVELS TO SEEK THE PERSON WHO WOULD TRULY LOVE HIM.
YEAH! WHEN WE LOOKED INSIDE THE HOUSE...
...THERE WERE MANY ANIMALS LIVING THERE!
GO BACK THERE AND TELL THEM THE DEAL'S OFF!!

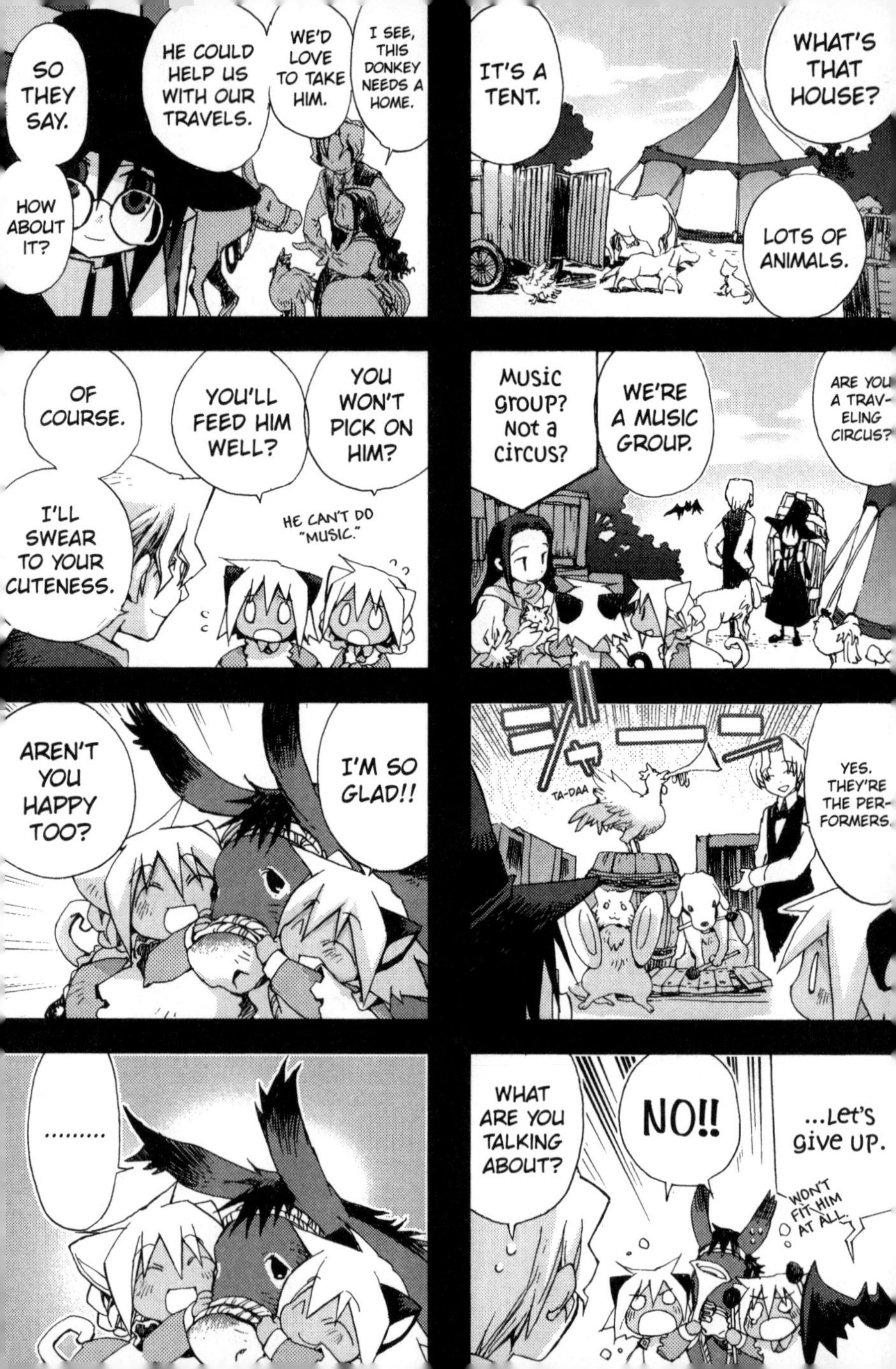
WHAT'S THAT HOUSE?
IT'S A TENT.
LOTS OF ANIMALS.
ARE YOU A TRAV-ELING CIRCUS?
WE'RE A MUSIC GROUP.
MUSIC GROUP? Not a circus?
YES. THEY'RE THE PER-FORMERS.
TA-DAA
...Let's give up.
NO!!
WHAT ARE YOU TALKING ABOUT?
WON'T FIT HIM AT ALL.
I SEE, THIS DONKEY NEEDS A HOME.
WE'D LOVE TO TAKE HIM.
HE COULD HELP US WITH OUR TRAVELS.
SO THEY SAY.
HOW ABOUT IT?
YOU WON'T PICK ON HIM?
YOU'LL FEED HIM WELL?
OF COURSE.
I'LL SWEAR TO YOUR CUTENESS.
HE CAN'T DO "MUSIC."
I'M SO GLAD!!
AREN'T YOU HAPPY TOO?
....

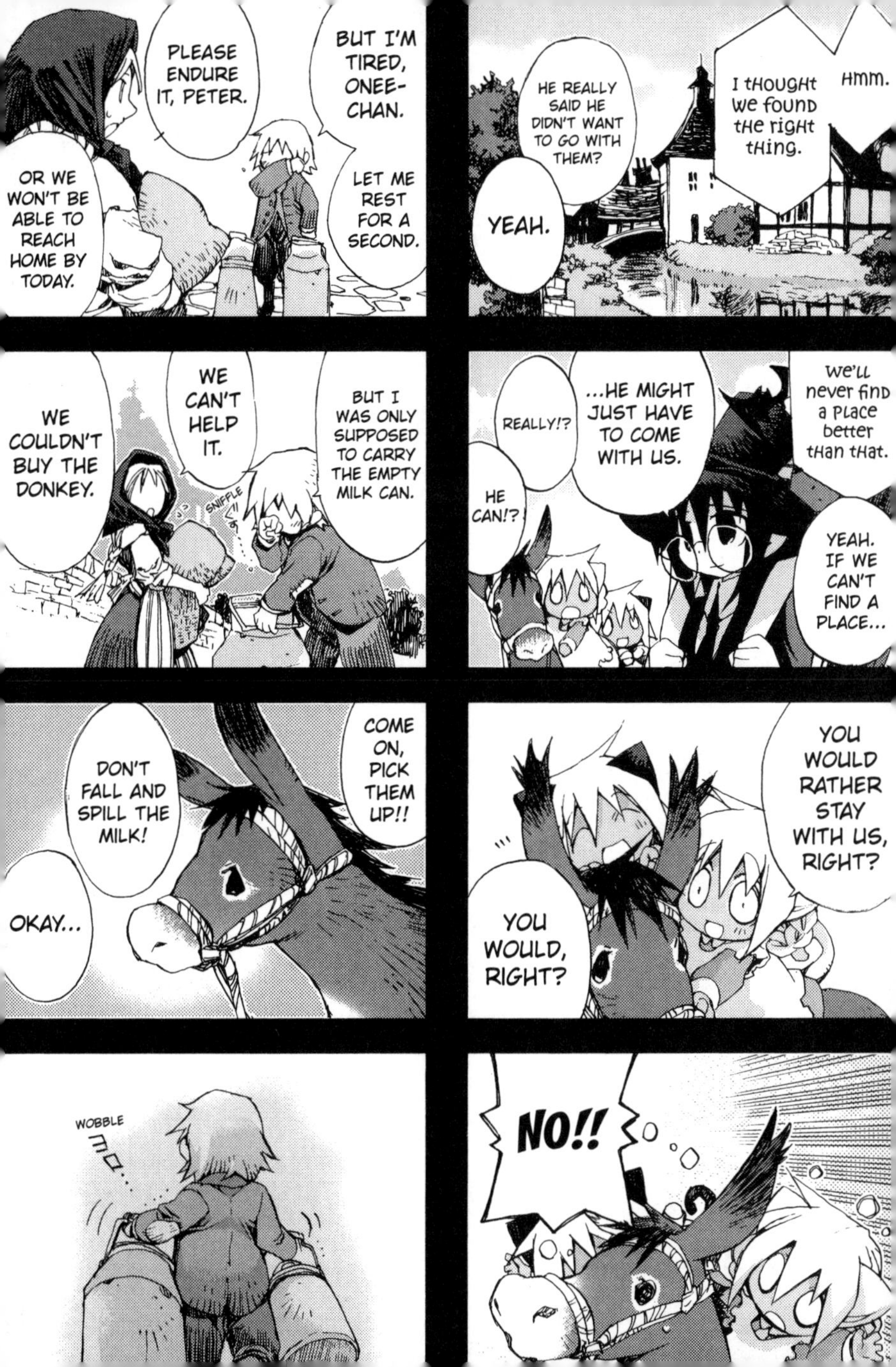

HMM.
I THOUGHT WE FOUND THE RIGHT THING.
HE REALLY SAID HE DIDN'T WANT TO GO WITH THEM?
YEAH.
WE'LL NEVER FIND A PLACE BETTER THAN THAT.
YEAH. IF WE CAN'T FIND A PLACE...
...HE MIGHT JUST HAVE TO COME WITH US.
REALLY!?
HE CAN!?
YOU WOULD RATHER STAY WITH US, RIGHT?
YOU WOULD, RIGHT?
NO!!
BUT I'M TIRED, ONEE-CHAN.
LET ME REST FOR A SECOND.
PLEASE ENDURE IT, PETER.
OR WE WON'T BE ABLE TO REACH HOME BY TODAY.
BUT I WAS ONLY SUPPOSED TO CARRY THE EMPTY MILK CAN.
WE CAN'T HELP IT.
SNIFFLE
WE COULDN'T BUY THE DONKEY.
COME ON, PICK THEM UP!!
DON'T FALL AND SPILL THE MILK!
OKAY...
WOBBLE

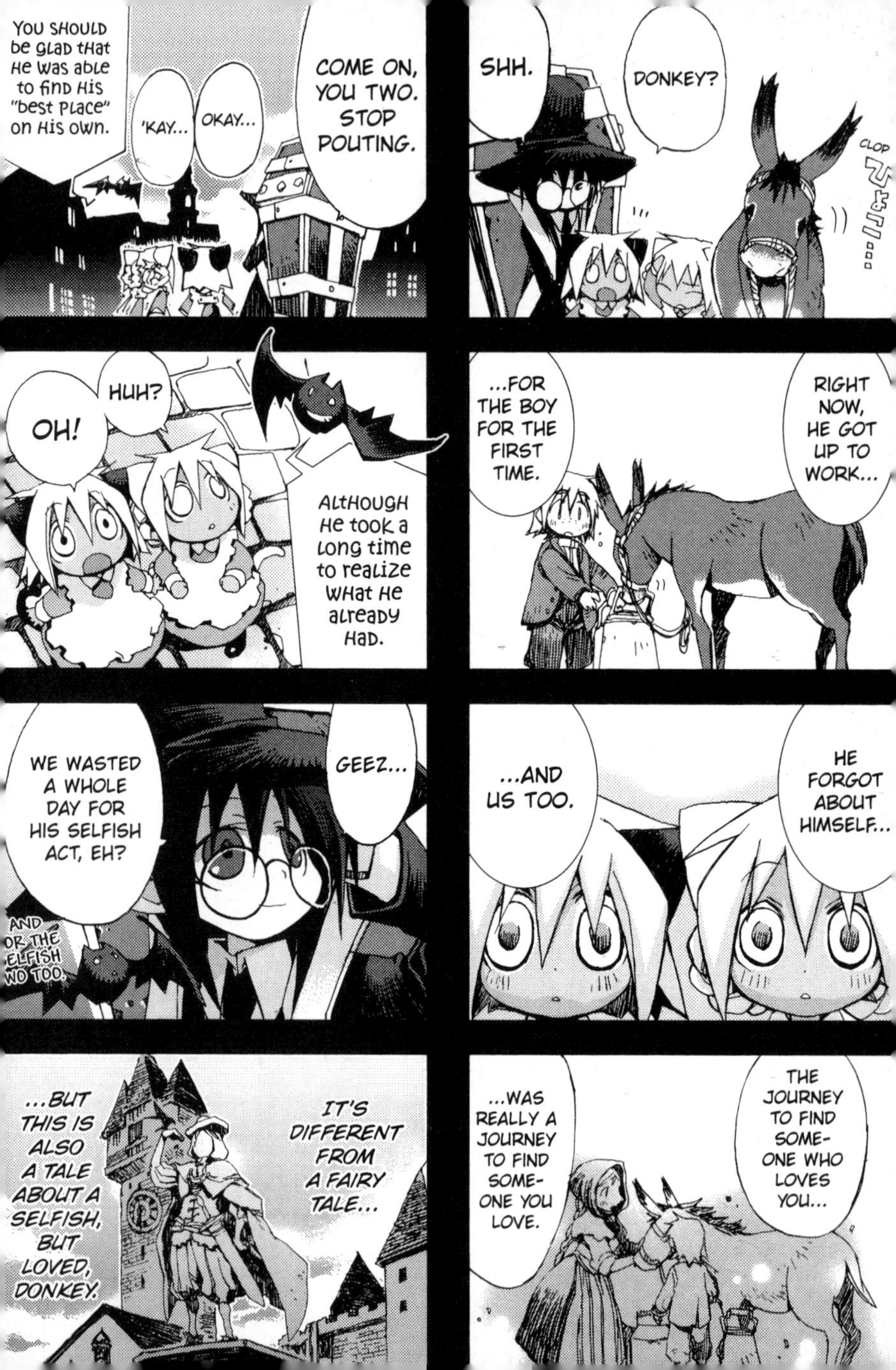
CLOP
DONKEY?
SHH.
COME ON, YOU TWO. STOP POUTING.
OKAY...
'KAY...
You should be glad that he was able to find his "best place" on his own.
RIGHT NOW, HE GOT UP TO WORK...
...FOR THE BOY FOR THE FIRST TIME.
HUH?
OH!
Although he took a long time to realize what he already had.
HE FORGOT ABOUT HIMSELF...
...AND US TOO.
GEEZ...
WE WASTED A WHOLE DAY FOR HIS SELFISH ACT, EH?
AND OR THE ELFISH WO TOO.
THE JOURNEY TO FIND SOME-ONE WHO LOVES YOU...
...WAS REALLY A JOURNEY TO FIND SOME-ONE YOU LOVE.
IT'S DIFFERENT FROM A FAIRY TALE...
...BUT THIS IS ALSO A TALE ABOUT A SELFISH, BUT LOVED, DONKEY.

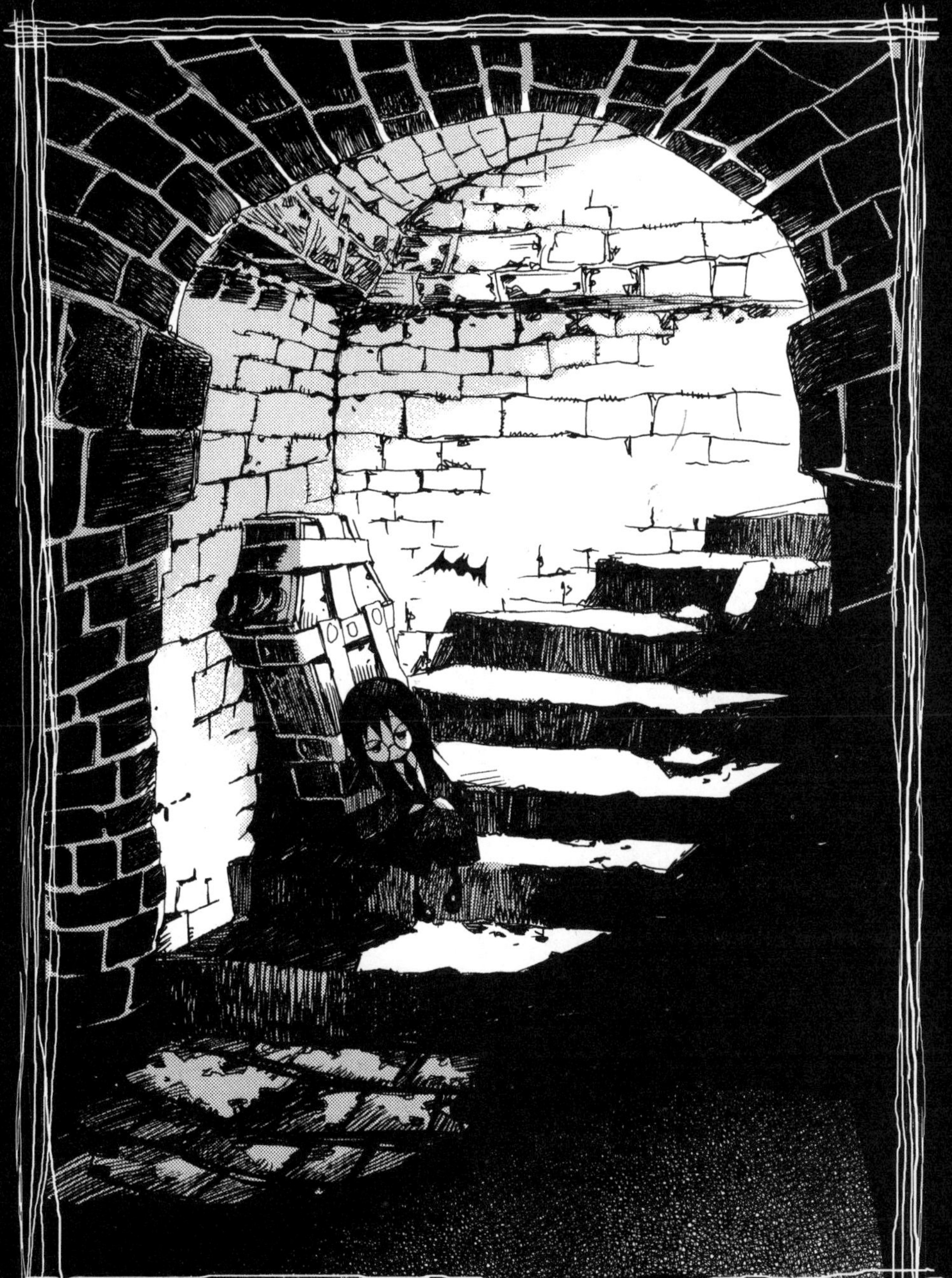

To walk into an unknown town and to meet unknown people—
it's what happens when you travel.
But it was not that easy for the young traveler to accept this.

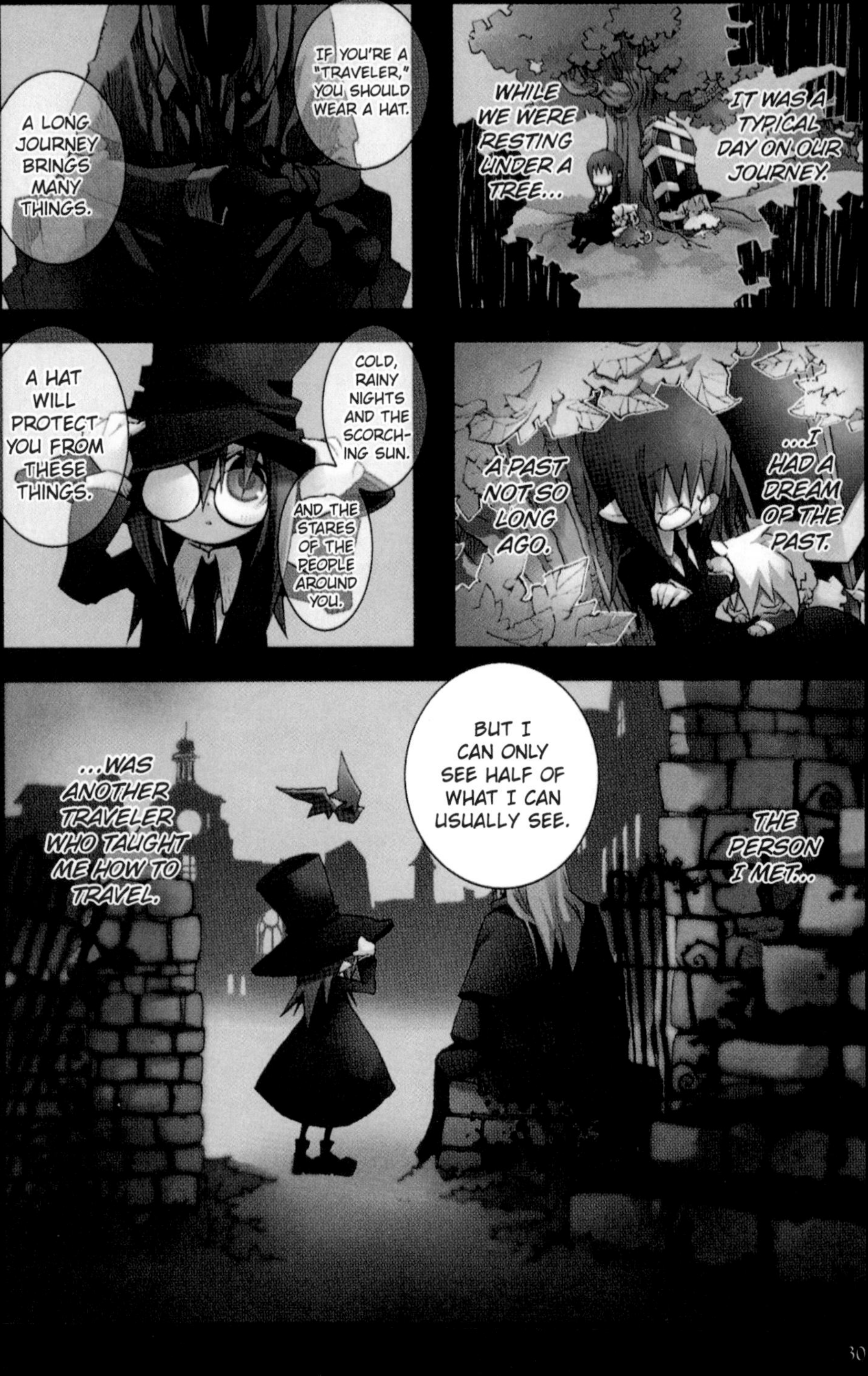
IT WAS A TYPICAL DAY ON OUR JOURNEY.
WHILE WE WERE RESTING UNDER A TREE...
IF YOU'RE A "TRAVELER," YOU SHOULD WEAR A HAT.
A LONG JOURNEY BRINGS MANY THINGS.
...I HAD A DREAM OF THE PAST.
A PAST NOT SO LONG AGO.
COLD, RAINY NIGHTS AND THE SCORCHING SUN.
AND THE STARES OF THE PEOPLE AROUND YOU.
A HAT WILL PROTECT YOU FROM THESE THINGS.
THE PERSON I MET...
BUT I CAN ONLY SEE HALF OF WHAT I CAN USUALLY SEE.
...WAS ANOTHER TRAVELER WHO TAUGHT ME HOW TO TRAVEL.

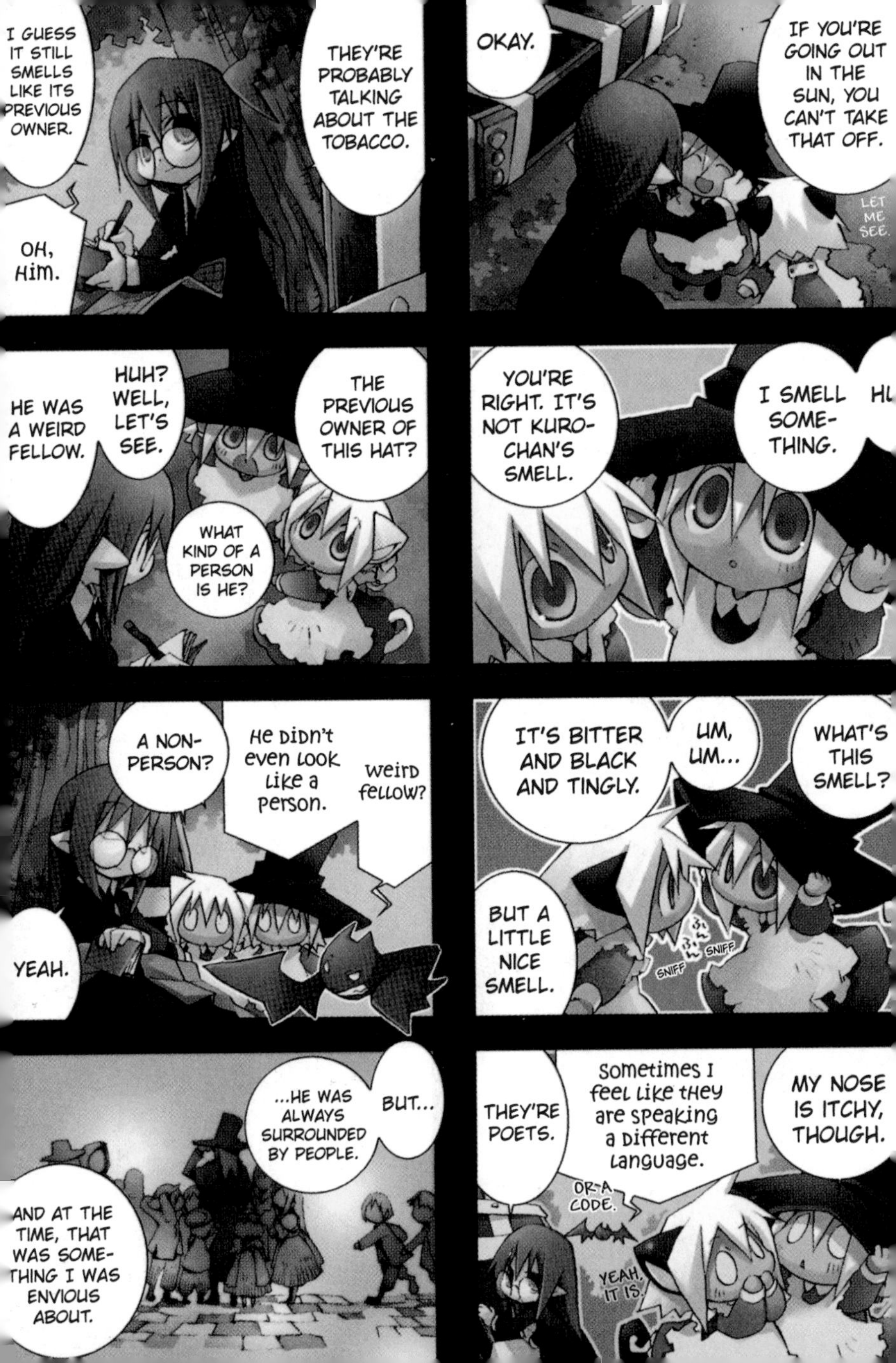
IF YOU'RE GOING OUT IN THE SUN, YOU CAN'T TAKE THAT OFF.
LET ME SEE.
OKAY.
THEY'RE PROBABLY TALKING ABOUT THE TOBACCO.
I GUESS IT STILL SMELLS LIKE ITS PREVIOUS OWNER.
OH, HIM.
I SMELL SOME-THING.
YOU'RE RIGHT. IT'S NOT KURO-CHAN'S SMELL.
THE PREVIOUS OWNER OF THIS HAT?
HUH? WELL, LET'S SEE.
HE WAS A WEIRD FELLOW.
WHAT KIND OF A PERSON IS HE?
WHAT'S THIS SMELL?
UM, UM...
IT'S BITTER AND BLACK AND TINGLY.
ふん ふん
SNIFF
SNIFF
BUT A LITTLE NICE SMELL.
weird fellow?
He didn't even look like a person.
A NON-PERSON?
YEAH.
MY NOSE IS ITCHY, THOUGH.
Sometimes I feel like they are speaking a different language.
THEY'RE POETS.
OR A CODE.
YEAH, IT IS.
BUT...
...HE WAS ALWAYS SURROUNDED BY PEOPLE.
AND AT THE TIME, THAT WAS SOMETHING I WAS ENVIOUS ABOUT.

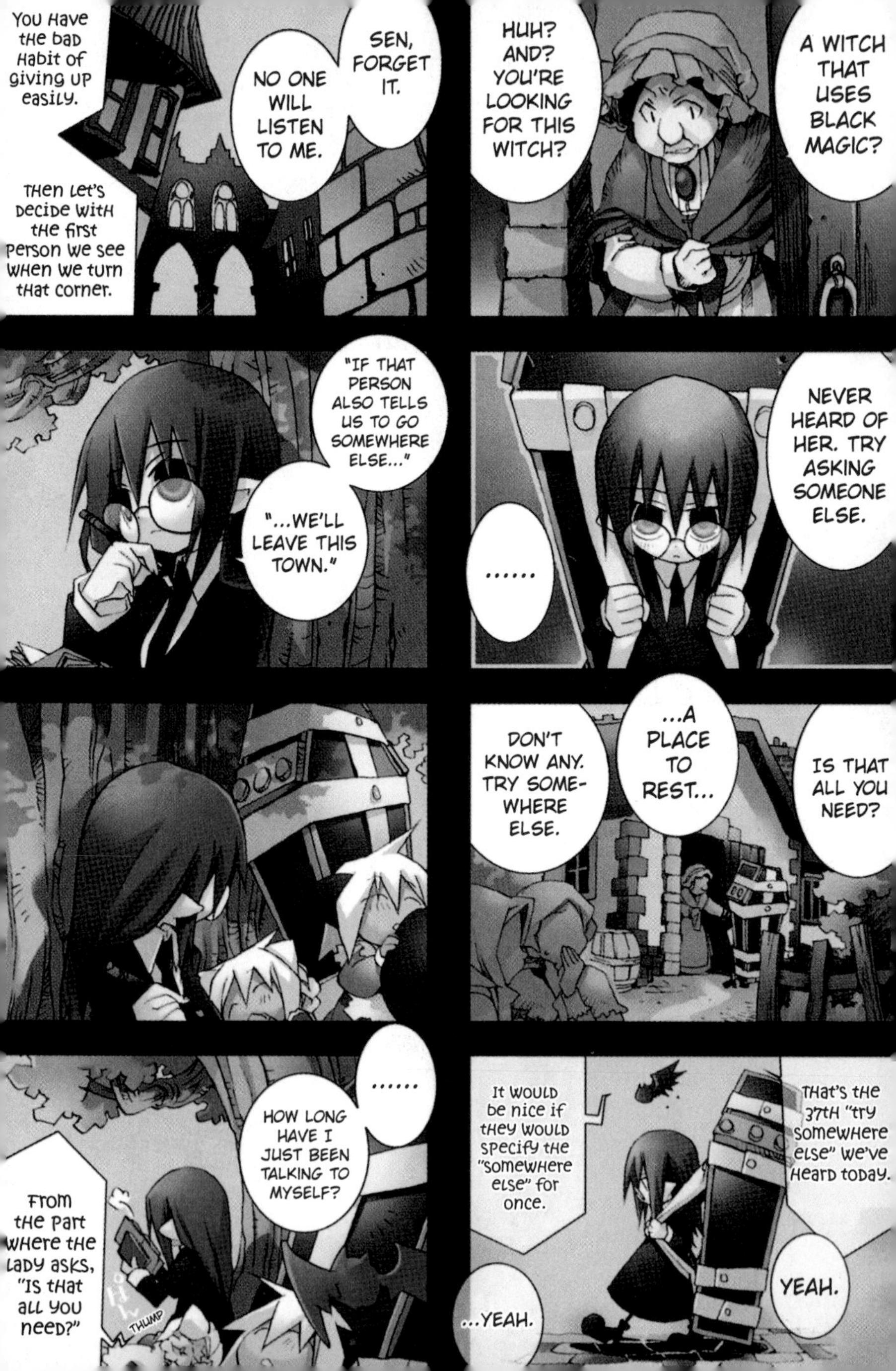
A WITCH THAT USES BLACK MAGIC?
HUH? AND? YOU'RE LOOKING FOR THIS WITCH?
SEN, FORGET IT.
NO ONE WILL LISTEN TO ME.
You have the bad habit of giving up easily.
Then let's decide with the first person we see when we turn that corner.
NEVER HEARD OF HER. TRY ASKING SOMEONE ELSE.
......
"IF THAT PERSON ALSO TELLS US TO GO SOMEWHERE ELSE..."
"...WE'LL LEAVE THIS TOWN."
IS THAT ALL YOU NEED?
...A PLACE TO REST...
DON'T KNOW ANY. TRY SOME-WHERE ELSE.
That's the 37th "try somewhere else" we've heard today.
It would be nice if they would specify the "somewhere else" for once.
YEAH.
...YEAH.
......
HOW LONG HAVE I JUST BEEN TALKING TO MYSELF?
From the part where the lady asks, "Is that all you need?"
THUMP

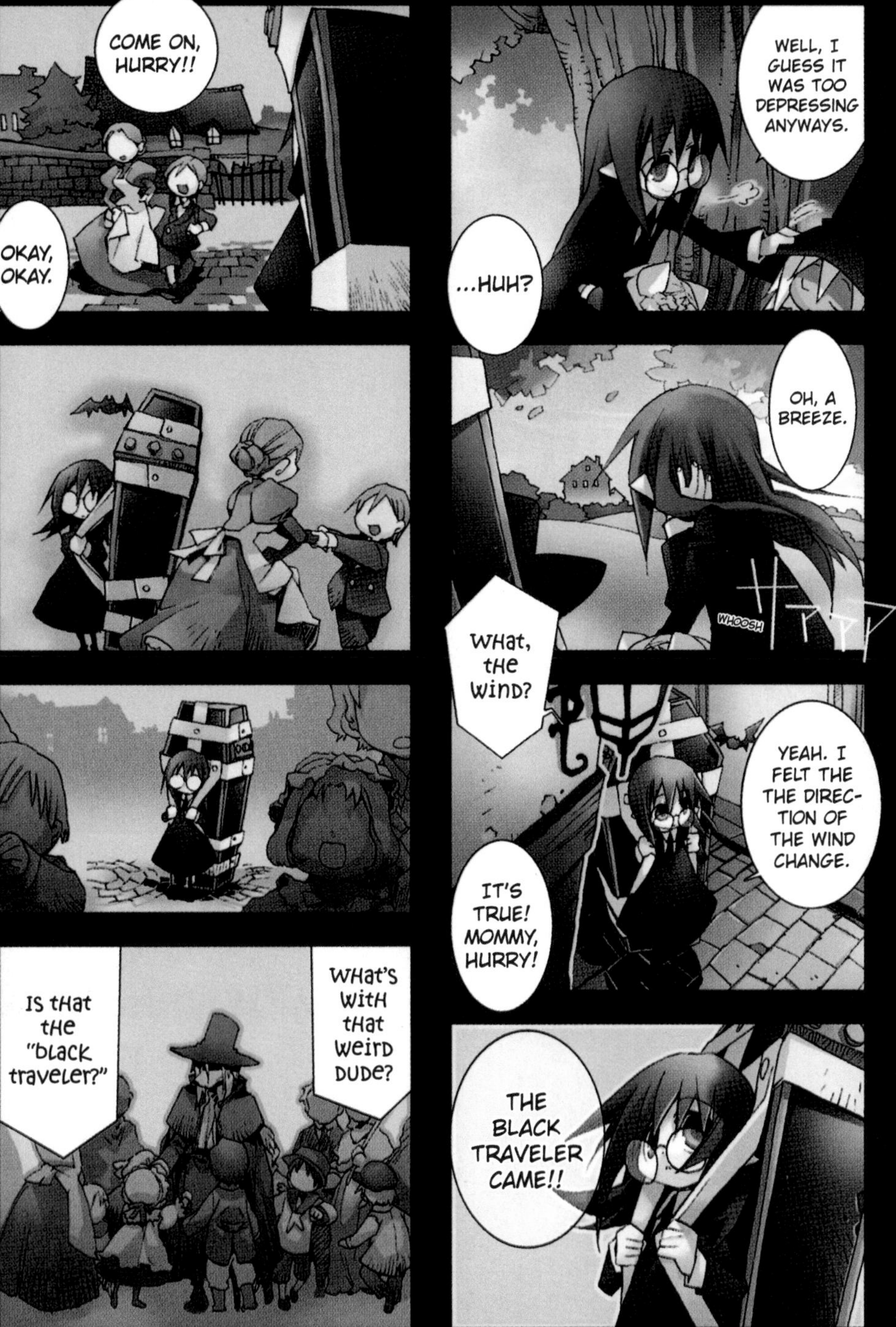
WELL, I GUESS IT WAS TOO DEPRESSING ANYWAYS.
...HUH?
COME ON, HURRY!!
OKAY, OKAY.
OH, A BREEZE.
WHOOSH
WHAT, THE WIND?
YEAH. I FELT THE THE DIREC-TION OF THE WIND CHANGE.
IT'S TRUE! MOMMY, HURRY!
THE BLACK TRAVELER CAME!!
WHAT'S WITH THAT WEIRD DUDE?
IS THAT THE "BLACK TRAVELER?"

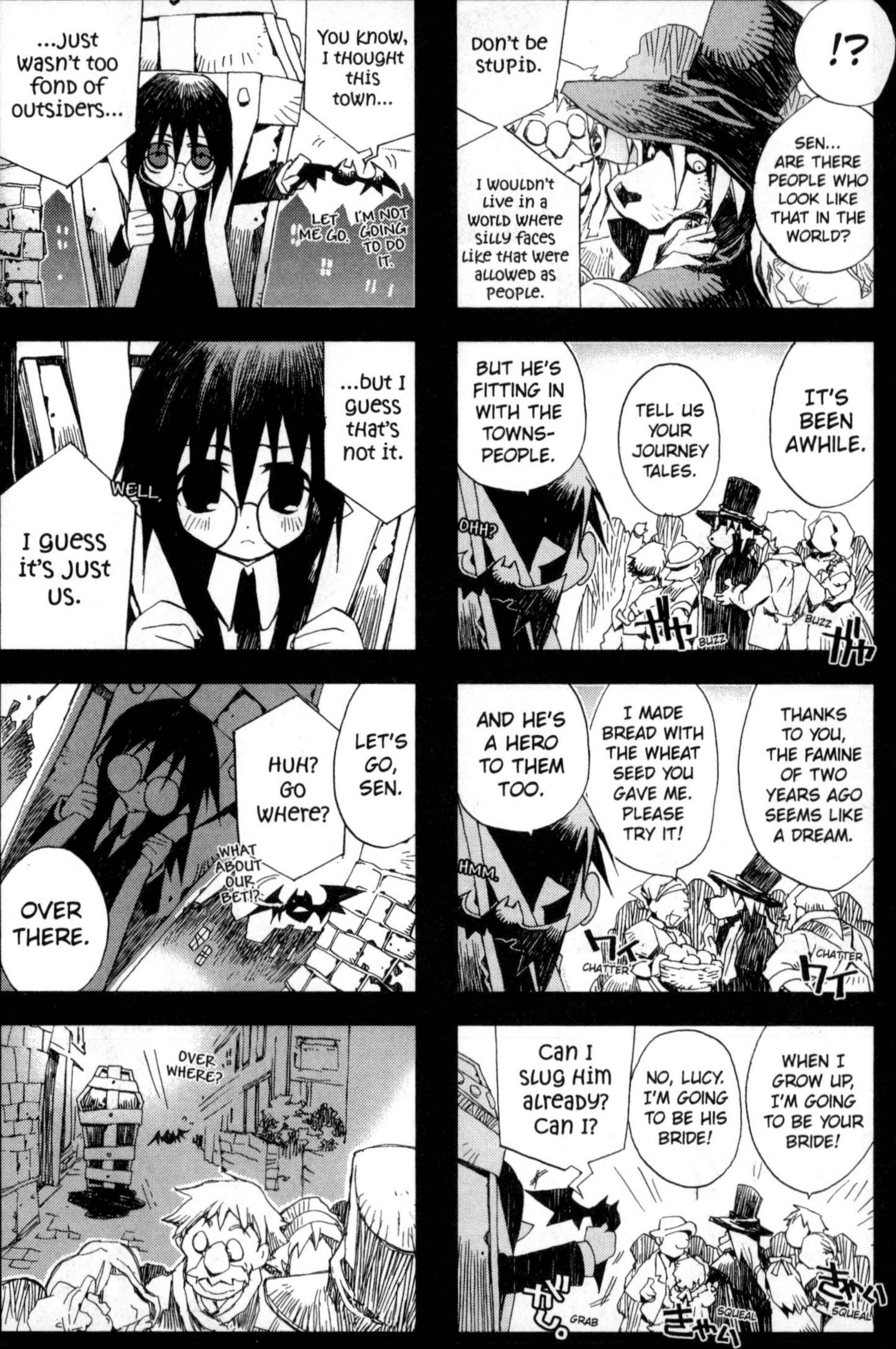
!?
SEN... ARE THERE PEOPLE WHO LOOK LIKE THAT IN THE WORLD?
Don't be stupid.
I wouldn't live in a world where silly faces like that were allowed as people.
You know, I thought this town...
...Just wasn't too fond of outsiders...
I'M NOT GOING TO DO IT.
LET ME GO.
IT'S BEEN AWHILE.
TELL US YOUR JOURNEY TALES.
BUT HE'S FITTING IN WITH THE TOWNS-PEOPLE.
OHH?
ガヤ BUZZ
ガヤ BUZZ
...but I guess that's not it.
WELL,
I guess it's just us.
THANKS TO YOU, THE FAMINE OF TWO YEARS AGO SEEMS LIKE A DREAM.
I MADE BREAD WITH THE WHEAT SEED YOU GAVE ME. PLEASE TRY IT!
AND HE'S A HERO TO THEM TOO.
HMM.
ワイ CHATTER
ワイ CHATTER
LET'S GO, SEN.
HUH? GO WHERE?
WHAT ABOUT OUR BET!?
OVER THERE.
WHEN I GROW UP, I'M GOING TO BE YOUR BRIDE!
NO, LUCY. I'M GOING TO BE HIS BRIDE!
Can I slug him already? Can I?
きゃい SQUEAL
きゃ SQUEAL
がし。GRAB
OVER WHERE?

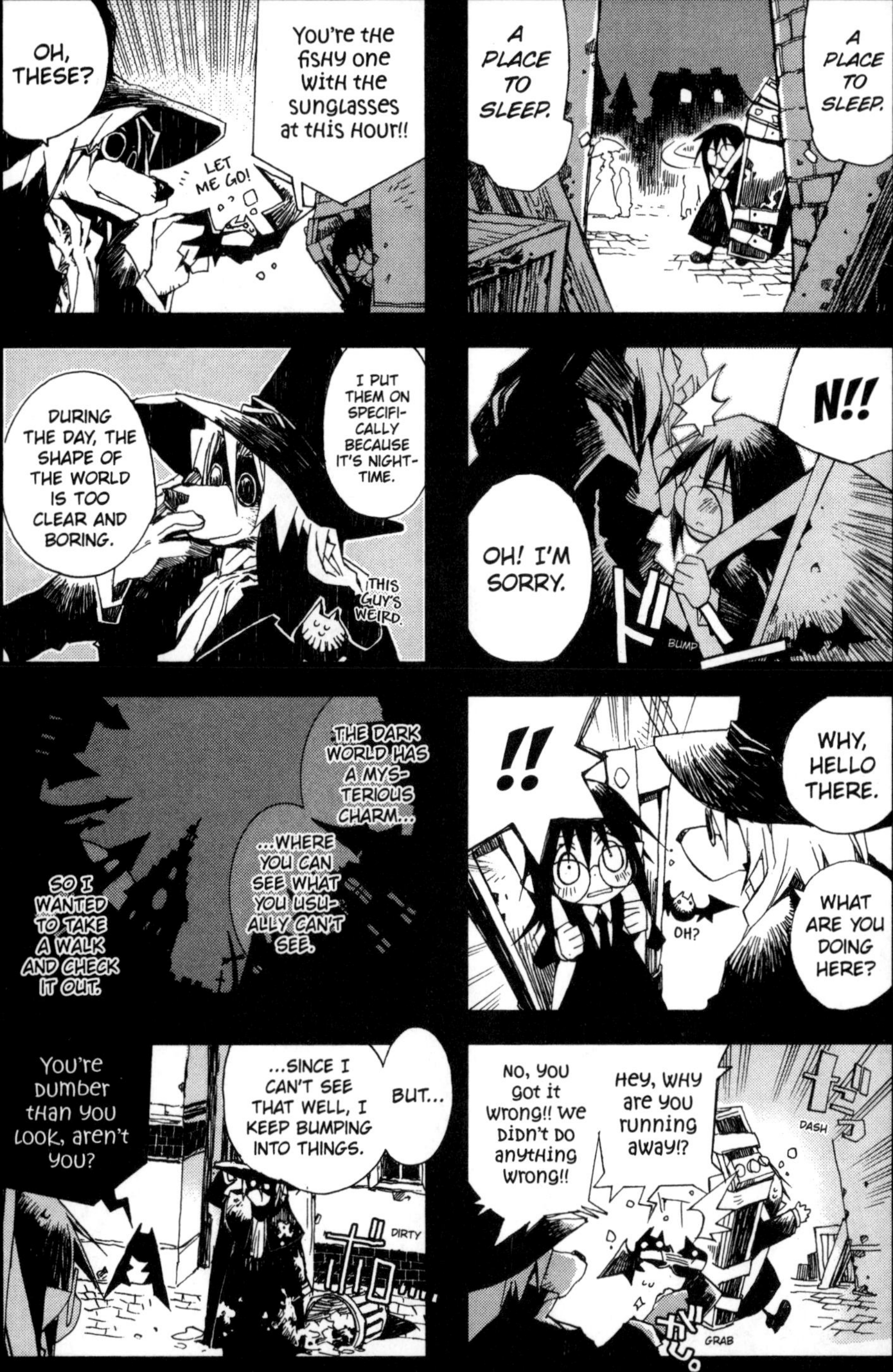
A PLACE TO SLEEP.
A PLACE TO SLEEP.
You're the fishy one with the sunglasses at this hour!!
LET ME GO!
OH, THESE?
N!!
OH! I'M SORRY.
BUMP
I PUT THEM ON SPECIFI-CALLY BECAUSE IT'S NIGHT-TIME.
DURING THE DAY, THE SHAPE OF THE WORLD IS TOO CLEAR AND BORING.
THIS GUY'S WEIRD.
WHY, HELLO THERE.
!!
WHAT ARE YOU DOING HERE?
OH?
THE DARK WORLD HAS A MYS-TERIOUS CHARM...
...WHERE YOU CAN SEE WHAT YOU USU-ALLY CAN'T SEE.
SO I WANTED TO TAKE A WALK AND CHECK IT OUT.
DASH
Hey, WHY are you running away!?
No, you got it wrong!! We didn't do anything wrong!!
GRAB
BUT...
...SINCE I CAN'T SEE THAT WELL, I KEEP BUMPING INTO THINGS.
DIRTY
You're dumber than you look, aren't you?

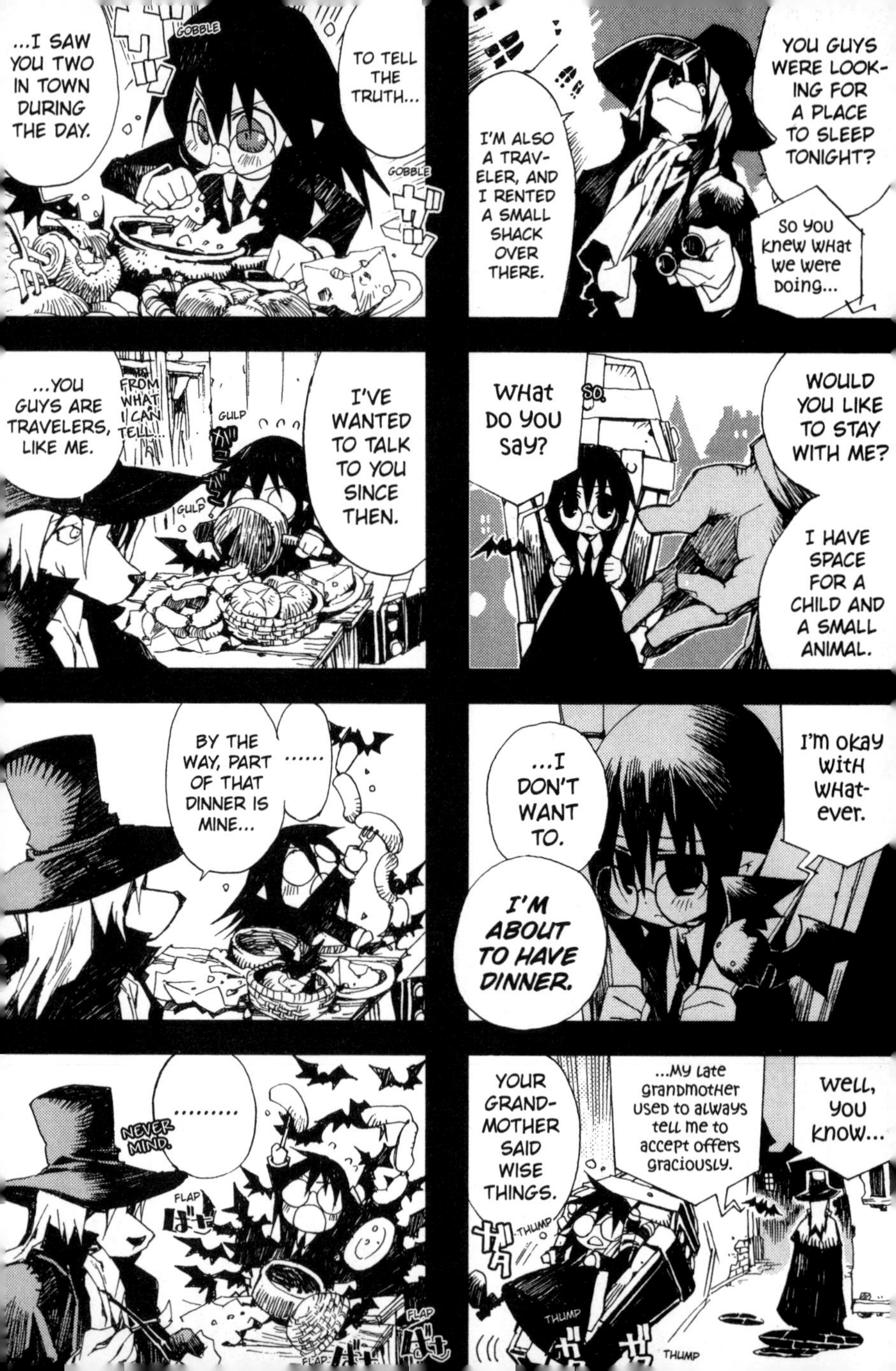
YOU GUYS WERE LOOKING FOR A PLACE TO SLEEP TONIGHT?
So you knew what we were doing...
I'M ALSO A TRAVELER, AND I RENTED A SMALL SHACK OVER THERE.
WOULD YOU LIKE TO STAY WITH ME?
I HAVE SPACE FOR A CHILD AND A SMALL ANIMAL.
What do you say?
SO.
I'm okay with whatever.
...I DON'T WANT TO.
I'M ABOUT TO HAVE DINNER.
Well, you know...
...My late grandmother used to always tell me to accept offers graciously.
YOUR GRANDMOTHER SAID WISE THINGS.
THUMP
THUMP
THUMP
TO TELL THE TRUTH...
GOBBLE
...I SAW YOU TWO IN TOWN DURING THE DAY.
GOBBLE
I'VE WANTED TO TALK TO YOU SINCE THEN.
GULP
FROM WHAT I CAN TELL...
...YOU GUYS ARE TRAVELERS, LIKE ME.
GULP
......
BY THE WAY, PART OF THAT DINNER IS MINE...
....
NEVER MIND.
FLAP
FLAP
FLAP

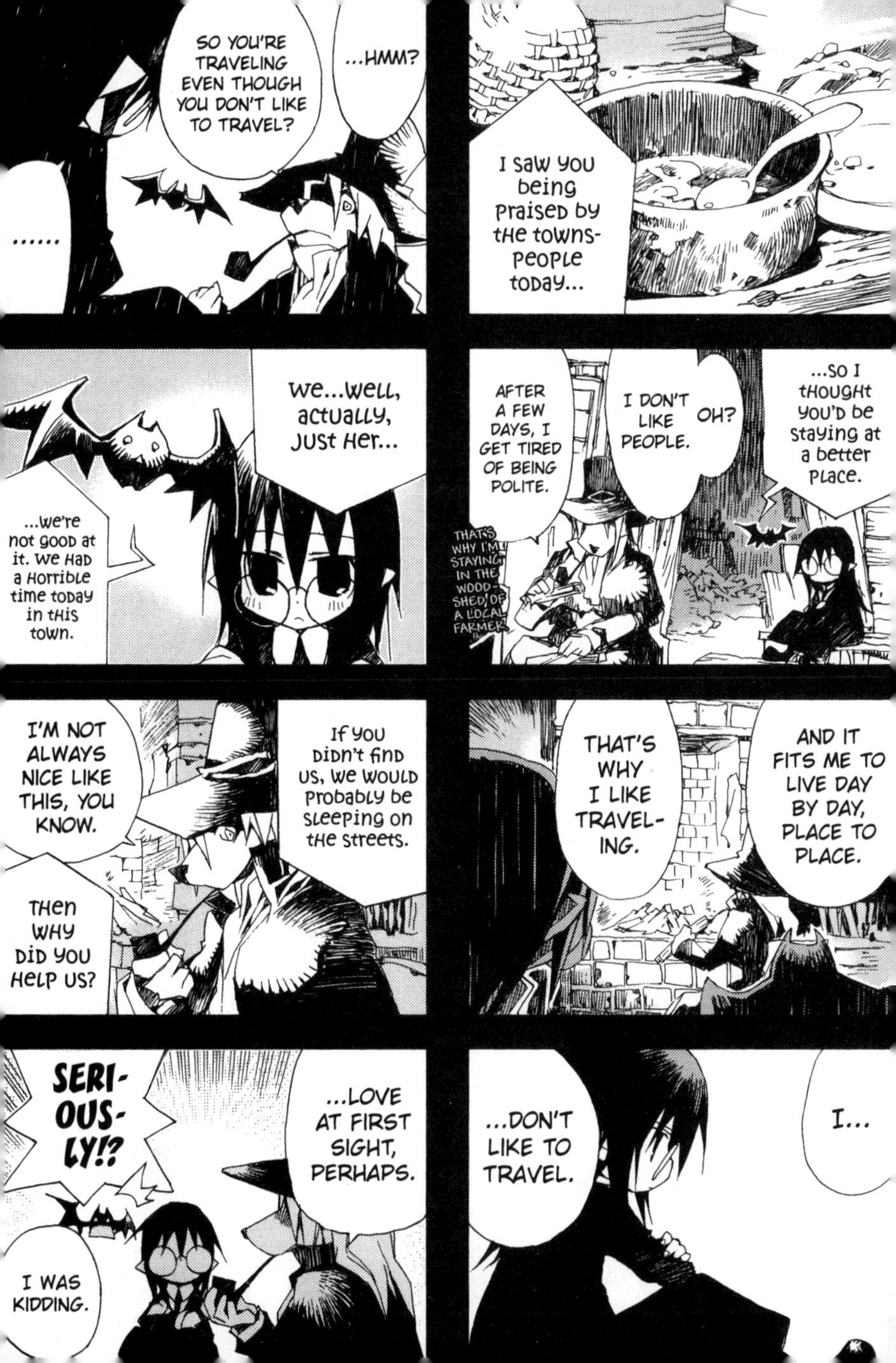
I saw you being praised by the towns-people today...
...HMM?
SO YOU'RE TRAVELING EVEN THOUGH YOU DON'T LIKE TO TRAVEL?
......
...so I thought you'd be staying at a better place.
OH?
I DON'T LIKE PEOPLE.
AFTER A FEW DAYS, I GET TIRED OF BEING POLITE.
THAT'S WHY I'M STAYING IN THE WOOD-SHED OF A LOCAL FARMER.
we...well, actually, just her...
...we're not good at it. We had a horrible time today in this town.
AND IT FITS ME TO LIVE DAY BY DAY, PLACE TO PLACE.
THAT'S WHY I LIKE TRAVEL-ING.
If you didn't find us, we would probably be sleeping on the streets.
I'M NOT ALWAYS NICE LIKE THIS, YOU KNOW.
Then why did you help us?
I...
...DON'T LIKE TO TRAVEL.
...LOVE AT FIRST SIGHT, PERHAPS.
SERI-OUS-LY!?
I WAS KIDDING.

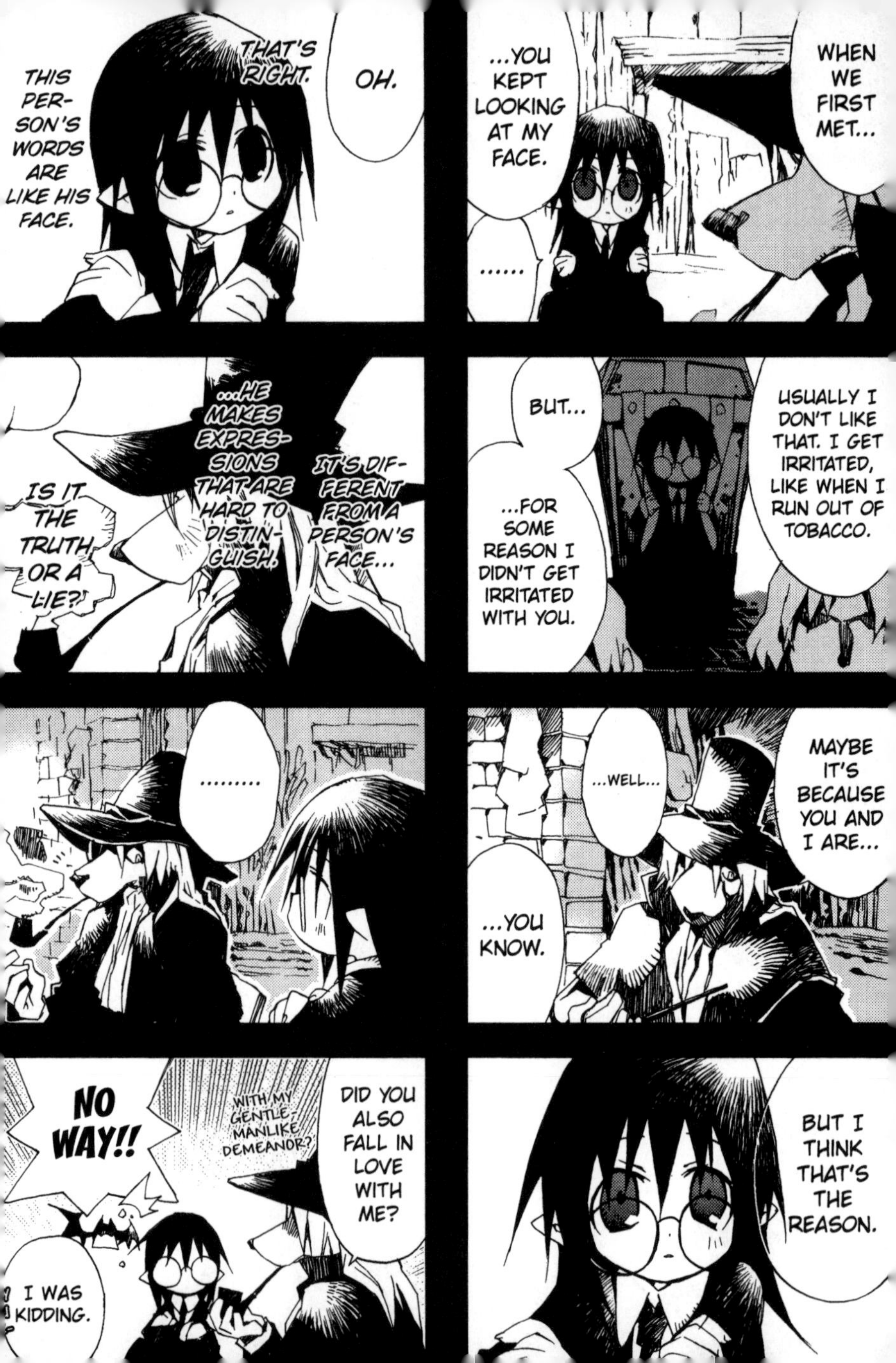
WHEN WE FIRST MET...
...YOU KEPT LOOKING AT MY FACE.
......
OH.
THAT'S RIGHT.
THIS PERSON'S WORDS ARE LIKE HIS FACE.
USUALLY I DON'T LIKE THAT. I GET IRRITATED, LIKE WHEN I RUN OUT OF TOBACCO.
BUT...
...FOR SOME REASON I DIDN'T GET IRRITATED WITH YOU.
IT'S DIFFERENT FROM A PERSON'S FACE...
...HE MAKES EXPRESSIONS THAT ARE HARD TO DISTINGUISH.
IS IT THE TRUTH OR A LIE?
MAYBE IT'S BECAUSE YOU AND I ARE...
...WELL...
...YOU KNOW.
....
BUT I THINK THAT'S THE REASON.
DID YOU ALSO FALL IN LOVE WITH ME?
WITH MY GENTLE, MANLIKE DEMEANOR?
NO WAY!!
I WAS KIDDING.

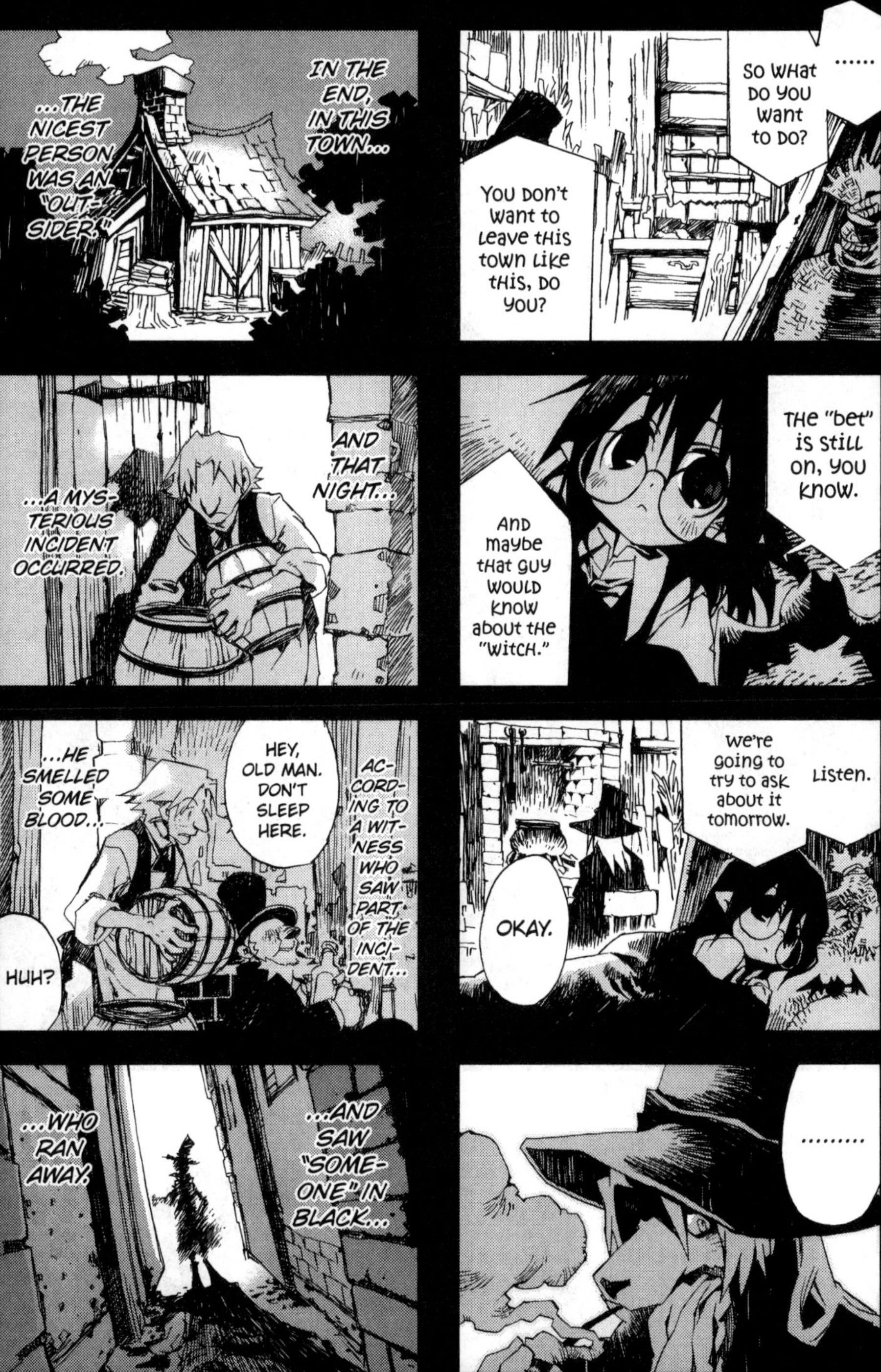
......
So what do you want to do?
You don't want to leave this town like this, do you?
IN THE END, IN THIS TOWN...
...THE NICEST PERSON WAS AN "OUTSIDER."
The "bet" is still on, you know.
And maybe that guy would know about the "witch."
AND THAT NIGHT...
...A MYSTERIOUS INCIDENT OCCURRED.
Listen.
We're going to try to ask about it tomorrow.
OKAY.
ACCORDING TO A WITNESS WHO SAW PART OF THE INCIDENT...
HEY, OLD MAN. DON'T SLEEP HERE.
...HE SMELLED SOME BLOOD...
HUH?
....
...AND SAW "SOMEONE" IN BLACK...
...WHO RAN AWAY.

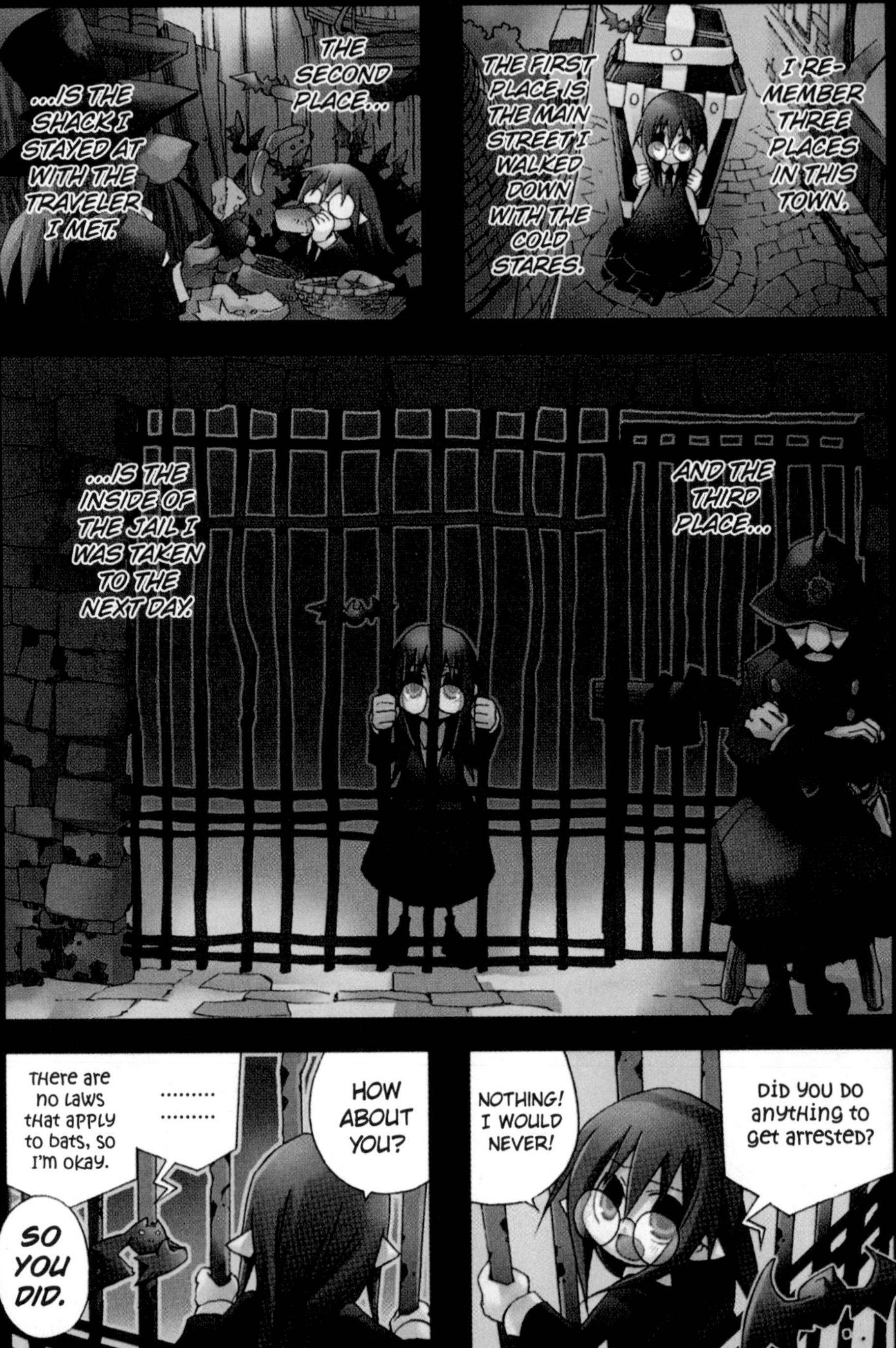
I RE-MEMBER THREE PLACES IN THIS TOWN.
THE FIRST PLACE IS THE MAIN STREET I WALKED DOWN WITH THE COLD STARES.
THE SECOND PLACE...
...IS THE SHACK I STAYED AT WITH THE TRAVELER I MET.
AND THE THIRD PLACE...
...IS THE INSIDE OF THE JAIL I WAS TAKEN TO THE NEXT DAY.
DID YOU DO anything to get arrested?
NOTHING! I WOULD NEVER!
HOW ABOUT YOU?
....
There are no laws that apply to bats, so I'm okay.
SO YOU DID.

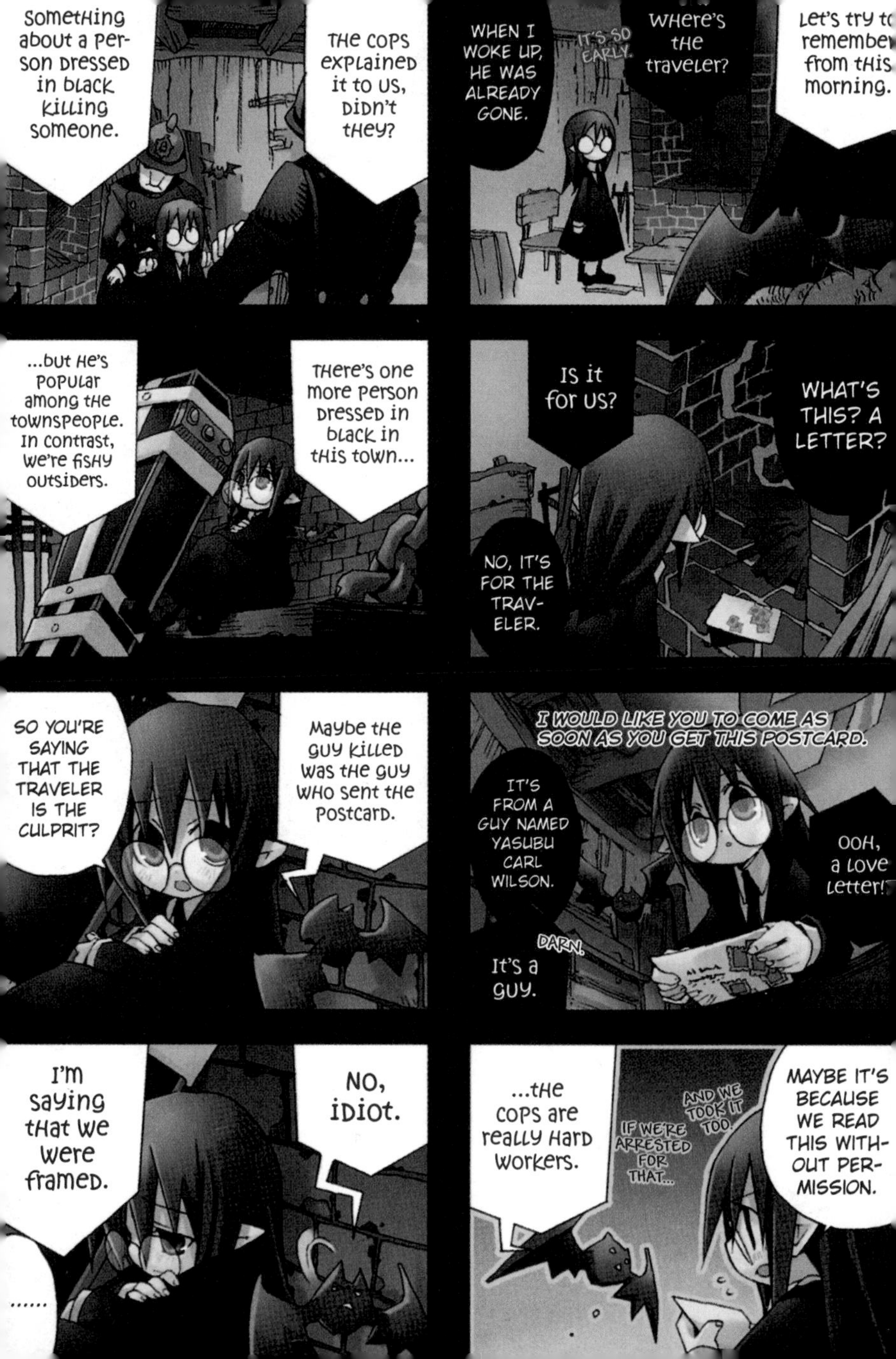
Let's try to remembe from this morning.
Where's the traveler?
IT'S SO EARLY.
WHEN I WOKE UP, HE WAS ALREADY GONE.
The cops explained it to us, didn't they?
Something about a person dressed in black killing someone.
WHAT'S THIS? A LETTER?
Is it for us?
NO, IT'S FOR THE TRAVELER.
There's one more person dressed in black in this town...
...but he's popular among the townspeople. In contrast, we're fishy outsiders.
I WOULD LIKE YOU TO COME AS SOON AS YOU GET THIS POSTCARD.
Ooh, a love letter!
IT'S FROM A GUY NAMED YASUBU CARL WILSON.
DARN.
It's a guy.
Maybe the guy killed was the guy who sent the postcard.
SO YOU'RE SAYING THAT THE TRAVELER IS THE CULPRIT?
MAYBE IT'S BECAUSE WE READ THIS WITHOUT PERMISSION.
AND WE TOOK IT TOO.
IF WE'RE ARRESTED FOR THAT...
...the cops are really hard workers.
NO, idiot.
I'm saying that we were framed.
......

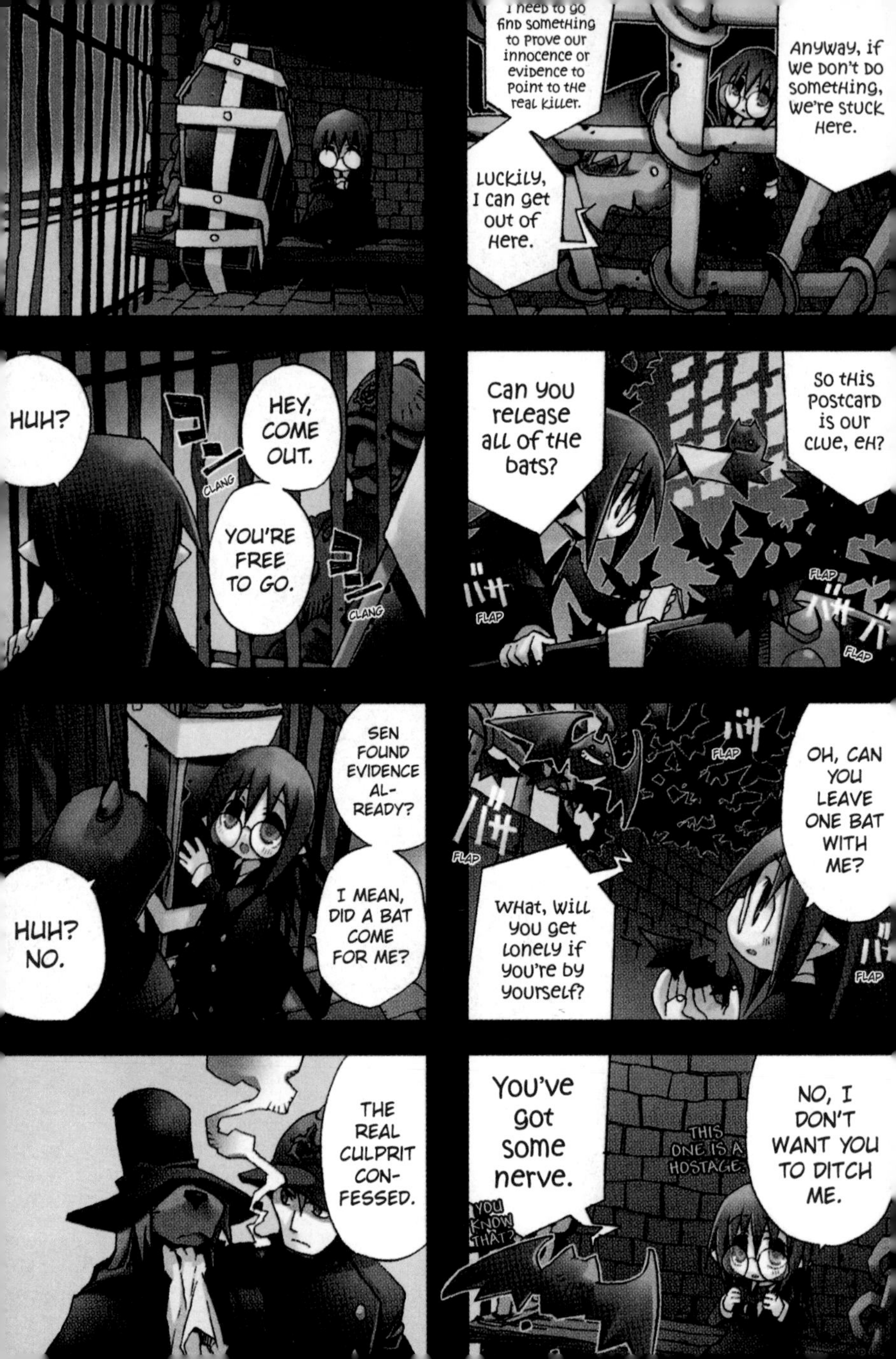
Anyway, if we don't do something, we're stuck here.
I need to go find something to prove our innocence or evidence to point to the real killer.
Luckily, I can get out of here.
So this postcard is our clue, eh?
Can you release all of the bats?
FLAP
FLAP
FLAP
HEY, COME OUT.
YOU'RE FREE TO GO.
CLANG
CLANG
HUH?
OH, CAN YOU LEAVE ONE BAT WITH ME?
FLAP
FLAP
What, will you get lonely if you're by yourself?
FLAP
SEN FOUND EVIDENCE AL-READY?
I MEAN, DID A BAT COME FOR ME?
HUH? NO.
NO, I DON'T WANT YOU TO DITCH ME.
THIS ONE IS A HOSTAGE.
You've got some nerve.
YOU KNOW THAT?
THE REAL CULPRIT CON-FESSED.

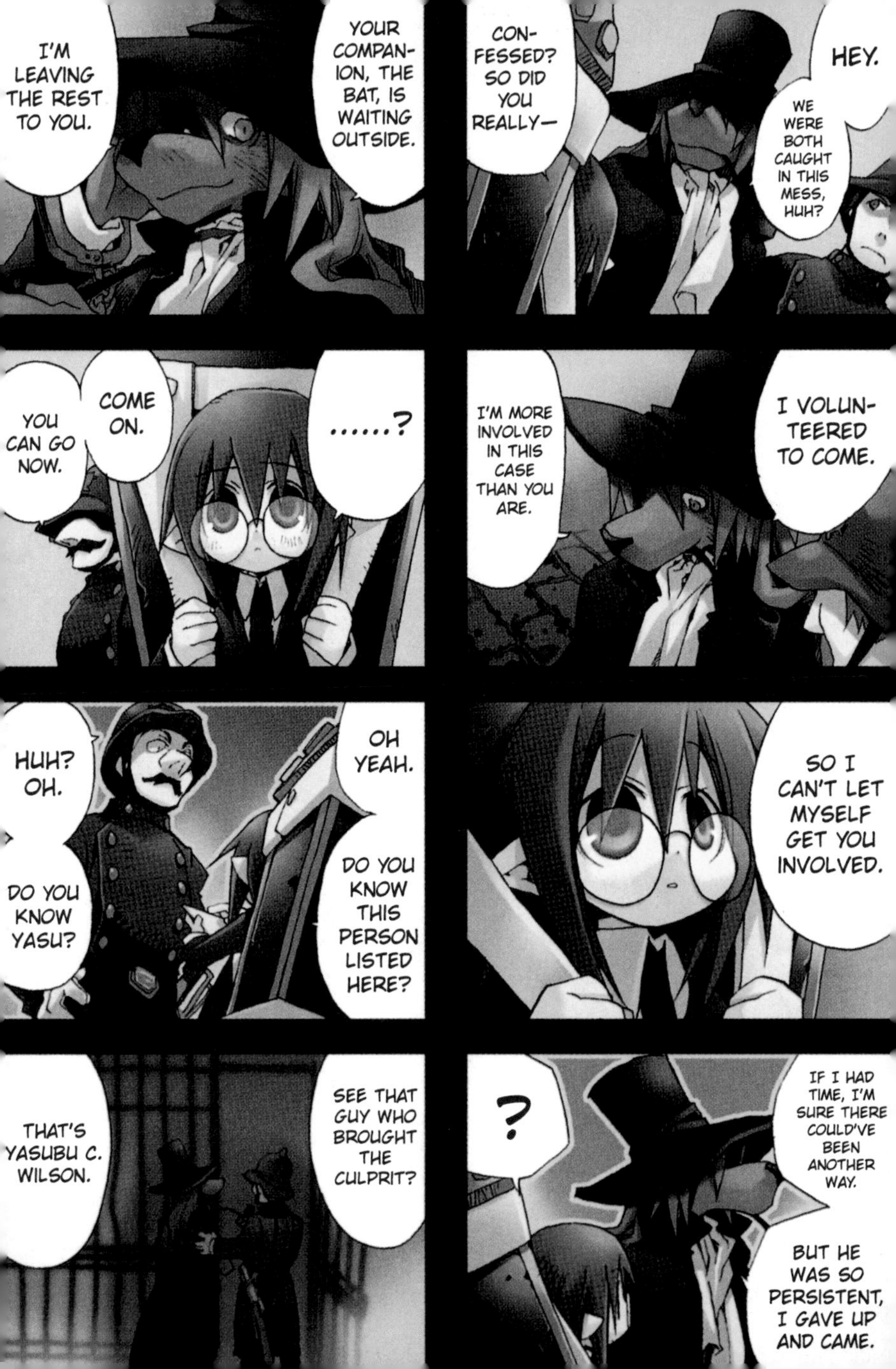
HEY.
WE WERE BOTH CAUGHT IN THIS MESS, HUH?
CONFESSED? SO DID YOU REALLY—
YOUR COMPANION, THE BAT, IS WAITING OUTSIDE.
I'M LEAVING THE REST TO YOU.
I VOLUNTEERED TO COME.
I'M MORE INVOLVED IN THIS CASE THAN YOU ARE.
......?
COME ON.
YOU CAN GO NOW.
SO I CAN'T LET MYSELF GET YOU INVOLVED.
OH YEAH.
DO YOU KNOW THIS PERSON LISTED HERE?
HUH? OH.
DO YOU KNOW YASU?
IF I HAD TIME, I'M SURE THERE COULD'VE BEEN ANOTHER WAY.
?
BUT HE WAS SO PERSISTENT, I GAVE UP AND CAME.
SEE THAT GUY WHO BROUGHT THE CULPRIT?
THAT'S YASUBU C. WILSON.

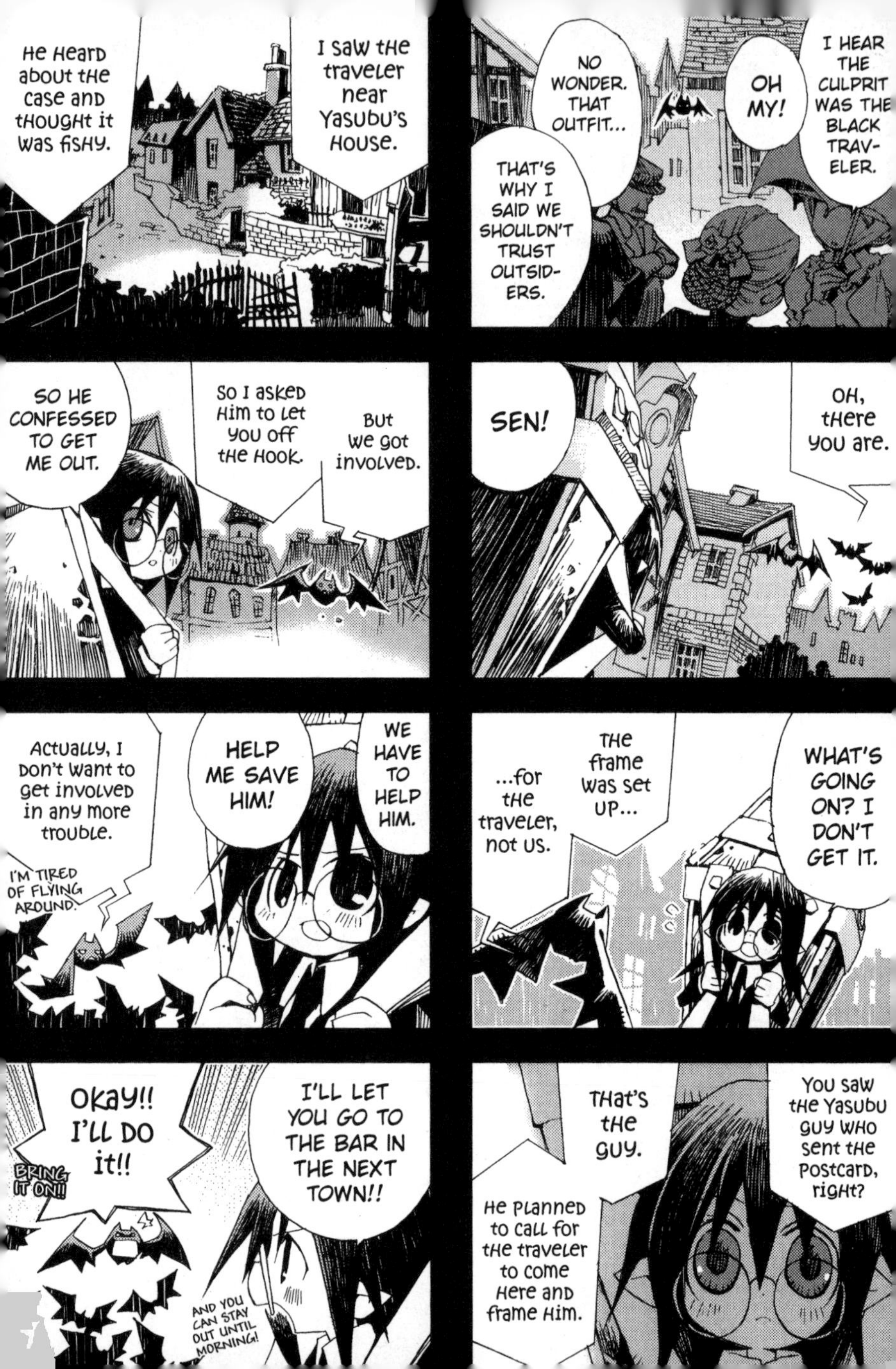
I HEAR THE CULPRIT WAS THE BLACK TRAVELER.
OH MY!
NO WONDER. THAT OUTFIT...
THAT'S WHY I SAID WE SHOULDN'T TRUST OUTSIDERS.
I saw the traveler near Yasubu's house.
He heard about the case and thought it was fishy.
Oh, there you are.
SEN!
SO HE CONFESSED TO GET ME OUT.
So I asked him to let you off the hook.
But we got involved.
WHAT'S GOING ON? I DON'T GET IT.
The frame was set up...
...for the traveler, not us.
WE HAVE TO HELP HIM.
HELP ME SAVE HIM!
Actually, I don't want to get involved in any more trouble.
I'M TIRED OF FLYING AROUND.
You saw the Yasubu guy who sent the postcard, right?
That's the guy.
He planned to call for the traveler to come here and frame him.
I'LL LET YOU GO TO THE BAR IN THE NEXT TOWN!!
AND YOU CAN STAY OUT UNTIL MORNING!
Okay!! I'll do it!!
BRING IT ON!!

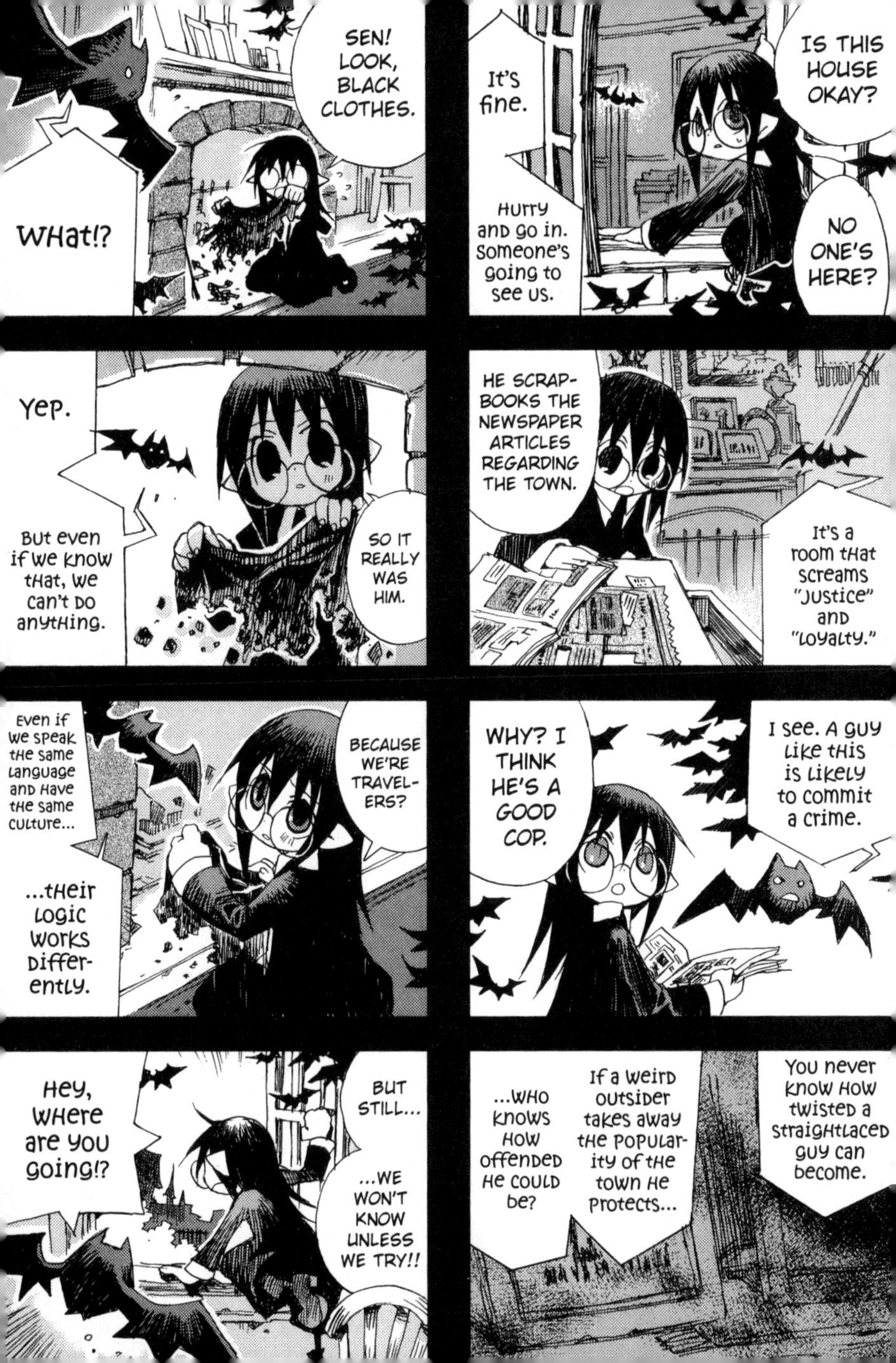

IS THIS HOUSE OKAY?
It's fine.
NO ONE'S HERE?
Hurry and go in. Someone's going to see us.
SEN! LOOK, BLACK CLOTHES.
WHAT!?
HE SCRAP-BOOKS THE NEWSPAPER ARTICLES REGARDING THE TOWN.
It's a room that screams "Justice" and "Loyalty."
SO IT REALLY WAS HIM.
Yep.
But even if we know that, we can't do anything.
I see. A guy like this is likely to commit a crime.
WHY? I THINK HE'S A GOOD COP.
BECAUSE WE'RE TRAVEL-ERS?
Even if we speak the same language and have the same culture...
...their logic works differ-ently.
You never know how twisted a straightlaced guy can become.
If a weird outsider takes away the popular-ity of the town he protects...
...who knows how offended he could be?
BUT STILL...
...WE WON'T KNOW UNLESS WE TRY!!
Hey, where are you going!?

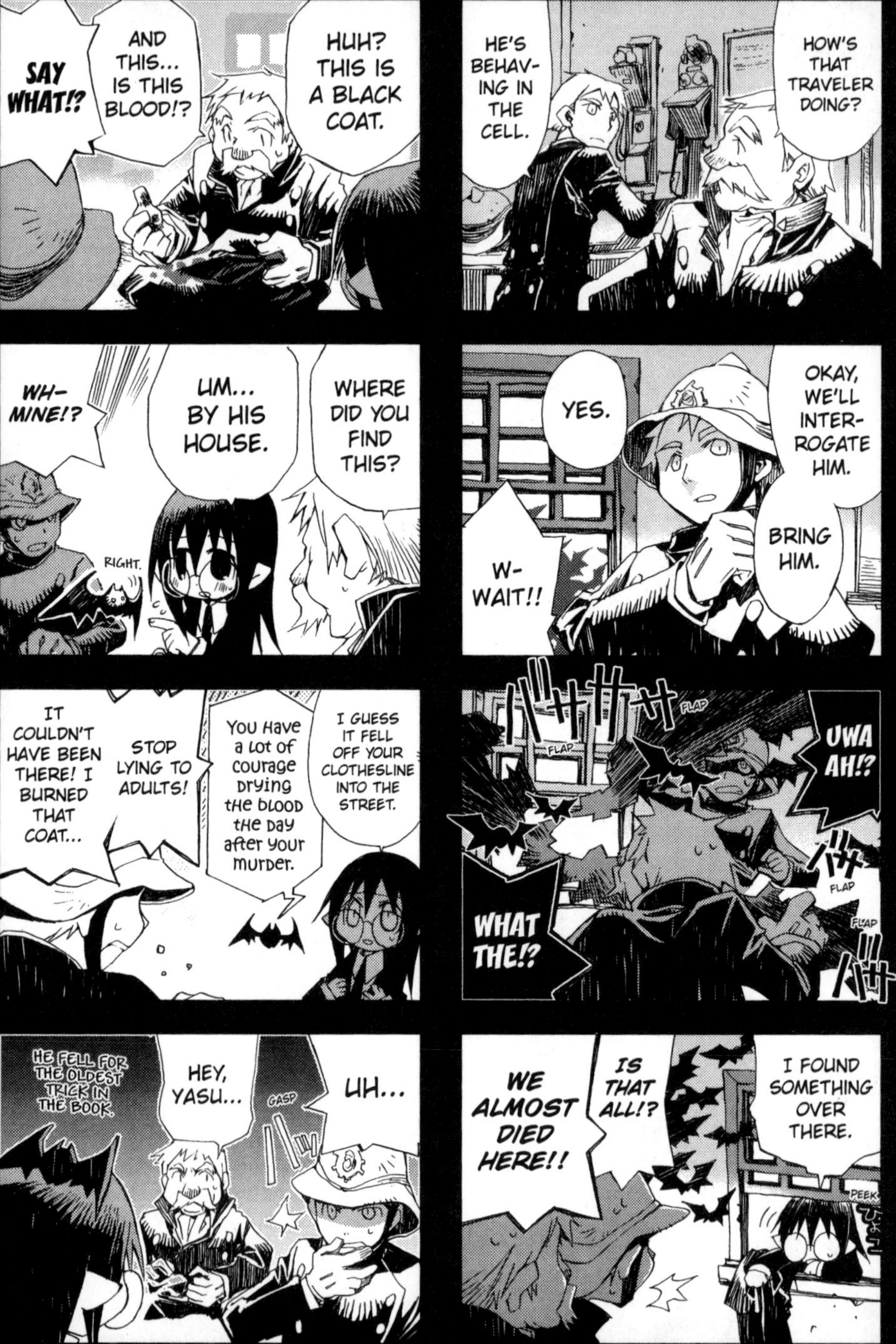
HOW'S THAT TRAVELER DOING?
HE'S BEHAV-ING IN THE CELL.
HUH? THIS IS A BLACK COAT.
AND THIS... IS THIS BLOOD!?
SAY WHAT!?
OKAY, WE'LL INTER-ROGATE HIM.
BRING HIM.
YES.
W- WAIT!!
WHERE DID YOU FIND THIS?
UM... BY HIS HOUSE.
WH- MINE!?
RIGHT.
UWA AH!?
FLAP
FLAP
FLAP
FLAP
WHAT THE!?
I GUESS IT FELL OFF YOUR CLOTHESLINE INTO THE STREET.
You Have a Lot of courage Drying the bLood the Day after your murder.
STOP LYING TO ADULTS!
IT COULDN'T HAVE BEEN THERE! I BURNED THAT COAT...
I FOUND SOMETHING OVER THERE.
IS THAT ALL!?
WE ALMOST DIED HERE!!
PEEK
UH...
GASP
HEY, YASU...
HE FELL FOR THE OLDEST TRICK IN THE BOOK.

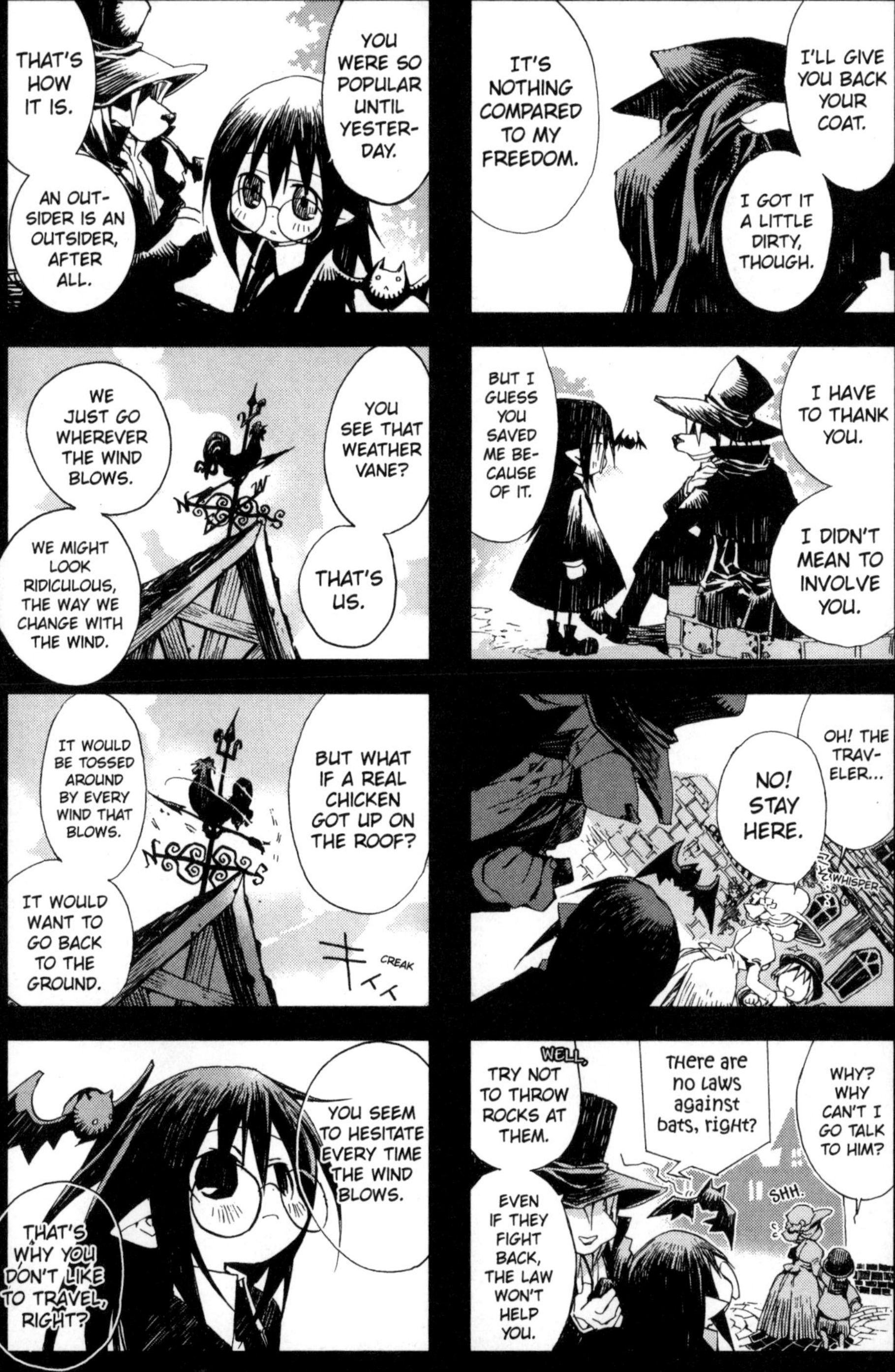
I'LL GIVE YOU BACK YOUR COAT.
I GOT IT A LITTLE DIRTY, THOUGH.
IT'S NOTHING COMPARED TO MY FREEDOM.
YOU WERE SO POPULAR UNTIL YESTERDAY.
THAT'S HOW IT IS.
AN OUTSIDER IS AN OUTSIDER, AFTER ALL.
I HAVE TO THANK YOU.
I DIDN'T MEAN TO INVOLVE YOU.
BUT I GUESS YOU SAVED ME BECAUSE OF IT.
YOU SEE THAT WEATHER VANE?
THAT'S US.
WE JUST GO WHEREVER THE WIND BLOWS.
WE MIGHT LOOK RIDICULOUS, THE WAY WE CHANGE WITH THE WIND.
OH! THE TRAVELER...
NO! STAY HERE.
WHISPER
BUT WHAT IF A REAL CHICKEN GOT UP ON THE ROOF?
IT WOULD BE TOSSED AROUND BY EVERY WIND THAT BLOWS.
IT WOULD WANT TO GO BACK TO THE GROUND.
CREAK
WHY? WHY CAN'T I GO TALK TO HIM?
SHH.
There are no laws against bats, right?
WELL, TRY NOT TO THROW ROCKS AT THEM.
EVEN IF THEY FIGHT BACK, THE LAW WON'T HELP YOU.
YOU SEEM TO HESITATE EVERY TIME THE WIND BLOWS.
THAT'S WHY YOU DON'T LIKE TO TRAVEL, RIGHT?

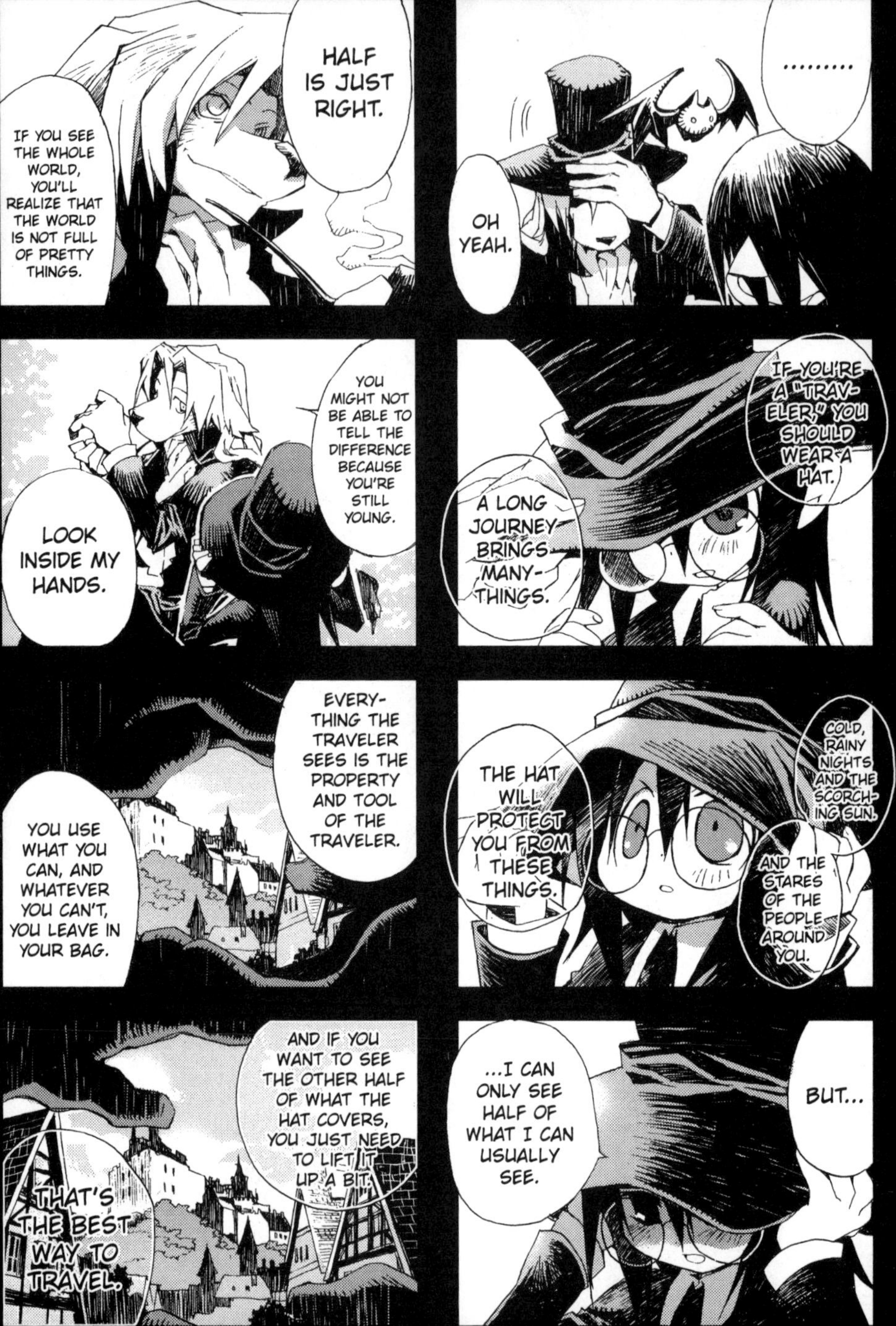
....
OH YEAH.
HALF IS JUST RIGHT.
IF YOU SEE THE WHOLE WORLD, YOU'LL REALIZE THAT THE WORLD IS NOT FULL OF PRETTY THINGS.
IF YOU'RE A "TRAVELER," YOU SHOULD WEAR A HAT.
A LONG JOURNEY BRINGS MANY THINGS.
YOU MIGHT NOT BE ABLE TO TELL THE DIFFERENCE BECAUSE YOU'RE STILL YOUNG.
LOOK INSIDE MY HANDS.
COLD, RAINY NIGHTS AND THE SCORCHING SUN.
AND THE STARES OF THE PEOPLE AROUND YOU.
THE HAT WILL PROTECT YOU FROM THESE THINGS.
EVERYTHING THE TRAVELER SEES IS THE PROPERTY AND TOOL OF THE TRAVELER.
YOU USE WHAT YOU CAN, AND WHATEVER YOU CAN'T, YOU LEAVE IN YOUR BAG.
BUT...
...I CAN ONLY SEE HALF OF WHAT I CAN USUALLY SEE.
AND IF YOU WANT TO SEE THE OTHER HALF OF WHAT THE HAT COVERS, YOU JUST NEED TO LIFT IT UP A BIT.
THAT'S THE BEST WAY TO TRAVEL.

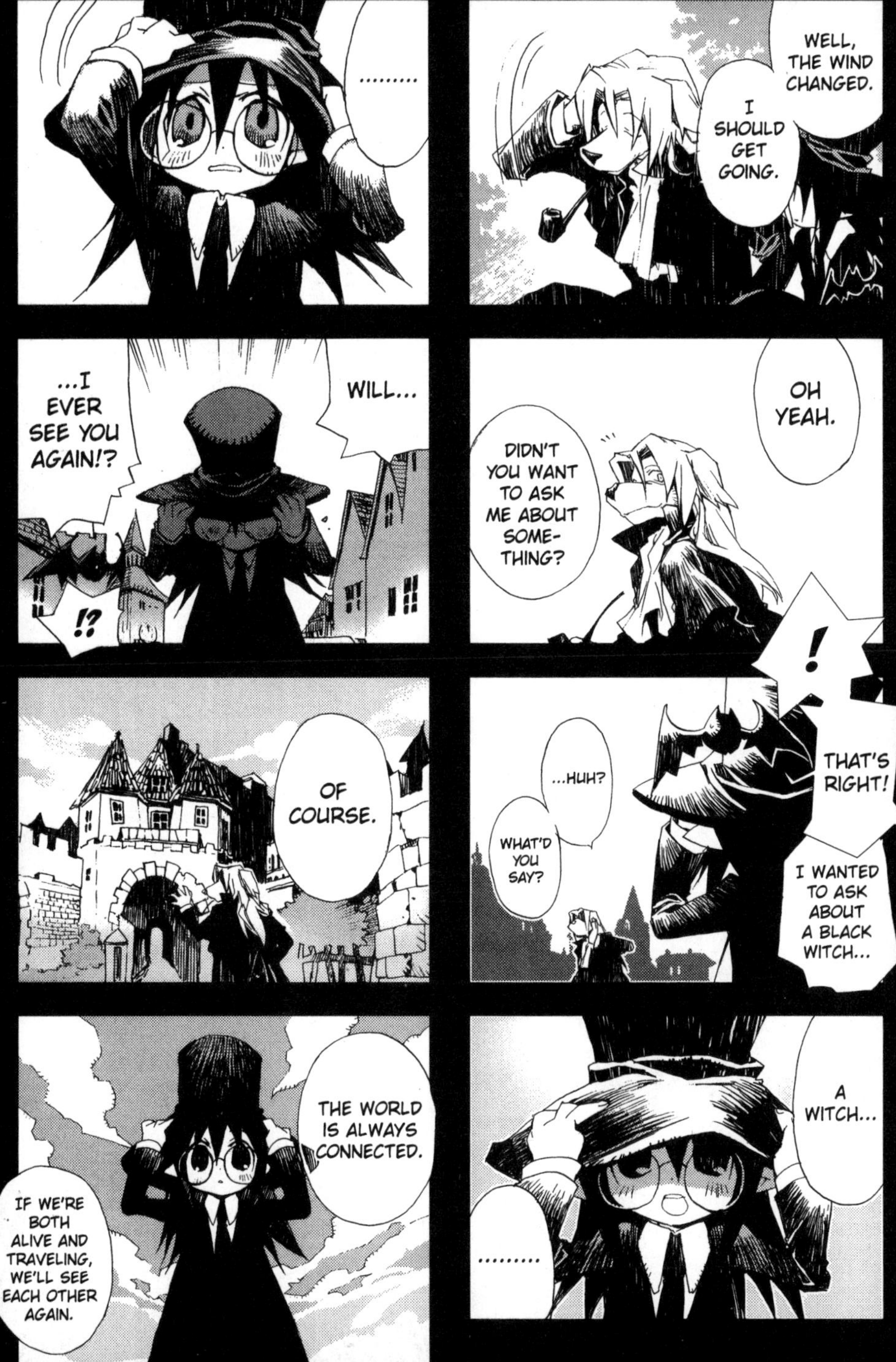
WELL, THE WIND CHANGED.
I SHOULD GET GOING.
....
OH YEAH.
DIDN'T YOU WANT TO ASK ME ABOUT SOME-THING?
WILL...
...I EVER SEE YOU AGAIN!?
!?
!
THAT'S RIGHT!
I WANTED TO ASK ABOUT A BLACK WITCH...
...HUH?
WHAT'D YOU SAY?
OF COURSE.
A WITCH...
....
THE WORLD IS ALWAYS CONNECTED.
IF WE'RE BOTH ALIVE AND TRAVELING, WE'LL SEE EACH OTHER AGAIN.

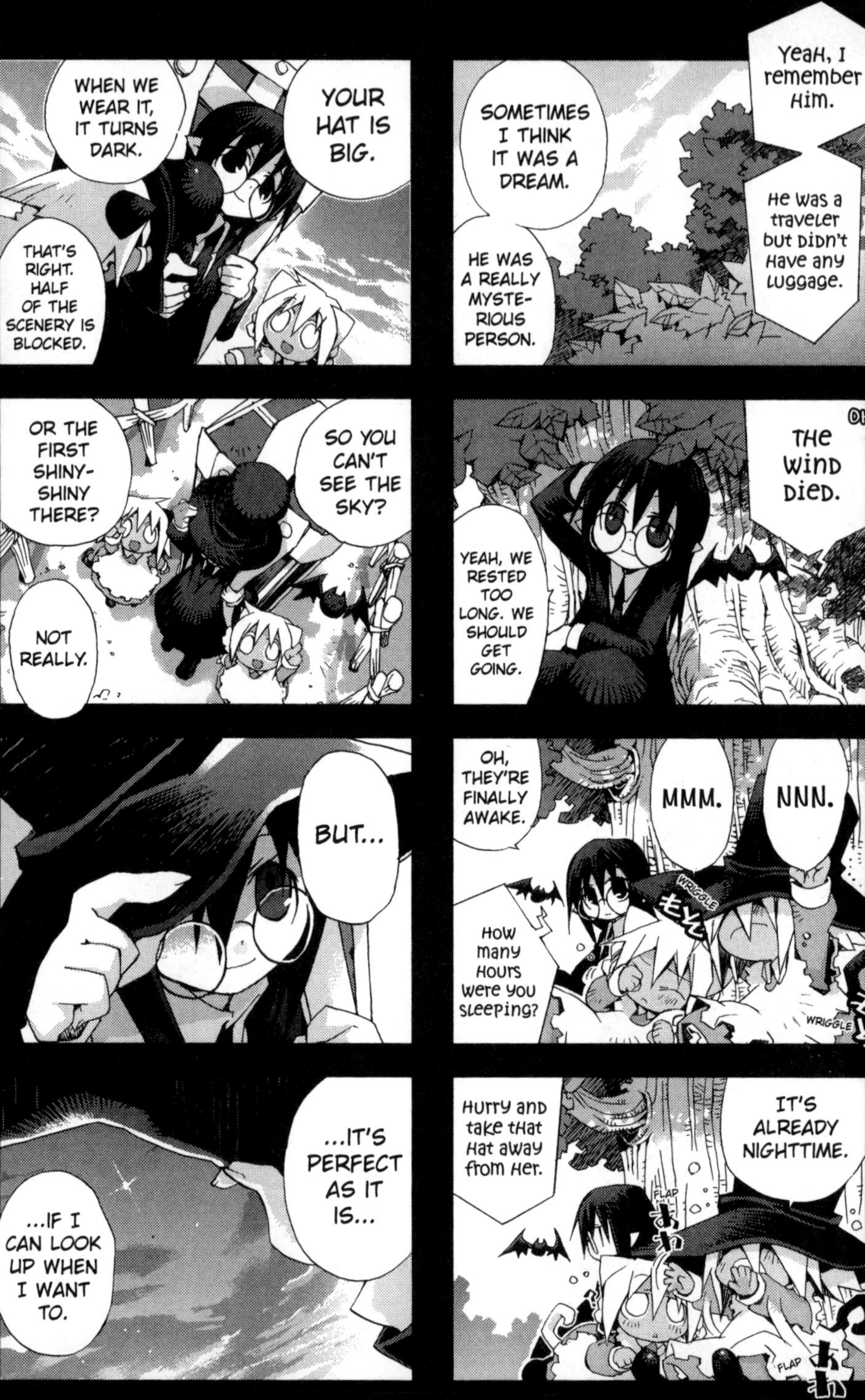
Yeah, I remember him.
He was a traveler but didn't have any luggage.
SOMETIMES I THINK IT WAS A DREAM.
HE WAS A REALLY MYSTE-RIOUS PERSON.
YOUR HAT IS BIG.
WHEN WE WEAR IT, IT TURNS DARK.
THAT'S RIGHT. HALF OF THE SCENERY IS BLOCKED.
The wind died.
YEAH, WE RESTED TOO LONG. WE SHOULD GET GOING.
SO YOU CAN'T SEE THE SKY?
OR THE FIRST SHINY-SHINY THERE?
NOT REALLY.
NNN.
MMM.
OH, THEY'RE FINALLY AWAKE.
WRIGGLE
How many hours were you sleeping?
WRIGGLE
BUT...
IT'S ALREADY NIGHTTIME.
Hurry and take that hat away from her.
FLAP
FLAP
...IT'S PERFECT AS IT IS...
...IF I CAN LOOK UP WHEN I WANT TO.

....

WHO IS THIS?

HERE'S A RIDDLE.

DIDN'T YOU JUST LOOK AT ME?

THAT'S easy. THE answer is, a pen.

HE JUST LEAVES HIS FOOTPRINTS ON WHITE GROUND.

HE'S A BLACK TRAVELER WHO DOESN'T TALK.

WHO ARE WE TALKING ABOUT?

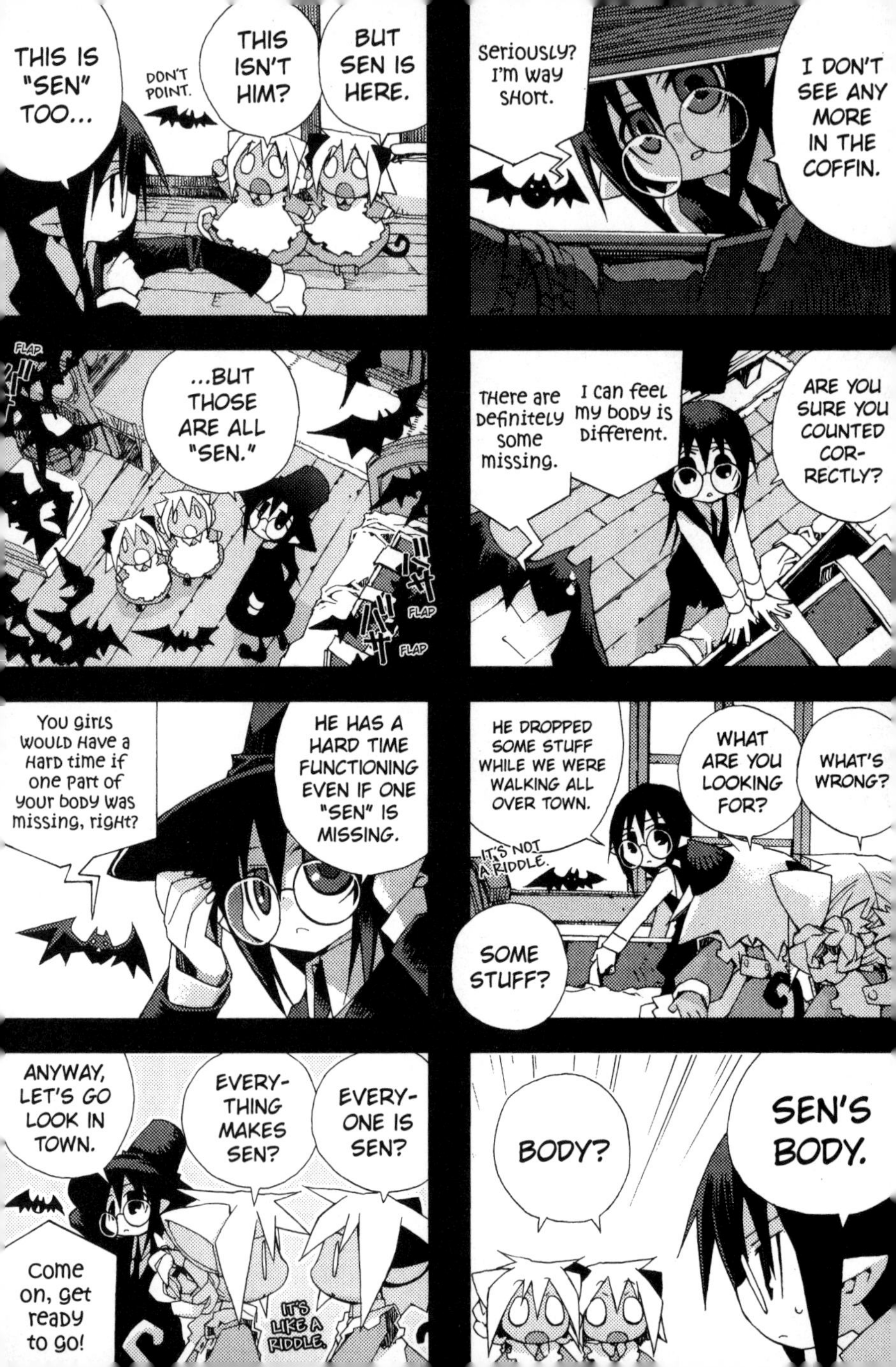
I DON'T SEE ANY MORE IN THE COFFIN.
Seriously? I'm way short.
BUT SEN IS HERE.
THIS ISN'T HIM?
DON'T POINT.
THIS IS "SEN" TOO...
ARE YOU SURE YOU COUNTED COR-RECTLY?
I can feel my body is different.
There are definitely some missing.
...BUT THOSE ARE ALL "SEN."
FLAP
FLAP
FLAP
WHAT'S WRONG?
WHAT ARE YOU LOOKING FOR?
HE DROPPED SOME STUFF WHILE WE WERE WALKING ALL OVER TOWN.
IT'S NOT A RIDDLE.
SOME STUFF?
HE HAS A HARD TIME FUNCTIONING EVEN IF ONE "SEN" IS MISSING.
You girls would have a hard time if one part of your body was missing, right?
SEN'S BODY.
BODY?
EVERY-ONE IS SEN?
EVERY-THING MAKES SEN?
ANYWAY, LET'S GO LOOK IN TOWN.
IT'S LIKE A RIDDLE.
Come on, get ready to go!

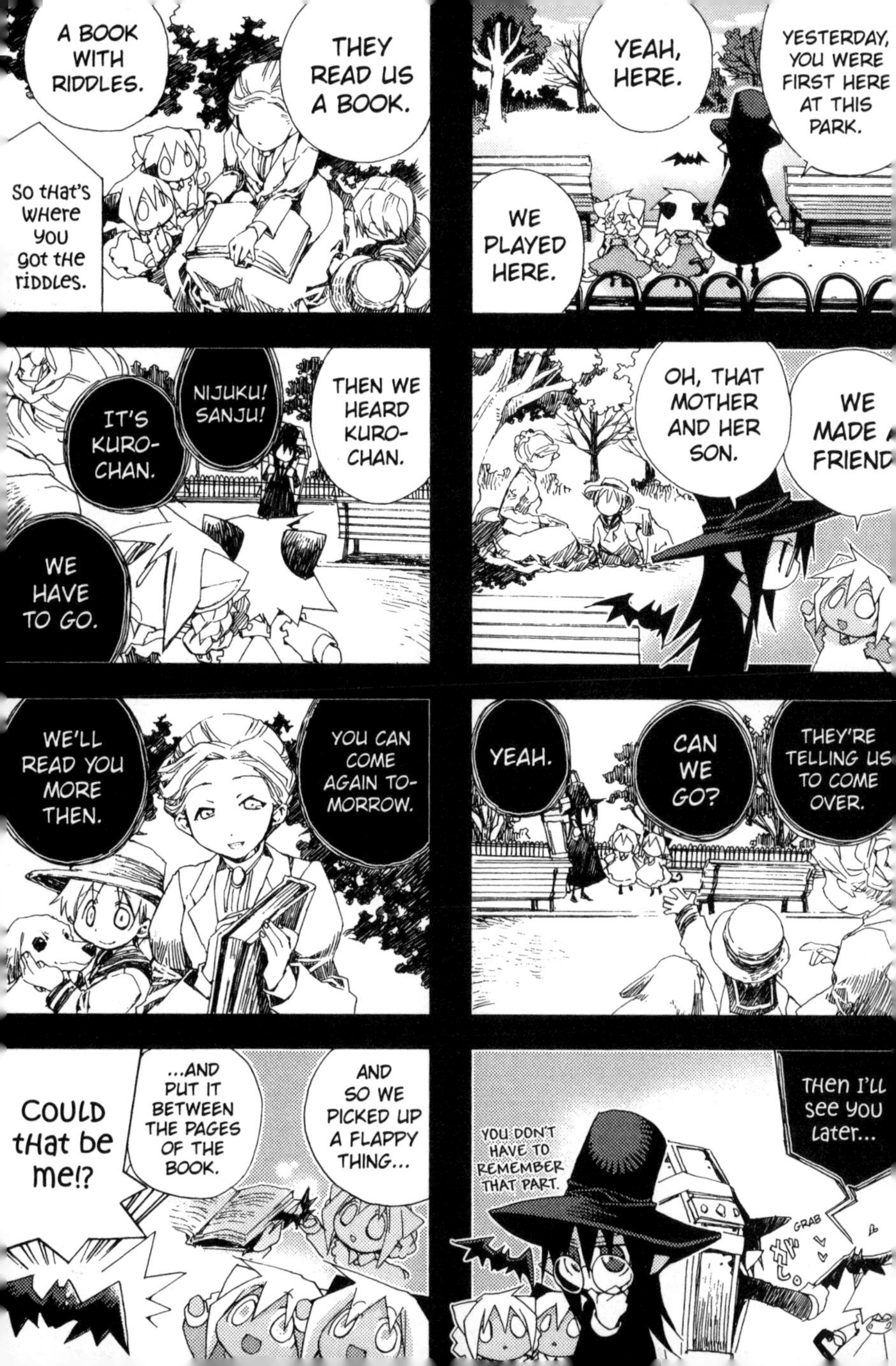

YESTERDAY, YOU WERE FIRST HERE AT THIS PARK.
YEAH, HERE.
WE PLAYED HERE.
WE MADE A FRIEND
OH, THAT MOTHER AND HER SON.
THEY'RE TELLING US TO COME OVER.
CAN WE GO?
YEAH.
Then I'll see you later...
YOU DON'T HAVE TO REMEMBER THAT PART.
GRAB
THEY READ US A BOOK.
A BOOK WITH RIDDLES.
So that's where you got the riddles.
THEN WE HEARD KURO-CHAN.
NIJUKU! SANJU!
IT'S KURO-CHAN.
WE HAVE TO GO.
YOU CAN COME AGAIN TO-MORROW.
WE'LL READ YOU MORE THEN.
AND SO WE PICKED UP A FLAPPY THING...
...AND PUT IT BETWEEN THE PAGES OF THE BOOK.
COULD that be me!?

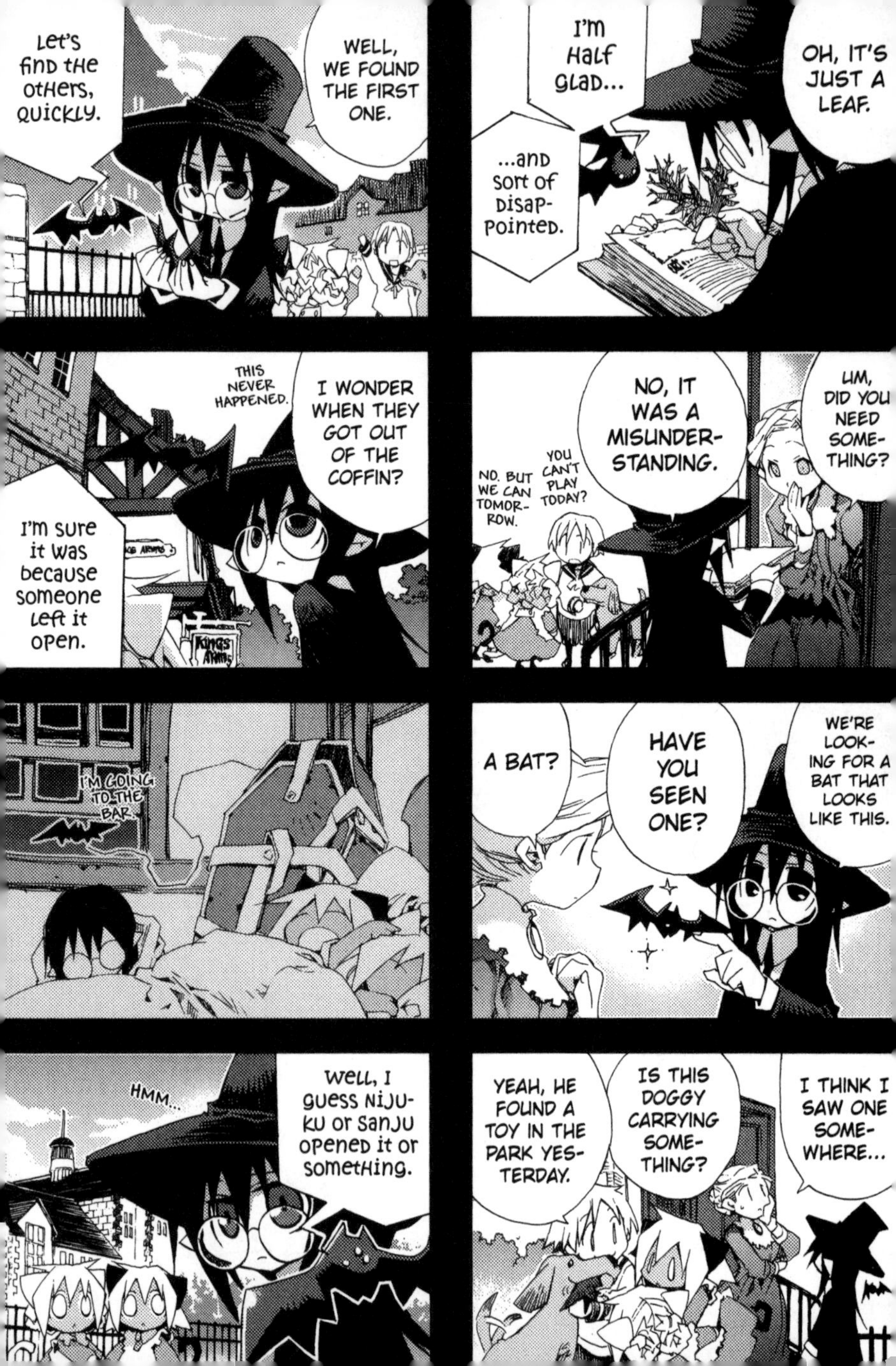

OH, IT'S JUST A LEAF.
I'M HALF GLAD...
...AND SORT OF DISAP-POINTED.
UM, DID YOU NEED SOME-THING?
NO, IT WAS A MISUNDER-STANDING.
YOU CAN'T PLAY TODAY?
NO. BUT WE CAN TOMOR-ROW.
WE'RE LOOK-ING FOR A BAT THAT LOOKS LIKE THIS.
HAVE YOU SEEN ONE?
A BAT?
I THINK I SAW ONE SOME-WHERE...
IS THIS DOGGY CARRYING SOME-THING?
YEAH, HE FOUND A TOY IN THE PARK YES-TERDAY.
WELL, WE FOUND THE FIRST ONE.
LET'S FIND THE OTHERS, QUICKLY.
I WONDER WHEN THEY GOT OUT OF THE COFFIN?
THIS NEVER HAPPENED.
I'M SURE IT WAS BECAUSE SOMEONE LEFT IT OPEN.
KINGS ARMS
I'M GOING TO THE BAR.
WELL, I GUESS NIJU-KU OR SANJU OPENED IT OR SOMETHING.
HMM...

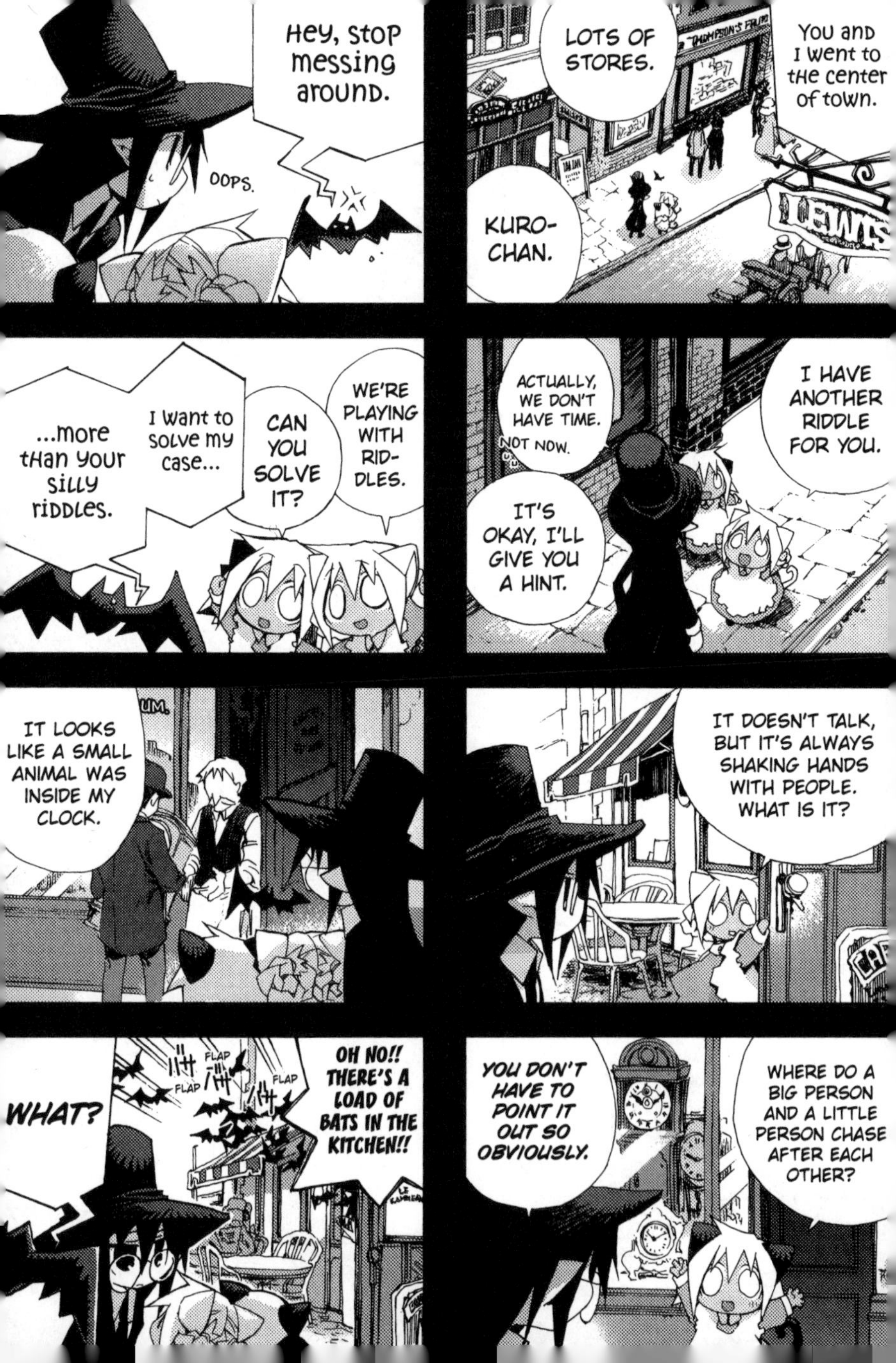
You and I went to the center of town.
LOTS OF STORES.
KURO-CHAN.
Hey, stop messing around.
OOPS.
I HAVE ANOTHER RIDDLE FOR YOU.
ACTUALLY, WE DON'T HAVE TIME.
NOT NOW.
IT'S OKAY, I'LL GIVE YOU A HINT.
WE'RE PLAYING WITH RID-DLES.
CAN YOU SOLVE IT?
I want to solve my case...
...more than your silly riddles.
IT DOESN'T TALK, BUT IT'S ALWAYS SHAKING HANDS WITH PEOPLE. WHAT IS IT?
IT LOOKS LIKE A SMALL ANIMAL WAS INSIDE MY CLOCK.
WHERE DO A BIG PERSON AND A LITTLE PERSON CHASE AFTER EACH OTHER?
YOU DON'T HAVE TO POINT IT OUT SO OBVIOUSLY.
OH NO!! THERE'S A LOAD OF BATS IN THE KITCHEN!!
FLAP
FLAP
FLAP
WHAT?

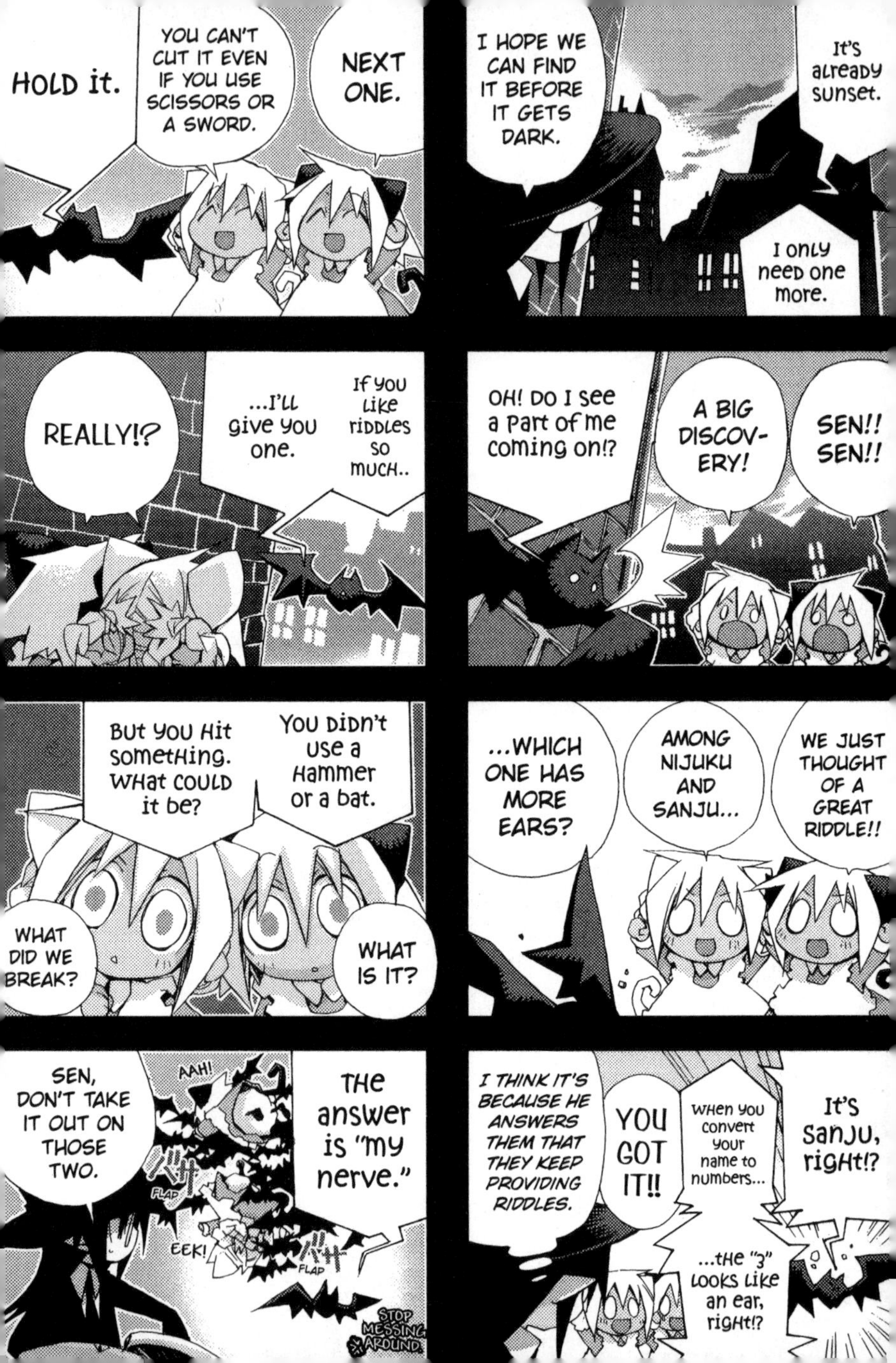
It's already sunset.
I HOPE WE CAN FIND IT BEFORE IT GETS DARK.
I only need one more.
NEXT ONE.
YOU CAN'T CUT IT EVEN IF YOU USE SCISSORS OR A SWORD.
HOLD it.
SEN!! SEN!!
A BIG DISCOV-ERY!
OH! DO I see a Part of me coming on!?
If you like riddles so much..
...I'll give you one.
REALLY!?
WE JUST THOUGHT OF A GREAT RIDDLE!!
AMONG NIJUKU AND SANJU...
...WHICH ONE HAS MORE EARS?
You didn't use a Hammer or a bat.
But you Hit something. What could it be?
WHAT IS IT?
WHAT DID WE BREAK?
It's sanju, right!?
When you convert your name to numbers...
YOU GOT IT!!
I THINK IT'S BECAUSE HE ANSWERS THEM THAT THEY KEEP PROVIDING RIDDLES.
...the "3" looks like an ear, right!?
The answer is "my nerve."
AAH!
FLAP
EEK!
FLAP
SEN, DON'T TAKE IT OUT ON THOSE TWO.
STOP MESSING AROUND.

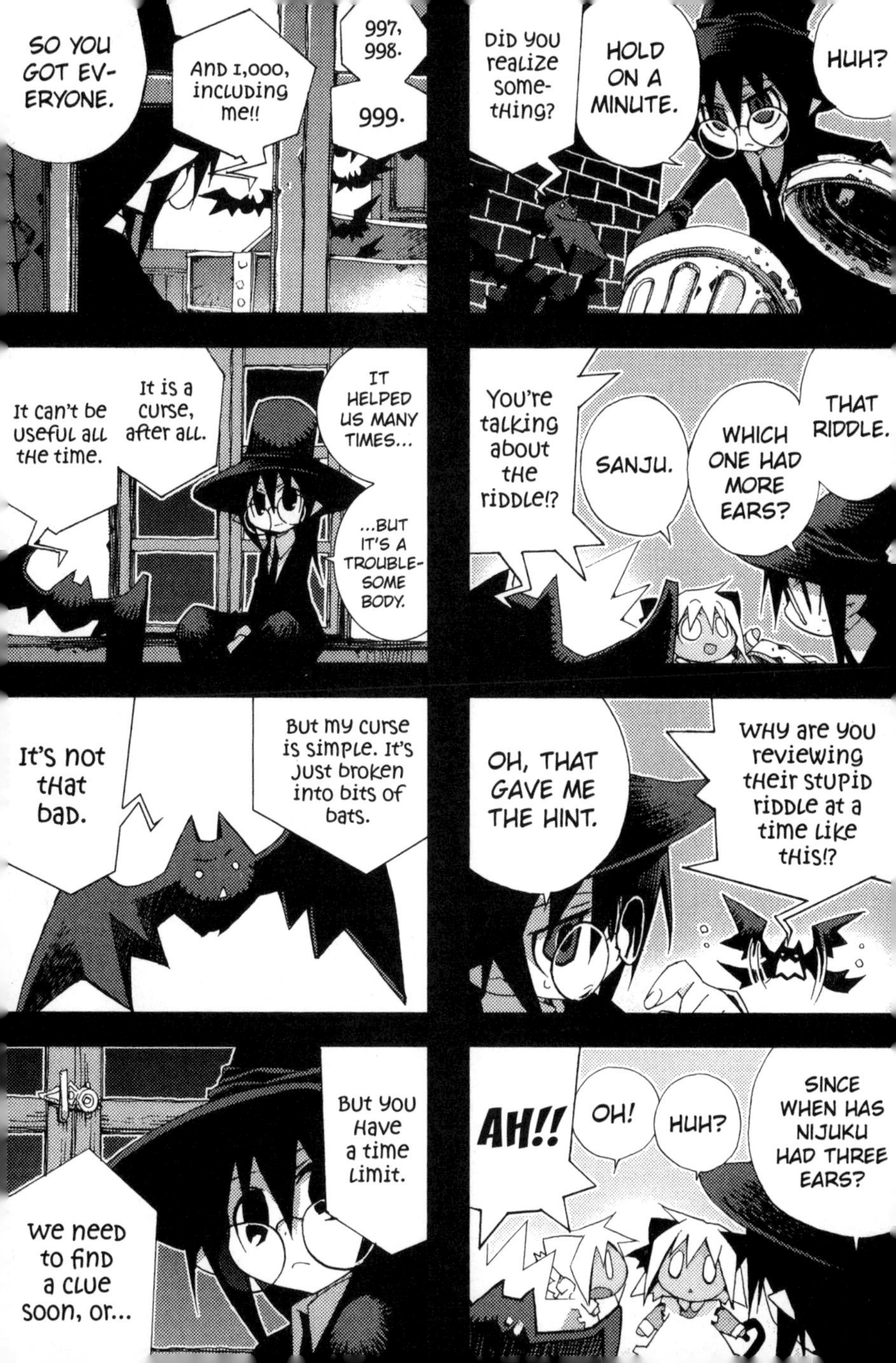
HUH?
HOLD ON A MINUTE.
DID YOU realize something?
997, 998.
999.
AND 1,000, including me!!
SO YOU GOT EVERYONE.
THAT RIDDLE.
WHICH ONE HAD MORE EARS?
SANJU.
You're talking about the riddle!?
IT HELPED US MANY TIMES...
...BUT IT'S A TROUBLESOME BODY.
It is a curse, after all.
It can't be useful all the time.
WHY are you reviewing their stupid riddle at a time like this!?
OH, THAT GAVE ME THE HINT.
But my curse is simple. It's just broken into bits of bats.
It's not that bad.
SINCE WHEN HAS NIJUKU HAD THREE EARS?
HUH?
OH!
AH!!
But you have a time limit.
We need to find a clue soon, or...

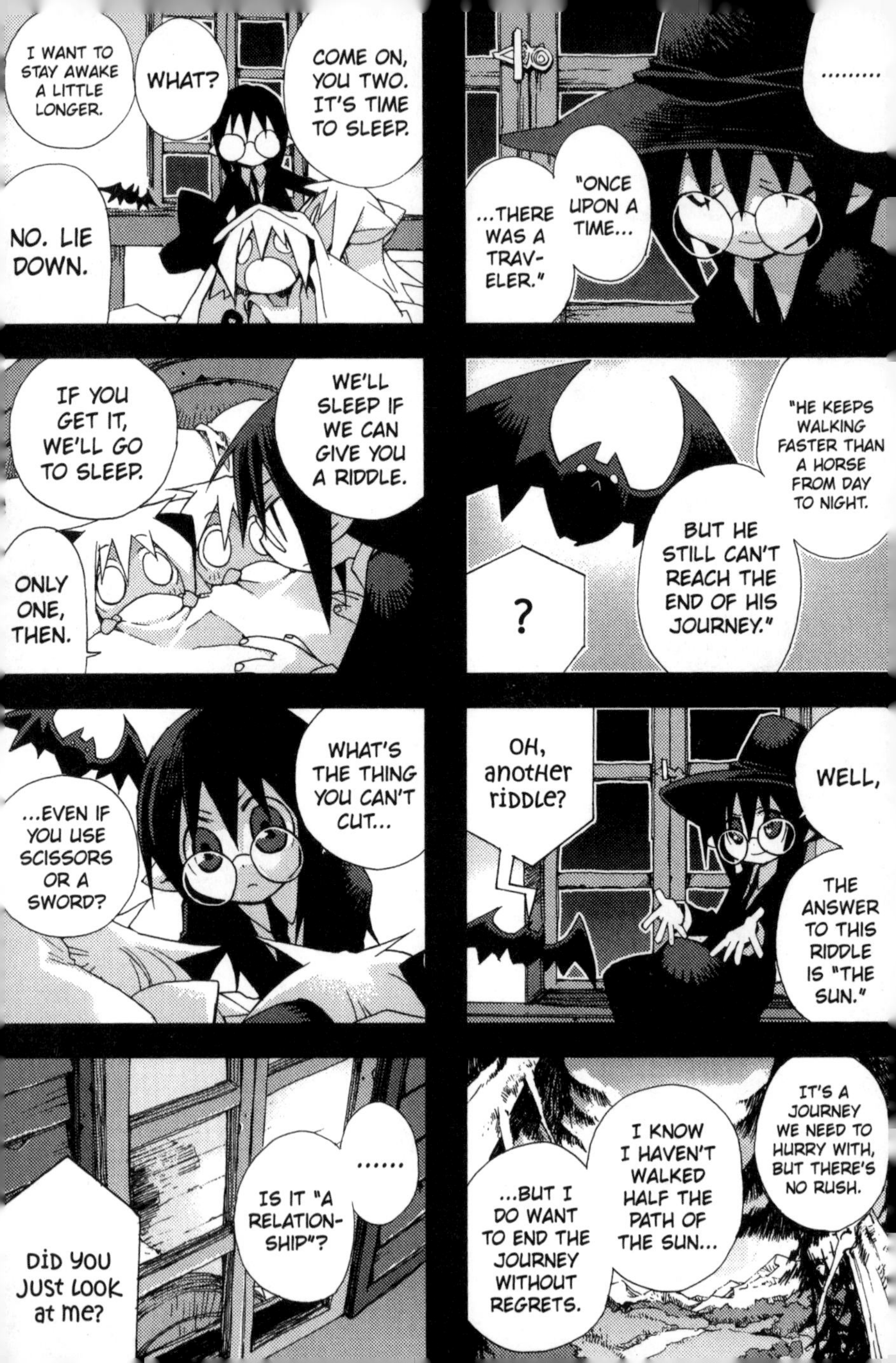
....
"ONCE UPON A TIME...
...THERE WAS A TRAVELER."
COME ON, YOU TWO. IT'S TIME TO SLEEP.
WHAT?
I WANT TO STAY AWAKE A LITTLE LONGER.
NO. LIE DOWN.
"HE KEEPS WALKING FASTER THAN A HORSE FROM DAY TO NIGHT.
BUT HE STILL CAN'T REACH THE END OF HIS JOURNEY."
?
WE'LL SLEEP IF WE CAN GIVE YOU A RIDDLE.
IF YOU GET IT, WE'LL GO TO SLEEP.
ONLY ONE, THEN.
WELL,
THE ANSWER TO THIS RIDDLE IS "THE SUN."
OH, another riddle?
WHAT'S THE THING YOU CAN'T CUT...
...EVEN IF YOU USE SCISSORS OR A SWORD?
IT'S A JOURNEY WE NEED TO HURRY WITH, BUT THERE'S NO RUSH.
I KNOW I HAVEN'T WALKED HALF THE PATH OF THE SUN...
...BUT I DO WANT TO END THE JOURNEY WITHOUT REGRETS.
......
IS IT "A RELATIONSHIP"?
DID YOU JUST LOOK at me?

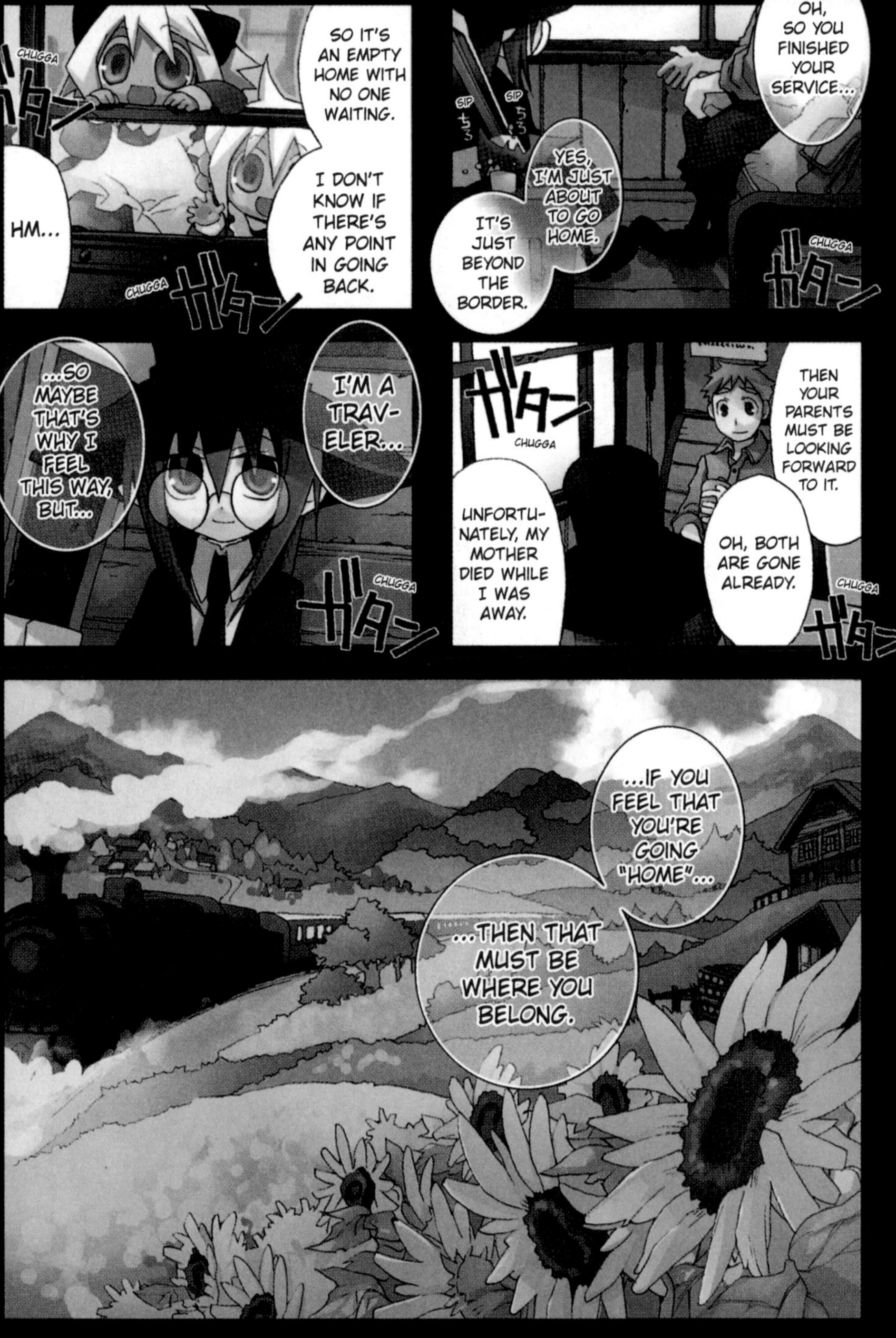
OH, SO YOU FINISHED YOUR SERVICE...
SIP
SIP
YES, I'M JUST ABOUT TO GO HOME.
IT'S JUST BEYOND THE BORDER.
CHUGGA
SO IT'S AN EMPTY HOME WITH NO ONE WAITING.
I DON'T KNOW IF THERE'S ANY POINT IN GOING BACK.
CHUGGA
HM...
CHUGGA
THEN YOUR PARENTS MUST BE LOOKING FORWARD TO IT.
OH, BOTH ARE GONE ALREADY.
CHUGGA
CHUGGA
UNFORTUNATELY, MY MOTHER DIED WHILE I WAS AWAY.
I'M A TRAVELER...
...SO MAYBE THAT'S WHY I FEEL THIS WAY, BUT...
CHUGGA
...IF YOU FEEL THAT YOU'RE GOING "HOME"...
...THEN THAT MUST BE WHERE YOU BELONG.

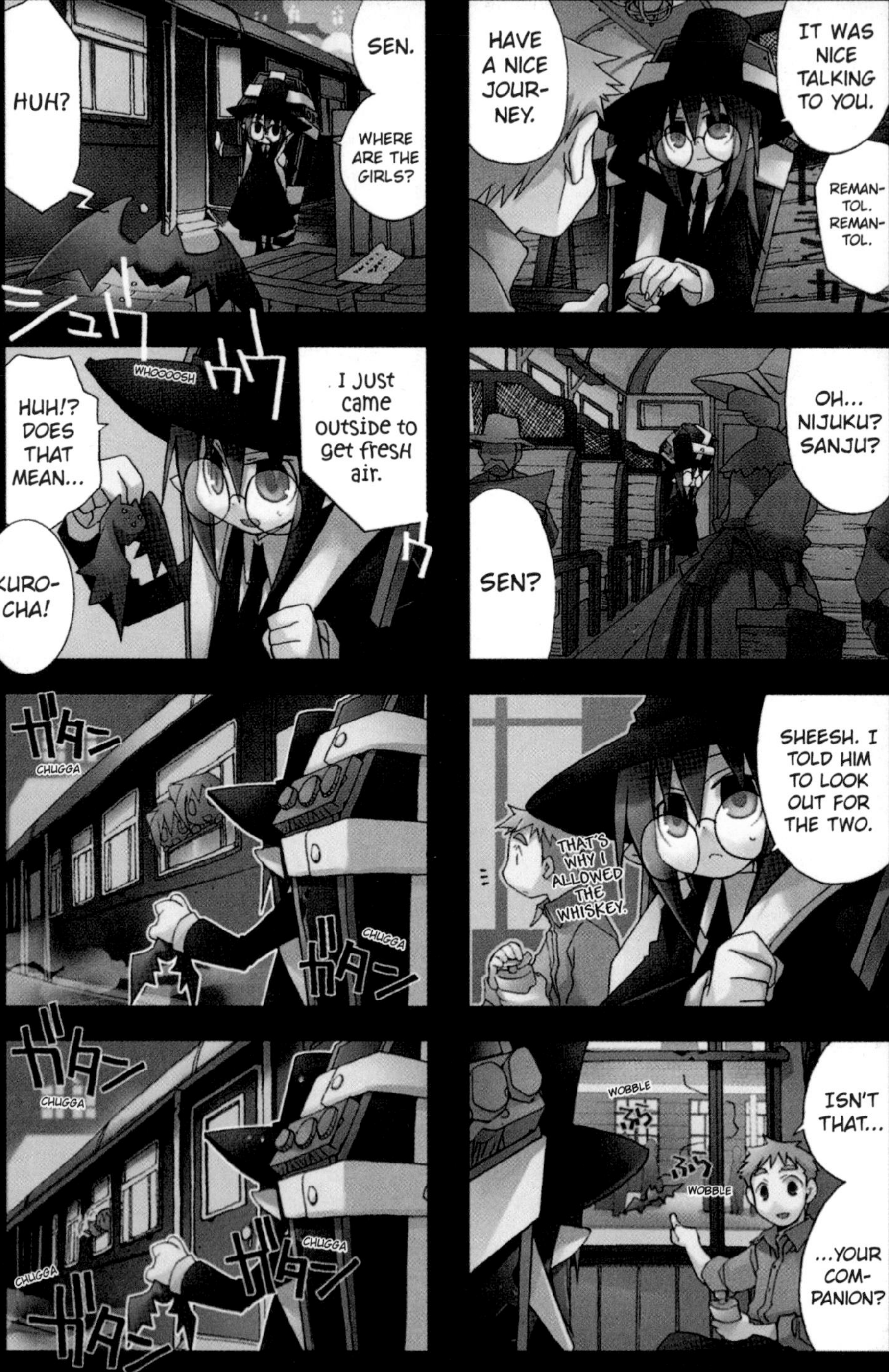
IT WAS NICE TALKING TO YOU.
HAVE A NICE JOURNEY.
REMANTOL. REMANTOL.
SEN.
WHERE ARE THE GIRLS?
HUH?
OH... NIJUKU? SANJU?
SEN?
I JUST came outside to get fresH air.
WHOOOOSH
HUH!? DOES THAT MEAN...
KURO-CHA!
SHEESH. I TOLD HIM TO LOOK OUT FOR THE TWO.
THAT'S WHY I ALLOWED THE WHISKEY.
CHUGGA
CHUGGA
ISN'T THAT...
WOBBLE
WOBBLE
...YOUR COMPANION?
CHUGGA
CHUGGA
CHUGGA

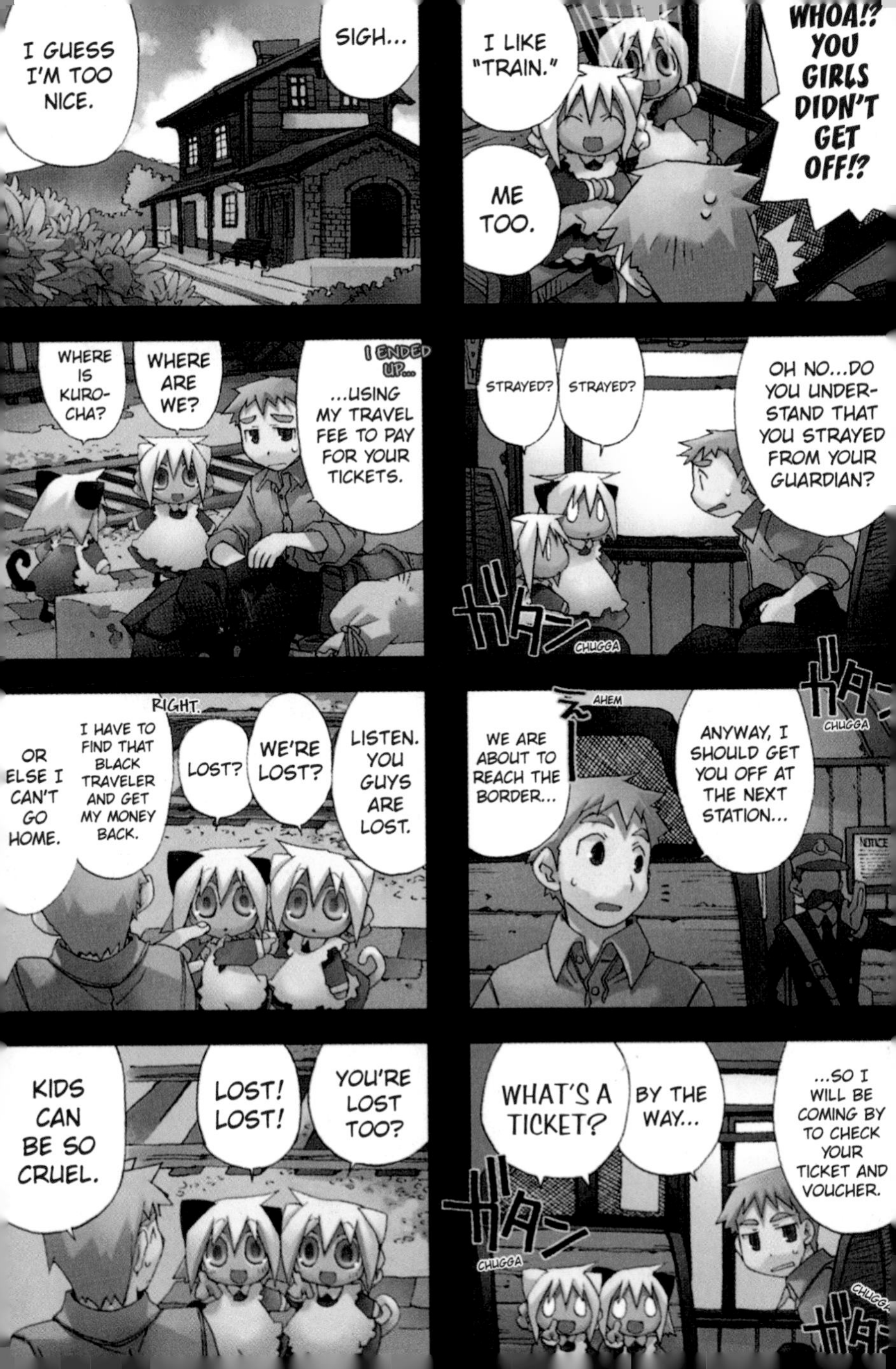
WHOA!? YOU GIRLS DIDN'T GET OFF!?
I LIKE "TRAIN."
ME TOO.
SIGH...
I GUESS I'M TOO NICE.
OH NO...DO YOU UNDERSTAND THAT YOU STRAYED FROM YOUR GUARDIAN?
STRAYED?
STRAYED?
CHUGGA
I ENDED UP...
...USING MY TRAVEL FEE TO PAY FOR YOUR TICKETS.
WHERE ARE WE?
WHERE IS KURO-CHA?
CHUGGA
ANYWAY, I SHOULD GET YOU OFF AT THE NEXT STATION...
AHEM
WE ARE ABOUT TO REACH THE BORDER...
NOTICE
LISTEN. YOU GUYS ARE LOST.
WE'RE LOST?
LOST?
RIGHT.
I HAVE TO FIND THAT BLACK TRAVELER AND GET MY MONEY BACK.
OR ELSE I CAN'T GO HOME.
...SO I WILL BE COMING BY TO CHECK YOUR TICKET AND VOUCHER.
BY THE WAY...
WHAT'S A TICKET?
CHUGGA
CHUGGA
YOU'RE LOST TOO?
LOST! LOST!
KIDS CAN BE SO CRUEL.

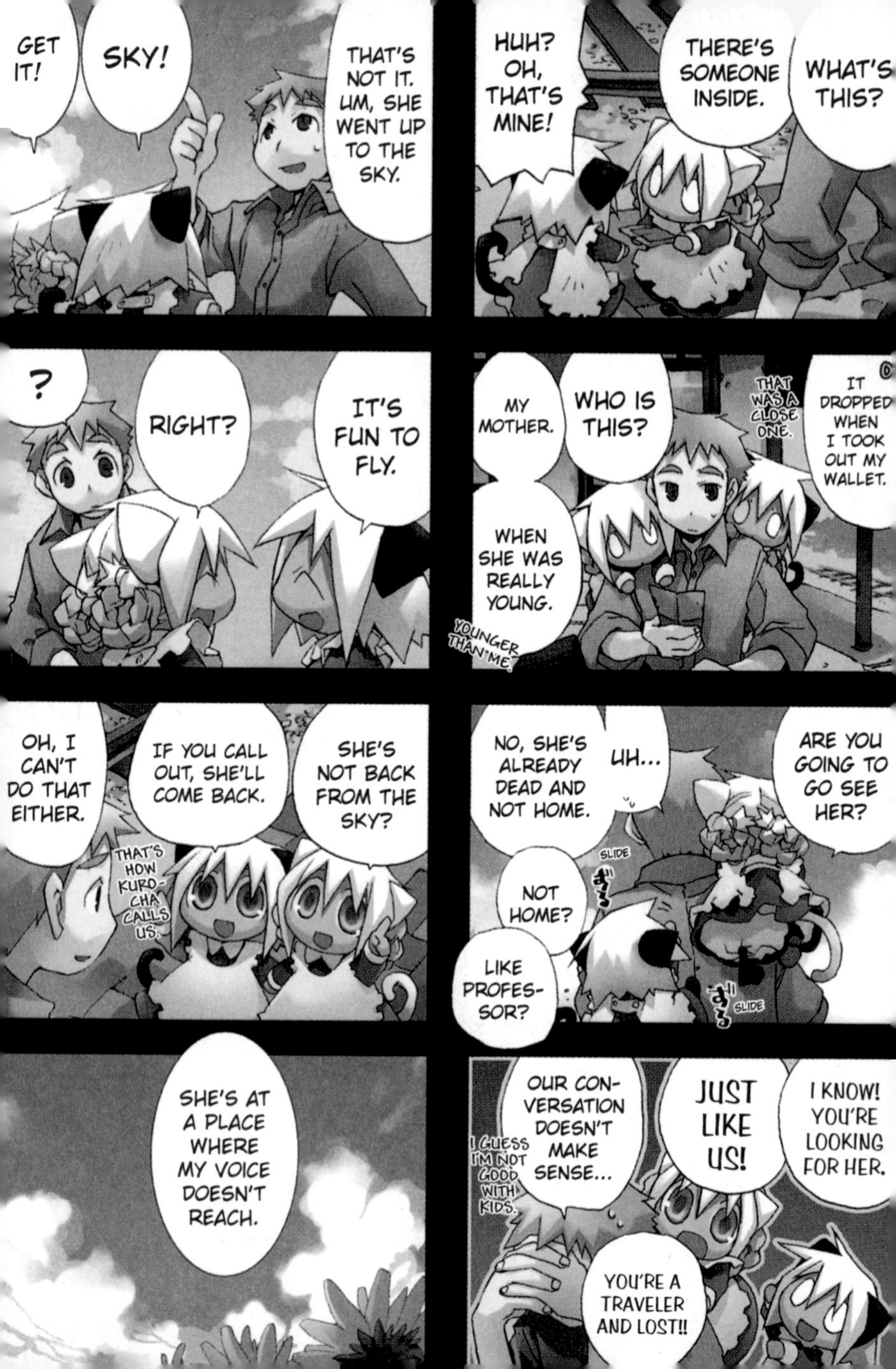
WHAT'S THIS?
THERE'S SOMEONE INSIDE.
HUH? OH, THAT'S MINE!
THAT'S NOT IT. UM, SHE WENT UP TO THE SKY.
SKY!
GET IT!
IT DROPPED WHEN I TOOK OUT MY WALLET.
THAT WAS A CLOSE ONE.
WHO IS THIS?
MY MOTHER.
WHEN SHE WAS REALLY YOUNG.
YOUNGER THAN ME.
IT'S FUN TO FLY.
RIGHT?
?
ARE YOU GOING TO GO SEE HER?
UH...
NO, SHE'S ALREADY DEAD AND NOT HOME.
SLIDE
NOT HOME?
LIKE PROFES-SOR?
SLIDE
SHE'S NOT BACK FROM THE SKY?
IF YOU CALL OUT, SHE'LL COME BACK.
THAT'S HOW KURO-CHA CALLS US.
OH, I CAN'T DO THAT EITHER.
I KNOW! YOU'RE LOOKING FOR HER.
JUST LIKE US!
OUR CON-VERSATION DOESN'T MAKE SENSE...
I GUESS I'M NOT GOOD WITH KIDS.
YOU'RE A TRAVELER AND LOST!!
SHE'S AT A PLACE WHERE MY VOICE DOESN'T REACH.

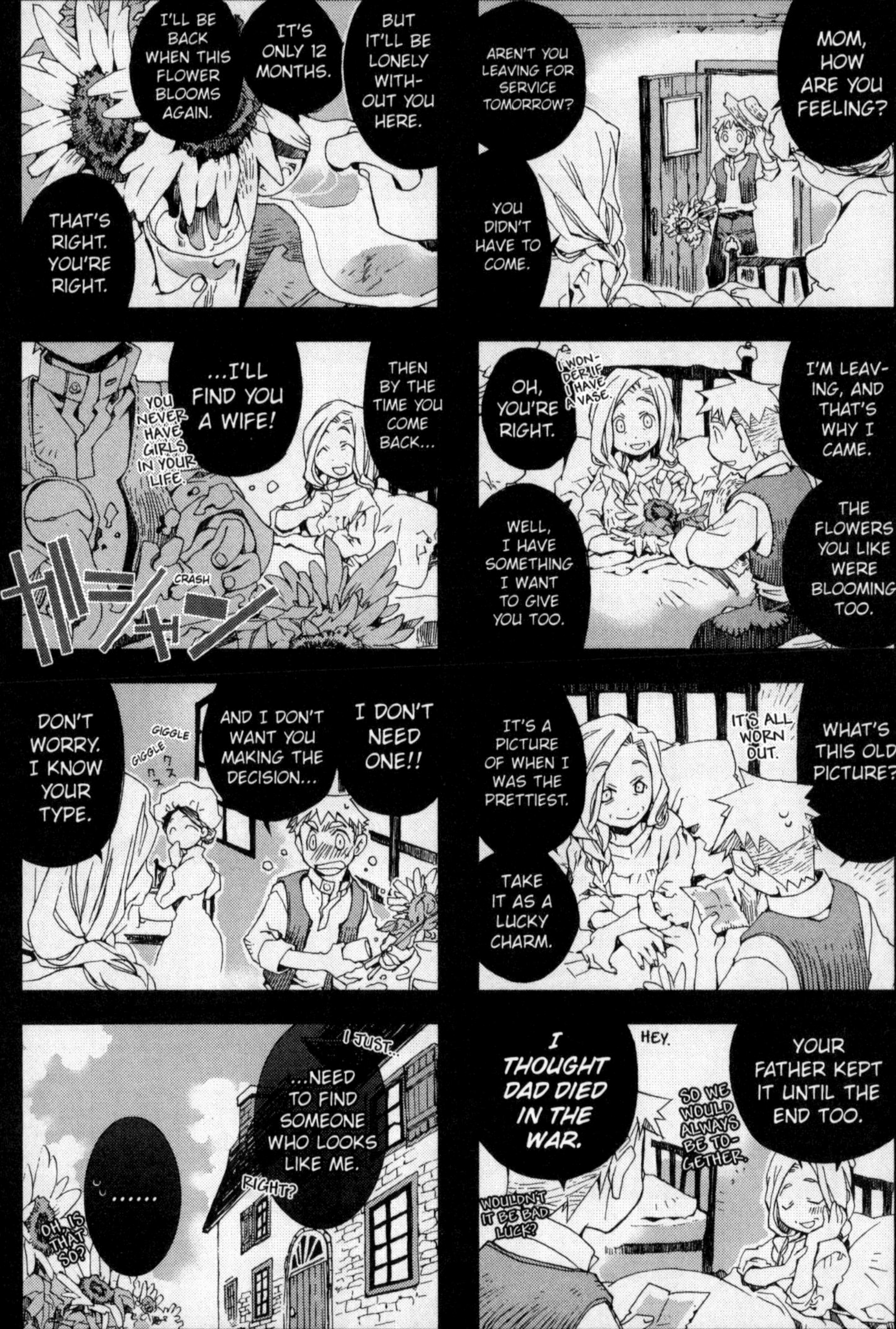
MOM, HOW ARE YOU FEELING?
AREN'T YOU LEAVING FOR SERVICE TOMORROW?
YOU DIDN'T HAVE TO COME.
BUT IT'LL BE LONELY WITHOUT YOU HERE.
IT'S ONLY 12 MONTHS.
I'LL BE BACK WHEN THIS FLOWER BLOOMS AGAIN.
THAT'S RIGHT. YOU'RE RIGHT.
I'M LEAVING, AND THAT'S WHY I CAME.
OH, YOU'RE RIGHT.
I WONDER IF I HAVE A VASE.
THE FLOWERS YOU LIKE WERE BLOOMING TOO.
WELL, I HAVE SOMETHING I WANT TO GIVE YOU TOO.
THEN BY THE TIME YOU COME BACK...
...I'LL FIND YOU A WIFE!
YOU NEVER HAVE GIRLS IN YOUR LIFE.
CRASH
WHAT'S THIS OLD PICTURE?
IT'S ALL WORN OUT.
IT'S A PICTURE OF WHEN I WAS THE PRETTIEST.
TAKE IT AS A LUCKY CHARM.
I DON'T NEED ONE!!
AND I DON'T WANT YOU MAKING THE DECISION...
GIGGLE
GIGGLE
DON'T WORRY. I KNOW YOUR TYPE.
YOUR FATHER KEPT IT UNTIL THE END TOO.
SO WE WOULD ALWAYS BE TOGETHER.
HEY.
I THOUGHT DAD DIED IN THE WAR.
WOULDN'T IT BE BAD LUCK?
I JUST...
...NEED TO FIND SOMEONE WHO LOOKS LIKE ME.
RIGHT?
......
OH, IS THAT SO?

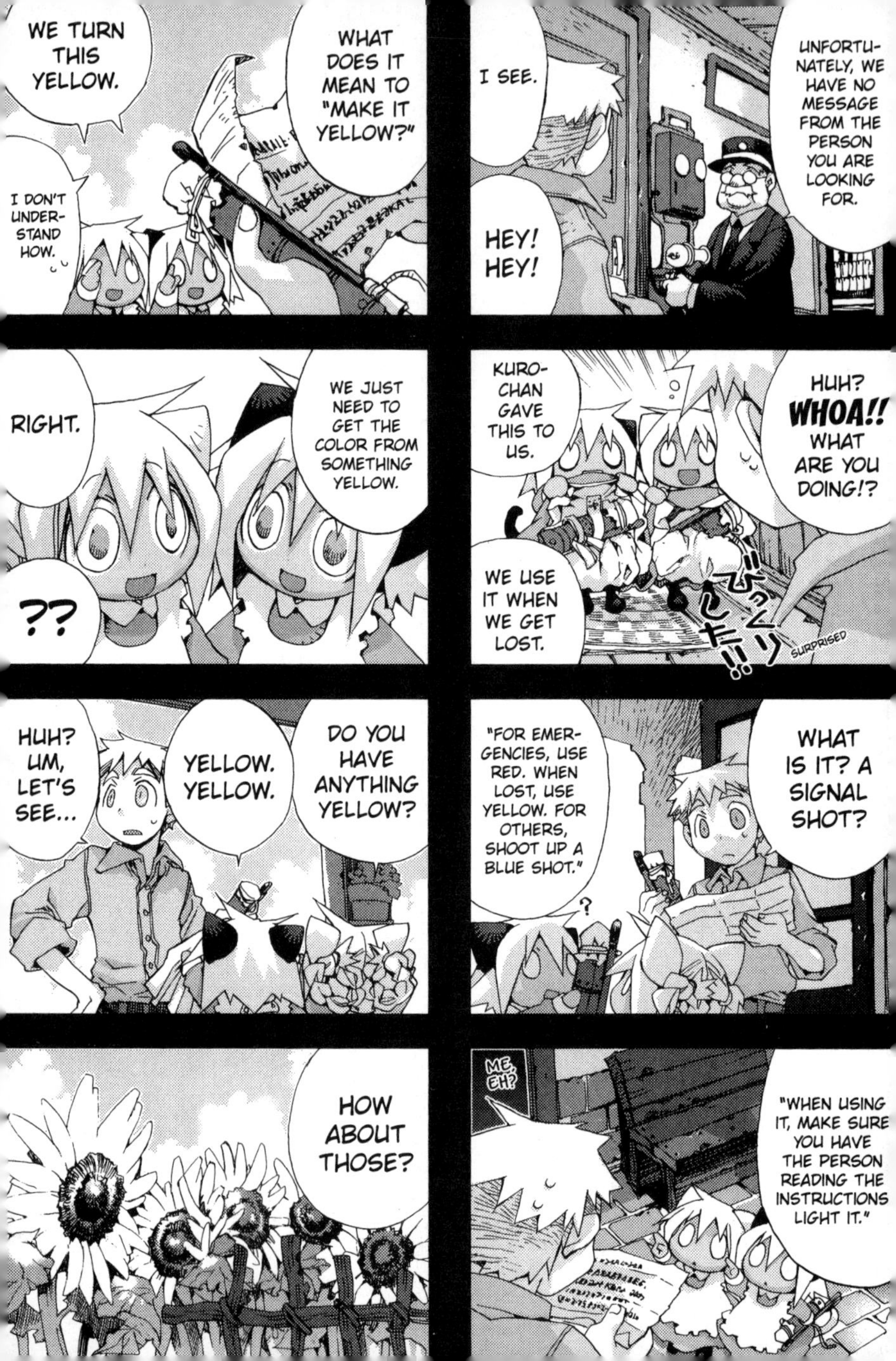
UNFORTUNATELY, WE HAVE NO MESSAGE FROM THE PERSON YOU ARE LOOKING FOR.
I SEE.
HEY! HEY!
WHAT DOES IT MEAN TO "MAKE IT YELLOW?"
WE TURN THIS YELLOW.
I DON'T UNDERSTAND HOW.
HUH? WHOA!! WHAT ARE YOU DOING!?
びっくり
SURPRISED
KURO-CHAN GAVE THIS TO US.
WE USE IT WHEN WE GET LOST.
WE JUST NEED TO GET THE COLOR FROM SOMETHING YELLOW.
RIGHT.
??
WHAT IS IT? A SIGNAL SHOT?
"FOR EMERGENCIES, USE RED. WHEN LOST, USE YELLOW. FOR OTHERS, SHOOT UP A BLUE SHOT."
?
DO YOU HAVE ANYTHING YELLOW?
YELLOW. YELLOW.
HUH? UM, LET'S SEE...
"WHEN USING IT, MAKE SURE YOU HAVE THE PERSON READING THE INSTRUCTIONS LIGHT IT."
ME, EH?
HOW ABOUT THOSE?

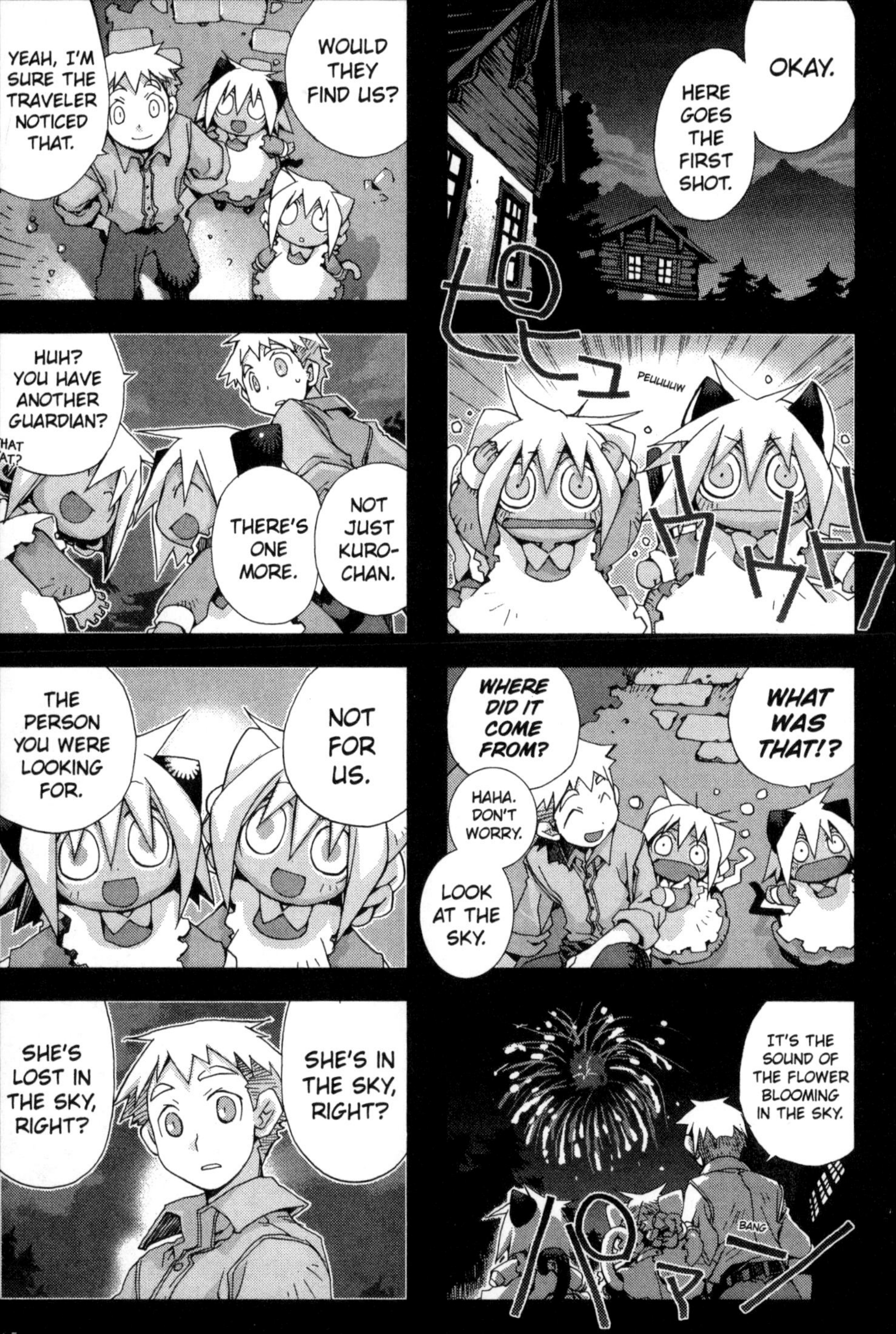
OKAY.
HERE GOES THE FIRST SHOT.
WOULD THEY FIND US?
YEAH, I'M SURE THE TRAVELER NOTICED THAT.
PEUUUUW
HUH? YOU HAVE ANOTHER GUARDIAN?
NOT JUST KURO-CHAN.
THERE'S ONE MORE.
WHAT WAS THAT!?
WHERE DID IT COME FROM?
HAHA. DON'T WORRY.
LOOK AT THE SKY.
NOT FOR US.
THE PERSON YOU WERE LOOKING FOR.
IT'S THE SOUND OF THE FLOWER BLOOMING IN THE SKY.
BANG
SHE'S IN THE SKY, RIGHT?
SHE'S LOST IN THE SKY, RIGHT?

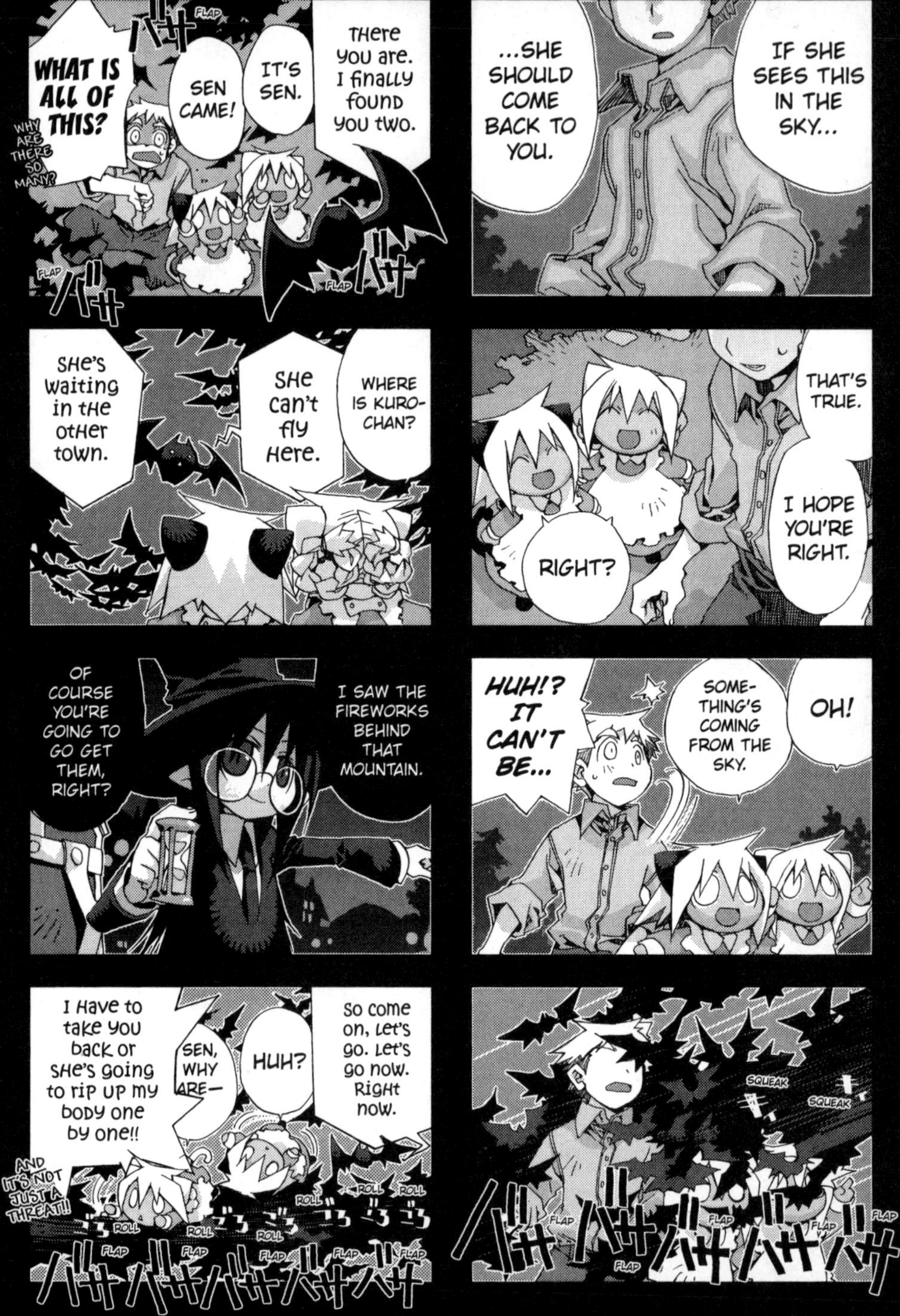
IF SHE SEES THIS IN THE SKY...
...SHE SHOULD COME BACK TO YOU.
THAT'S TRUE.
I HOPE YOU'RE RIGHT.
RIGHT?
OH!
SOME-THING'S COMING FROM THE SKY.
HUH!? IT CAN'T BE...
SQUEAK
SQUEAK
FLAP
FLAP
FLAP
FLAP
There you are. I finally found you two.
IT'S SEN.
SEN CAME!
WHAT IS ALL OF THIS?
WHY ARE THERE SO MANY?
FLAP
FLAP
FLAP
WHERE IS KURO-CHAN?
SHE can't fly Here.
SHE's waiting in tHe otHer town.
I SAW THE FIREWORKS BEHIND THAT MOUNTAIN.
OF COURSE YOU'RE GOING TO GO GET THEM, RIGHT?
So come on, let's go. Let's go now. Right now.
HUH?
SEN, WHY ARE—
I Have to take you back or sHe's going to rip up my body one by one!!
AND IT'S NOT JUST A THREAT!!
ROLL
ROLL
ROLL
ROLL
ROLL
ROLL
FLAP
FLAP
FLAP
FLAP
FLAP

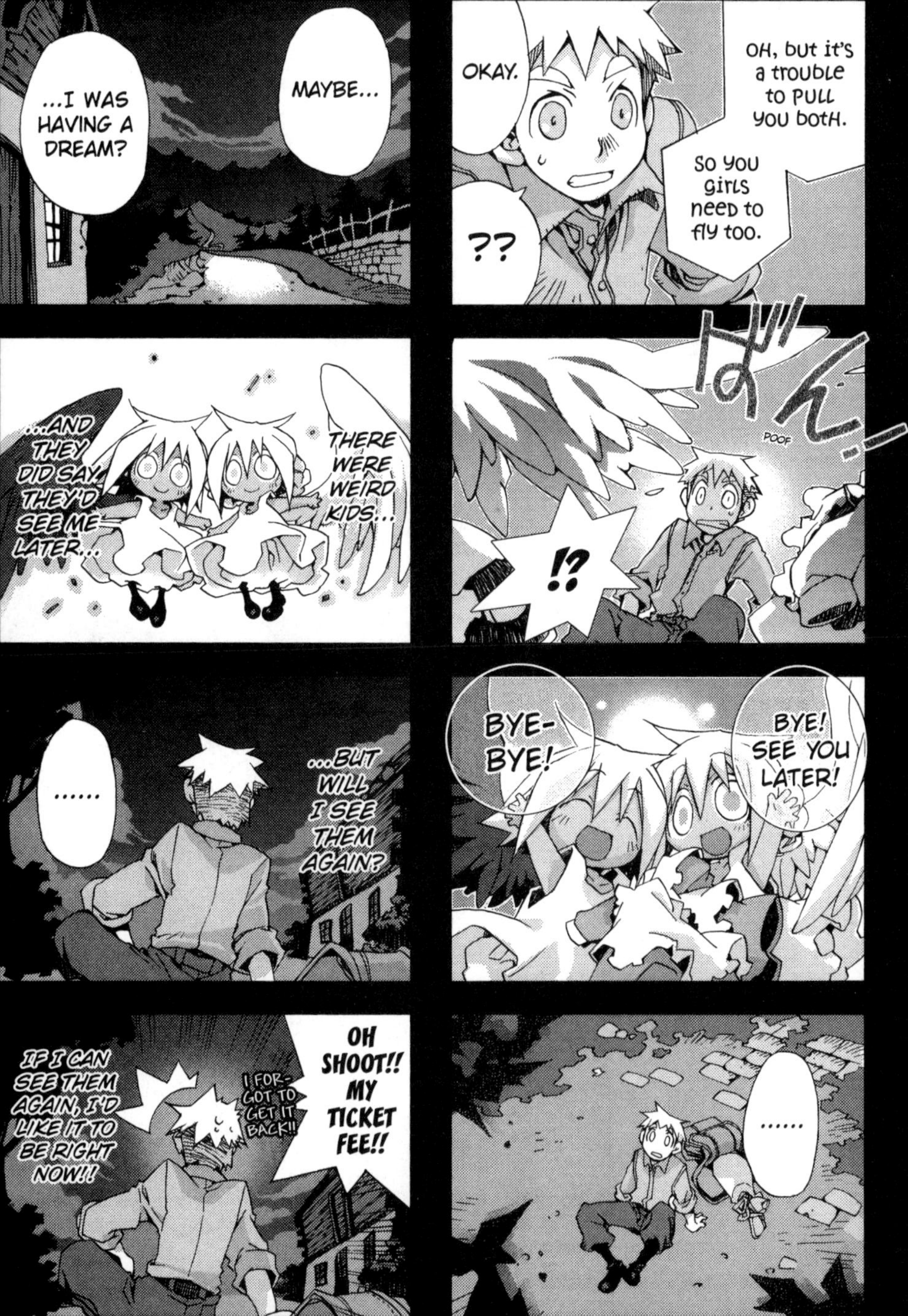
OKAY.
OH, but it's a trouble to PULL you both.
So you girls need to fly too.
??
MAYBE...
...I WAS HAVING A DREAM?
ばん
POOF
!?
THERE WERE WEIRD KIDS...
...AND THEY DID SAY THEY'D SEE ME LATER...
BYE! SEE YOU LATER!
BYE-BYE!
...BUT WILL I SEE THEM AGAIN?
......
......
OH SHOOT!! MY TICKET FEE!!
I FORGOT TO GET IT BACK!!
IF I CAN SEE THEM AGAIN, I'D LIKE IT TO BE RIGHT NOW!!

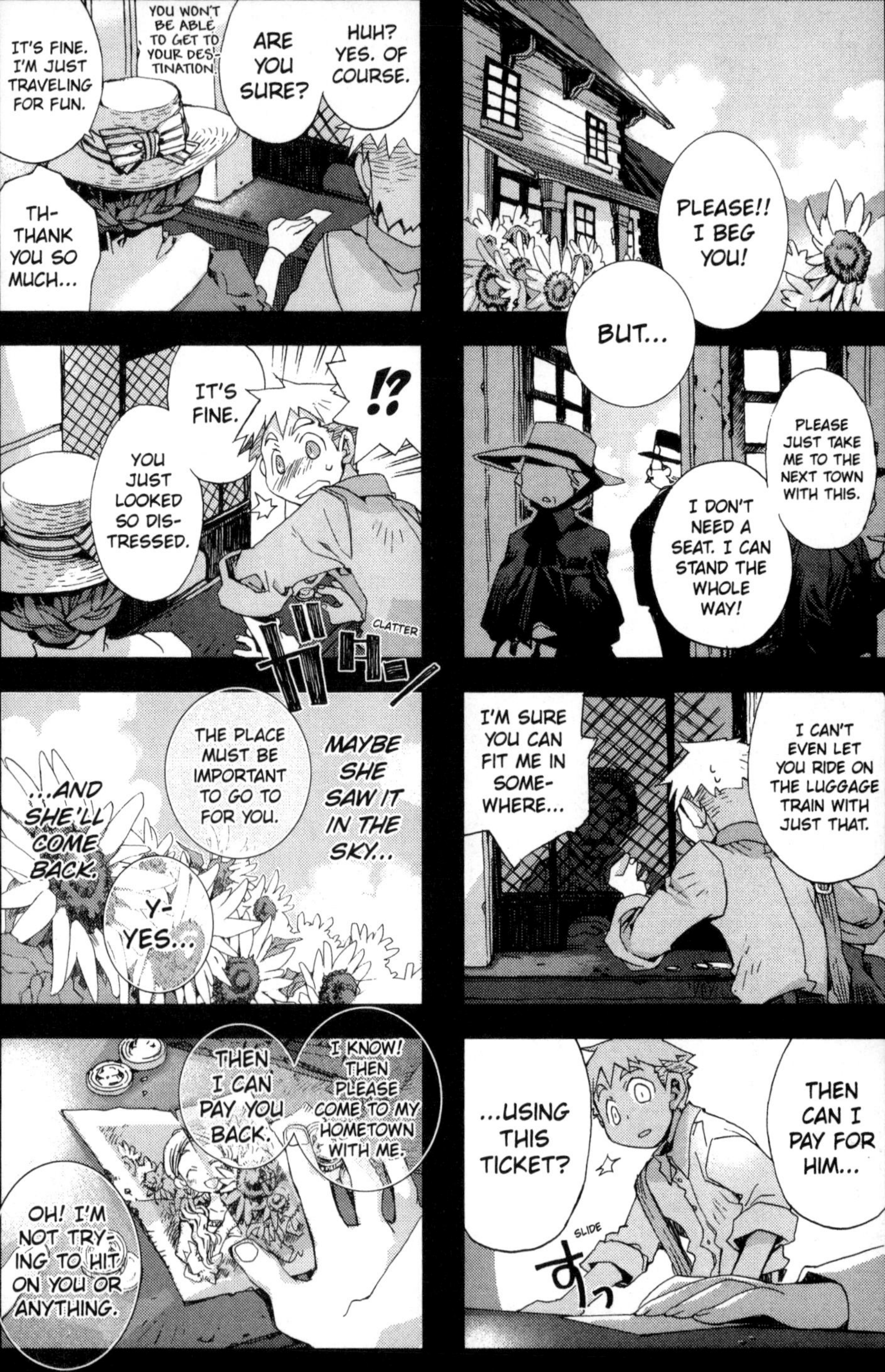
PLEASE!! I BEG YOU!
BUT...
PLEASE JUST TAKE ME TO THE NEXT TOWN WITH THIS.
I DON'T NEED A SEAT. I CAN STAND THE WHOLE WAY!
I CAN'T EVEN LET YOU RIDE ON THE LUGGAGE TRAIN WITH JUST THAT.
I'M SURE YOU CAN FIT ME IN SOME-WHERE...
THEN CAN I PAY FOR HIM...
SLIDE
...USING THIS TICKET?
HUH? YES. OF COURSE.
ARE YOU SURE?
YOU WON'T BE ABLE TO GET TO YOUR DES-TINATION.
IT'S FINE. I'M JUST TRAVELING FOR FUN.
TH- THANK YOU SO MUCH...
!?
IT'S FINE.
YOU JUST LOOKED SO DIS-TRESSED.
CLATTER
MAYBE SHE SAW IT IN THE SKY...
THE PLACE MUST BE IMPORTANT TO GO TO FOR YOU.
...AND SHE'LL COME BACK.
Y-YES...
I KNOW! THEN PLEASE COME TO MY HOMETOWN WITH ME.
THEN I CAN PAY YOU BACK.
OH! I'M NOT TRYING TO HIT ON YOU OR ANYTHING.

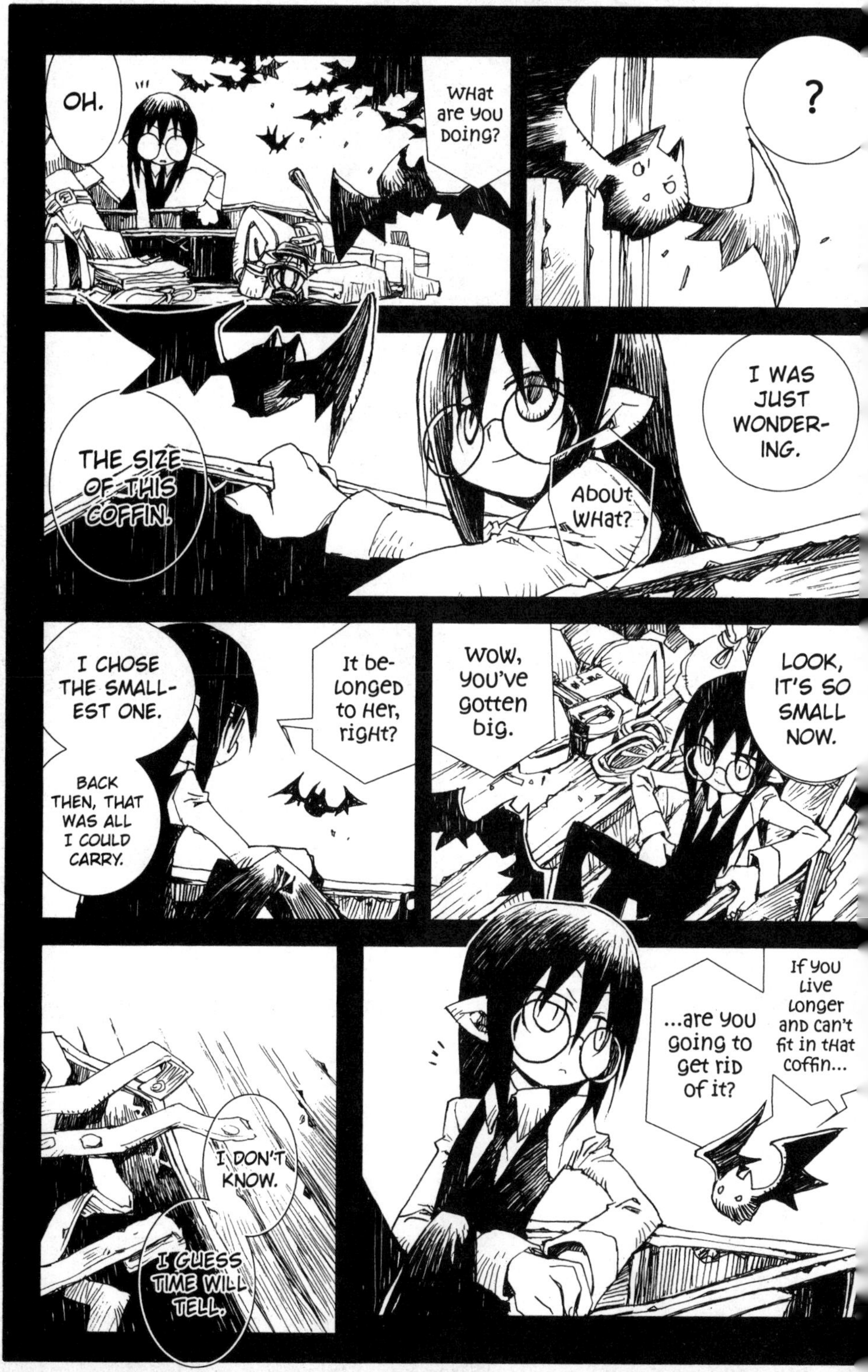
?
What are you doing?
OH.
I WAS JUST WONDERING.
About what?
THE SIZE OF THIS COFFIN.
LOOK, IT'S SO SMALL NOW.
WOW, YOU'VE GOTTEN BIG.
It belonged to her, right?
I CHOSE THE SMALLEST ONE.
BACK THEN, THAT WAS ALL I COULD CARRY.
If you live longer and can't fit in that coffin...
...are you going to get rid of it?
I DON'T KNOW.
I GUESS TIME WILL TELL.

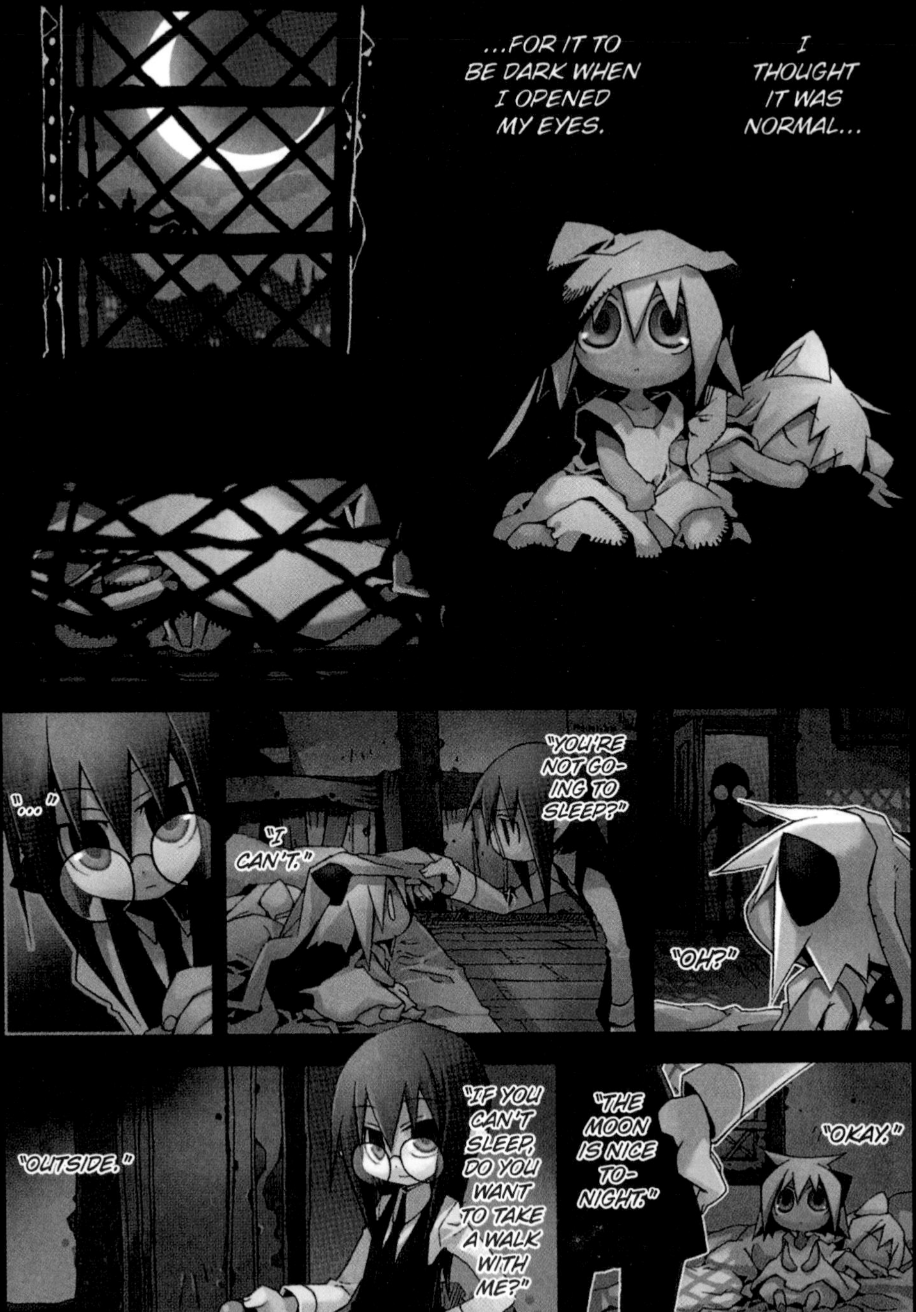
I THOUGHT IT WAS NORMAL...
...FOR IT TO BE DARK WHEN I OPENED MY EYES.
"OH?"
"YOU'RE NOT GOING TO SLEEP?"
"I CAN'T."
"..."
"THE MOON IS NICE TONIGHT."
"OKAY."
"IF YOU CAN'T SLEEP, DO YOU WANT TO TAKE A WALK WITH ME?"
"OUTSIDE."

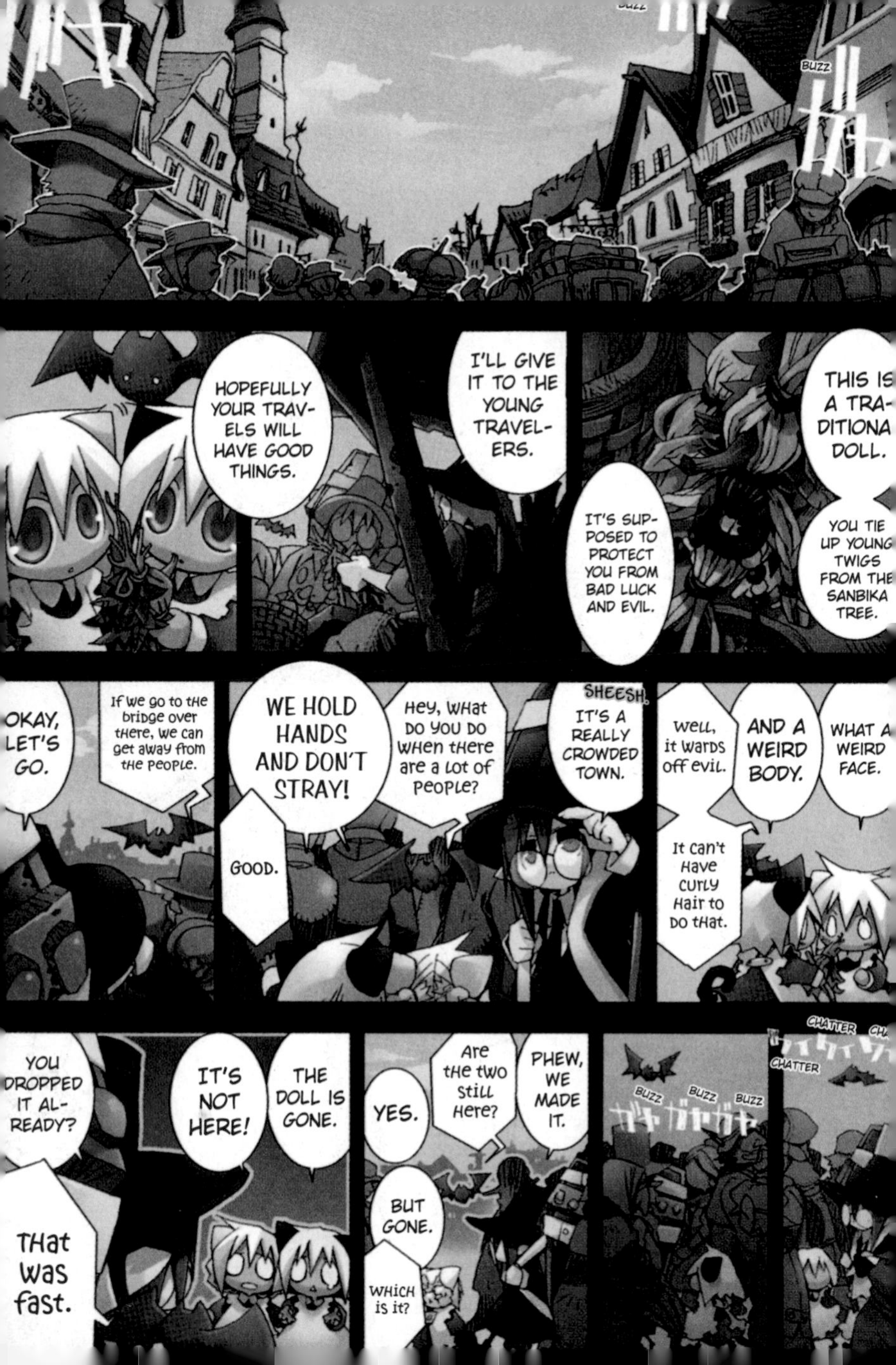
BUZZ
BUZZ
THIS IS A TRADITIONA DOLL.
YOU TIE UP YOUNG TWIGS FROM THE SANBIKA TREE.
IT'S SUPPOSED TO PROTECT YOU FROM BAD LUCK AND EVIL.
I'LL GIVE IT TO THE YOUNG TRAVELERS.
HOPEFULLY YOUR TRAVELS WILL HAVE GOOD THINGS.
WHAT A WEIRD FACE.
AND A WEIRD BODY.
Well, it wards off evil.
It can't have curly hair to do that.
SHEESH.
IT'S A REALLY CROWDED TOWN.
Hey, what do you do when there are a lot of people?
WE HOLD HANDS AND DON'T STRAY!
GOOD.
If we go to the bridge over there, we can get away from the people.
OKAY, LET'S GO.
CHATTER
CHATTER
BUZZ BUZZ BUZZ
PHEW, WE MADE IT.
Are the two still here?
YES.
BUT GONE.
WHICH is it?
THE DOLL IS GONE.
IT'S NOT HERE!
YOU DROPPED IT ALREADY?
That was fast.

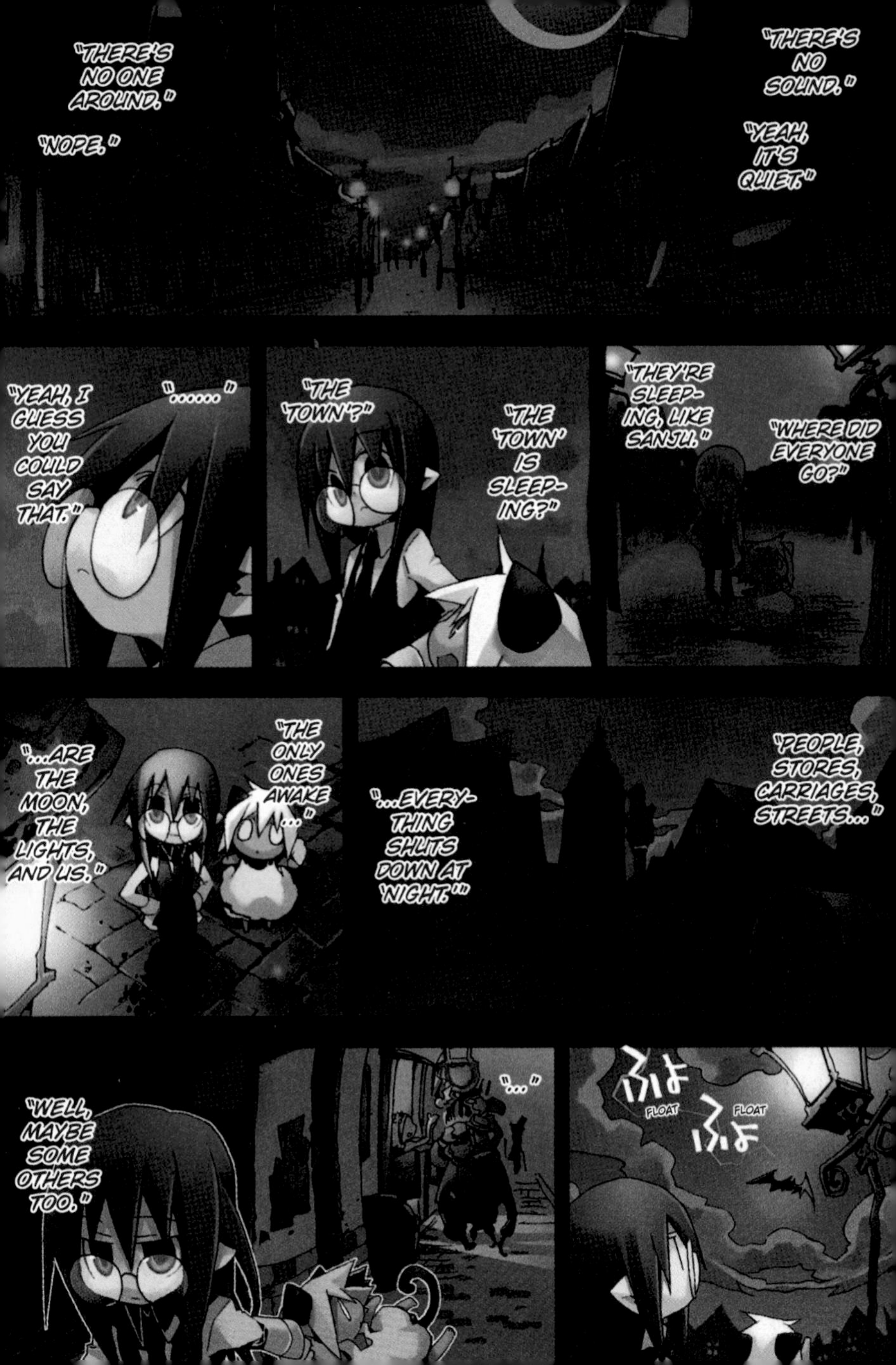
"THERE'S NO SOUND."
"YEAH, IT'S QUIET."
"THERE'S NO ONE AROUND."
"NOPE."
"WHERE DID EVERYONE GO?"
"THEY'RE SLEEPING, LIKE SANJU."
"THE 'TOWN' IS SLEEPING?"
"THE 'TOWN'?"
"......"
"YEAH, I GUESS YOU COULD SAY THAT."
"PEOPLE, STORES, CARRIAGES, STREETS..."
"...EVERYTHING SHUTS DOWN AT 'NIGHT.'"
"THE ONLY ONES AWAKE..."
"...ARE THE MOON, THE LIGHTS, AND US."
ふよ
FLOAT
ふよ
FLOAT
"..."
"WELL, MAYBE SOME OTHERS TOO."

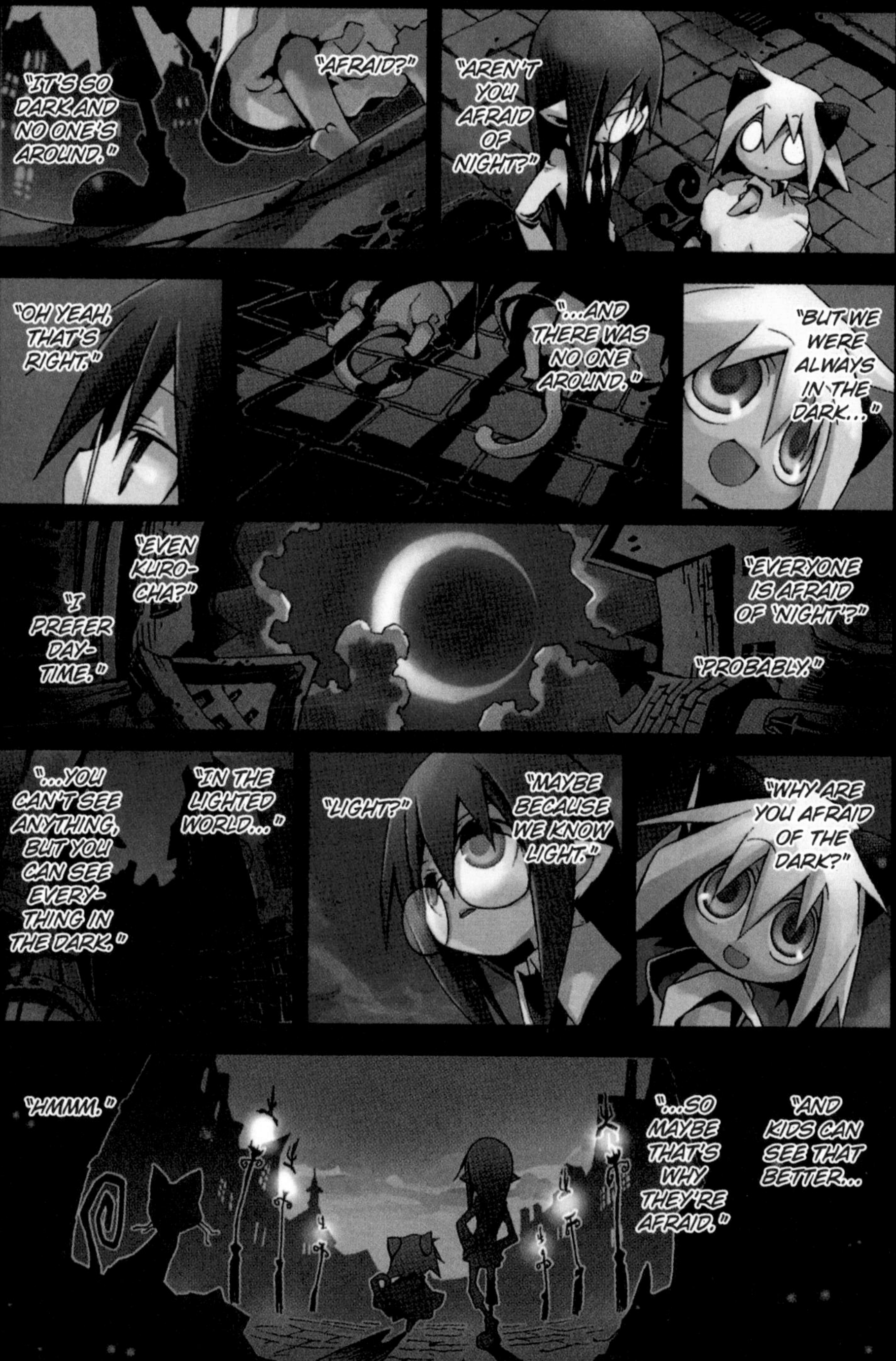
"AREN'T YOU AFRAID OF NIGHT?"
"AFRAID?"
"IT'S SO DARK AND NO ONE'S AROUND."
"BUT WE WERE ALWAYS IN THE DARK..."
"...AND THERE WAS NO ONE AROUND."
"OH YEAH, THAT'S RIGHT."
"EVERYONE IS AFRAID OF 'NIGHT'?"
"PROBABLY."
"EVEN KURO-CHA?"
"I PREFER DAY-TIME."
"WHY ARE YOU AFRAID OF THE DARK?"
"MAYBE BECAUSE WE KNOW LIGHT."
"LIGHT?"
"IN THE LIGHTED WORLD..."
"...YOU CAN'T SEE ANYTHING, BUT YOU CAN SEE EVERY-THING IN THE DARK."
"AND KIDS CAN SEE THAT BETTER...
"...SO MAYBE THAT'S WHY THEY'RE AFRAID."
"HMMM."

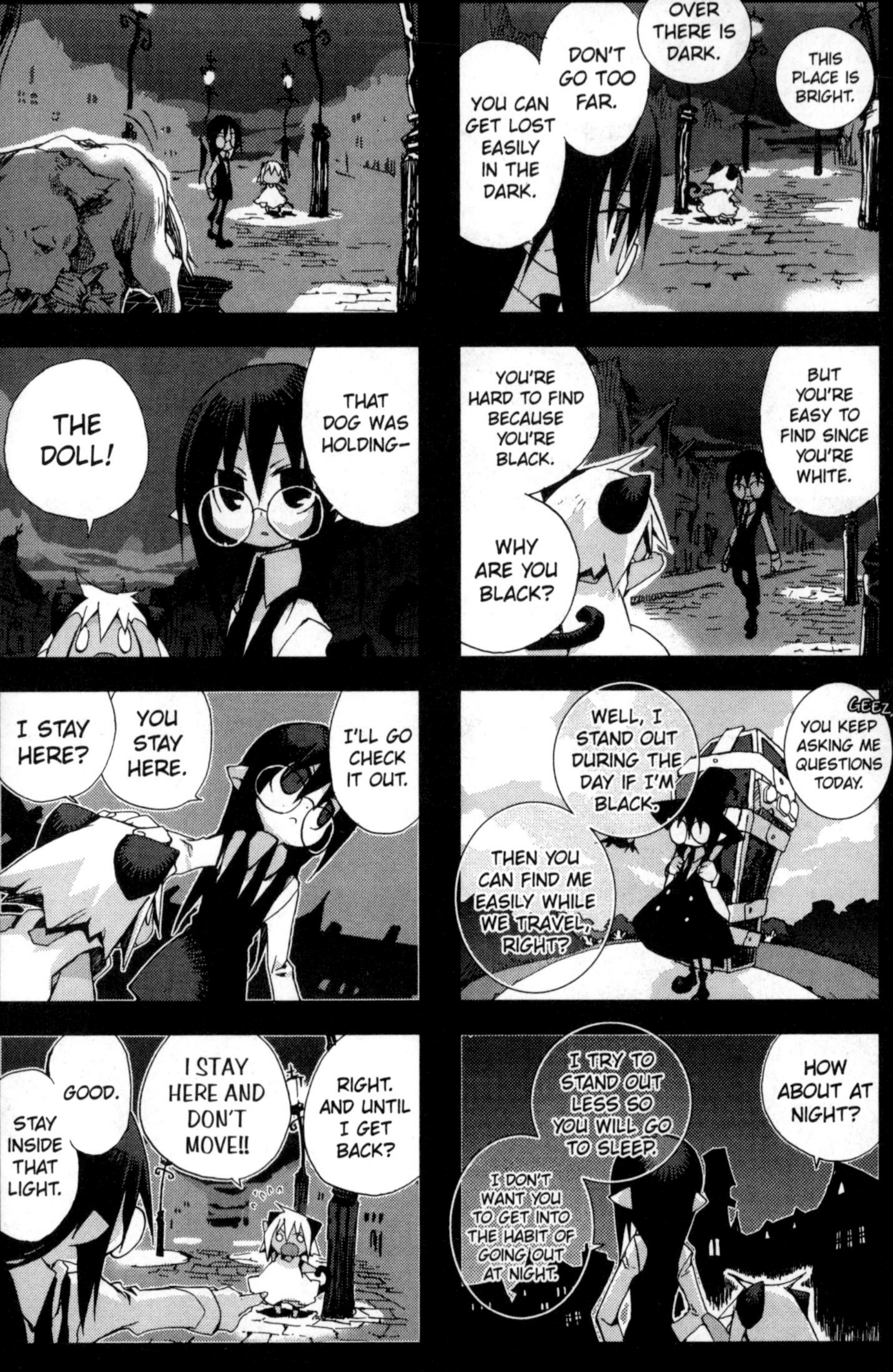
THIS PLACE IS BRIGHT.
OVER THERE IS DARK.
DON'T GO TOO FAR.
YOU CAN GET LOST EASILY IN THE DARK.
BUT YOU'RE EASY TO FIND SINCE YOU'RE WHITE.
YOU'RE HARD TO FIND BECAUSE YOU'RE BLACK.
WHY ARE YOU BLACK?
THAT DOG WAS HOLDING-
THE DOLL!
GEEZ,
YOU KEEP ASKING ME QUESTIONS TODAY.
WELL, I STAND OUT DURING THE DAY IF I'M BLACK.
THEN YOU CAN FIND ME EASILY WHILE WE TRAVEL, RIGHT?
I'LL GO CHECK IT OUT.
YOU STAY HERE.
I STAY HERE?
HOW ABOUT AT NIGHT?
I TRY TO STAND OUT LESS SO YOU WILL GO TO SLEEP.
I DON'T WANT YOU TO GET INTO THE HABIT OF GOING OUT AT NIGHT.
RIGHT. AND UNTIL I GET BACK?
I STAY HERE AND DON'T MOVE!!
GOOD.
STAY INSIDE THAT LIGHT.

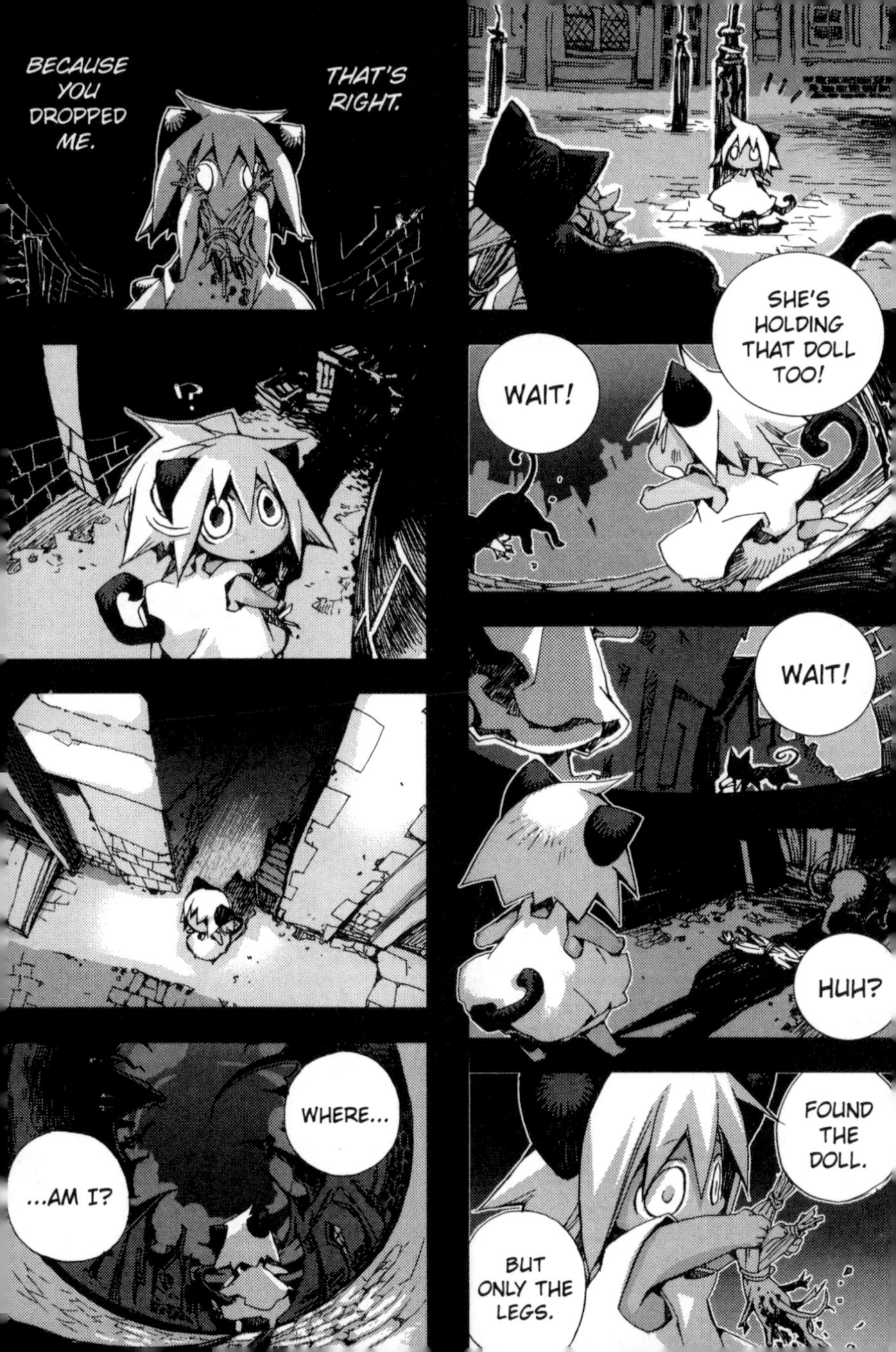
SHE'S HOLDING THAT DOLL TOO!
WAIT!
WAIT!
HUH?
FOUND THE DOLL.
BUT ONLY THE LEGS.
THAT'S RIGHT.
BECAUSE YOU DROPPED ME.
!?
WHERE...
...AM I?

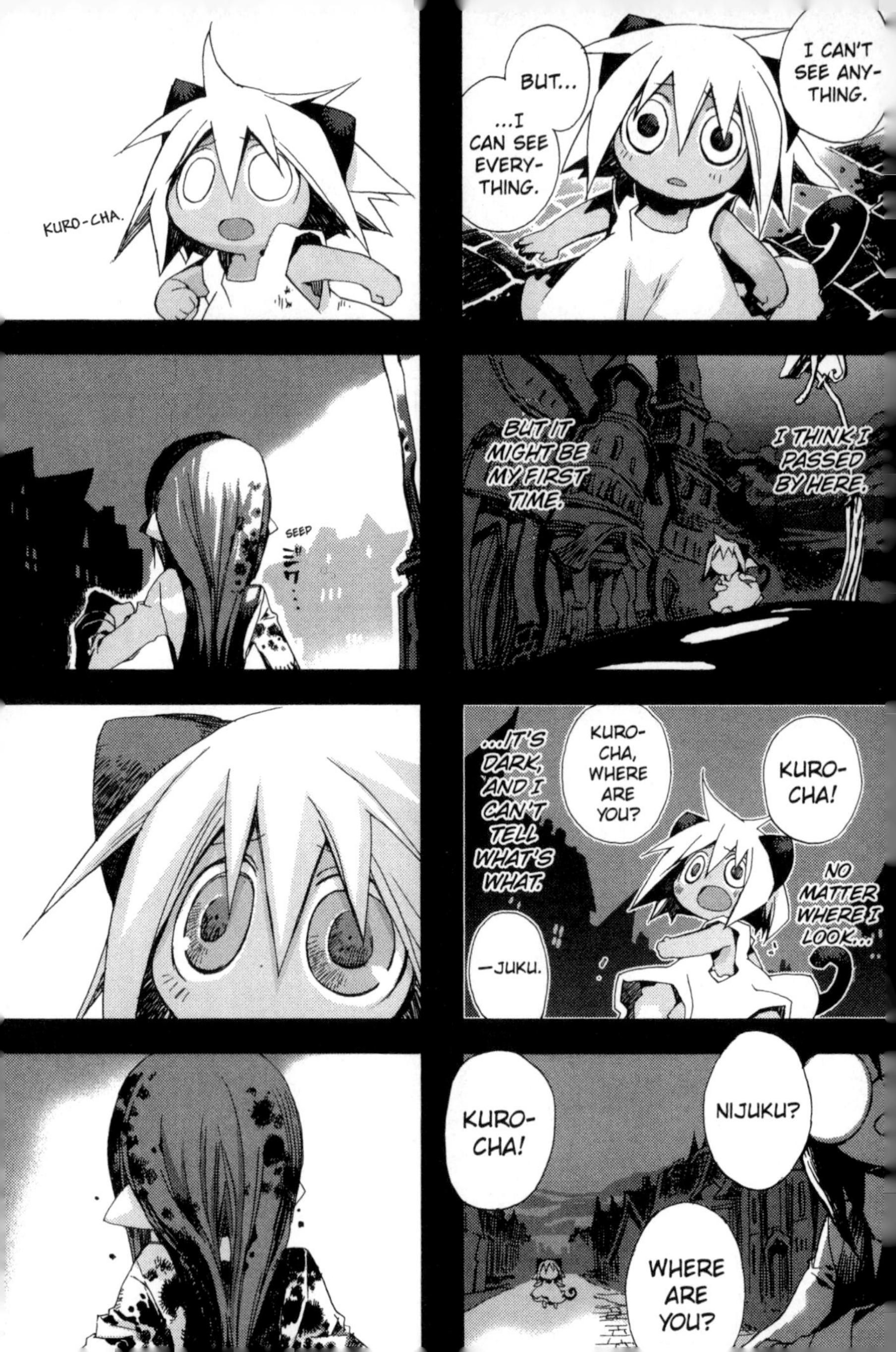
I CAN'T SEE ANY-THING.
BUT...
...I CAN SEE EVERY-THING.
KURO-CHA.
I THINK I PASSED BY HERE.
BUT IT MIGHT BE MY FIRST TIME.
SEEP
KURO-CHA!
KURO-CHA, WHERE ARE YOU?
...IT'S DARK, AND I CAN'T TELL WHAT'S WHAT.
NO MATTER WHERE I LOOK...
—JUKU.
NIJUKU?
KURO-CHA!
WHERE ARE YOU?

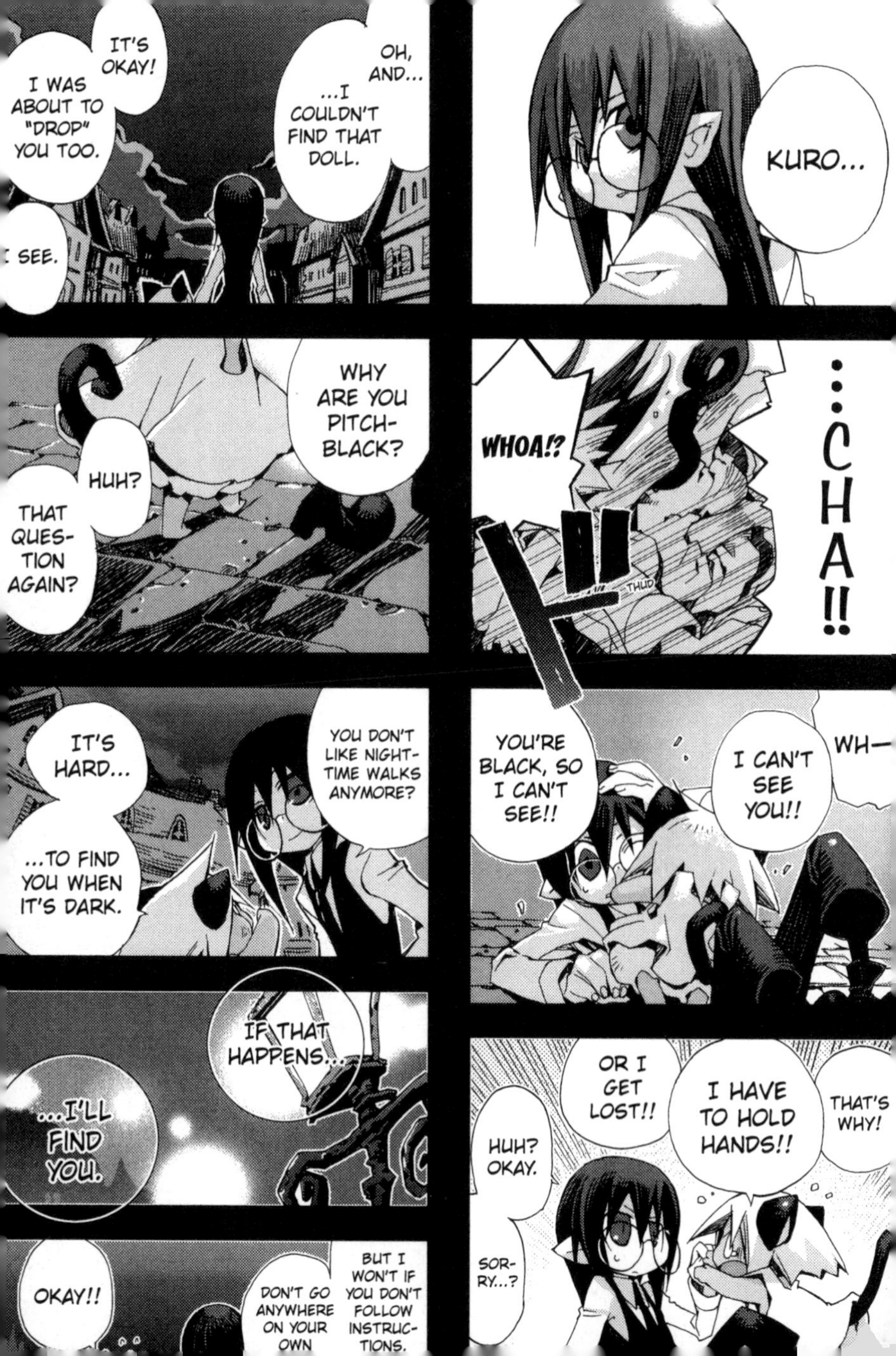
KURO...
...CHA!!
WHOA!?
THUD
WH—
I CAN'T SEE YOU!!
YOU'RE BLACK, SO I CAN'T SEE!!
THAT'S WHY!
I HAVE TO HOLD HANDS!!
OR I GET LOST!!
HUH? OKAY.
SOR-RY...?
OH, AND...
...I COULDN'T FIND THAT DOLL.
IT'S OKAY!
I WAS ABOUT TO "DROP" YOU TOO.
I SEE.
WHY ARE YOU PITCH-BLACK?
HUH?
THAT QUES-TION AGAIN?
YOU DON'T LIKE NIGHT-TIME WALKS ANYMORE?
IT'S HARD...
...TO FIND YOU WHEN IT'S DARK.
IF THAT HAPPENS...
...I'LL FIND YOU.
BUT I WON'T IF YOU DON'T FOLLOW INSTRUC-TIONS.
DON'T GO ANYWHERE ON YOUR OWN
OKAY!!

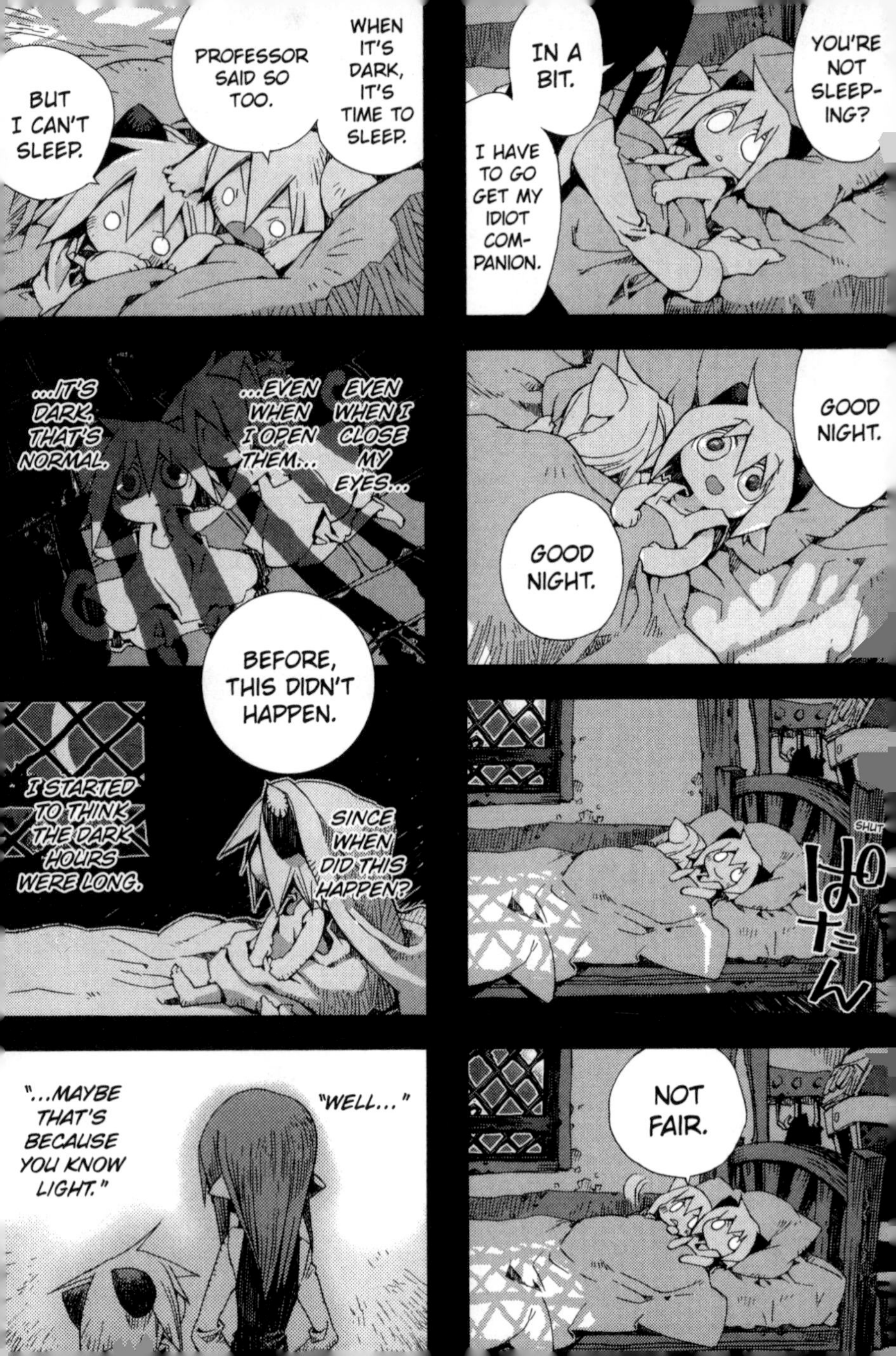
YOU'RE NOT SLEEP-ING?
IN A BIT.
I HAVE TO GO GET MY IDIOT COM-PANION.
WHEN IT'S DARK, IT'S TIME TO SLEEP.
PROFESSOR SAID SO TOO.
BUT I CAN'T SLEEP.
GOOD NIGHT.
GOOD NIGHT.
EVEN WHEN I CLOSE MY EYES...
...EVEN WHEN I OPEN THEM...
...IT'S DARK, THAT'S NORMAL.
BEFORE, THIS DIDN'T HAPPEN.
SHUT
ぱたん
SINCE WHEN DID THIS HAPPEN?
I STARTED TO THINK THE DARK HOURS WERE LONG.
NOT FAIR.
"WELL..."
"...MAYBE THAT'S BECAUSE YOU KNOW LIGHT."

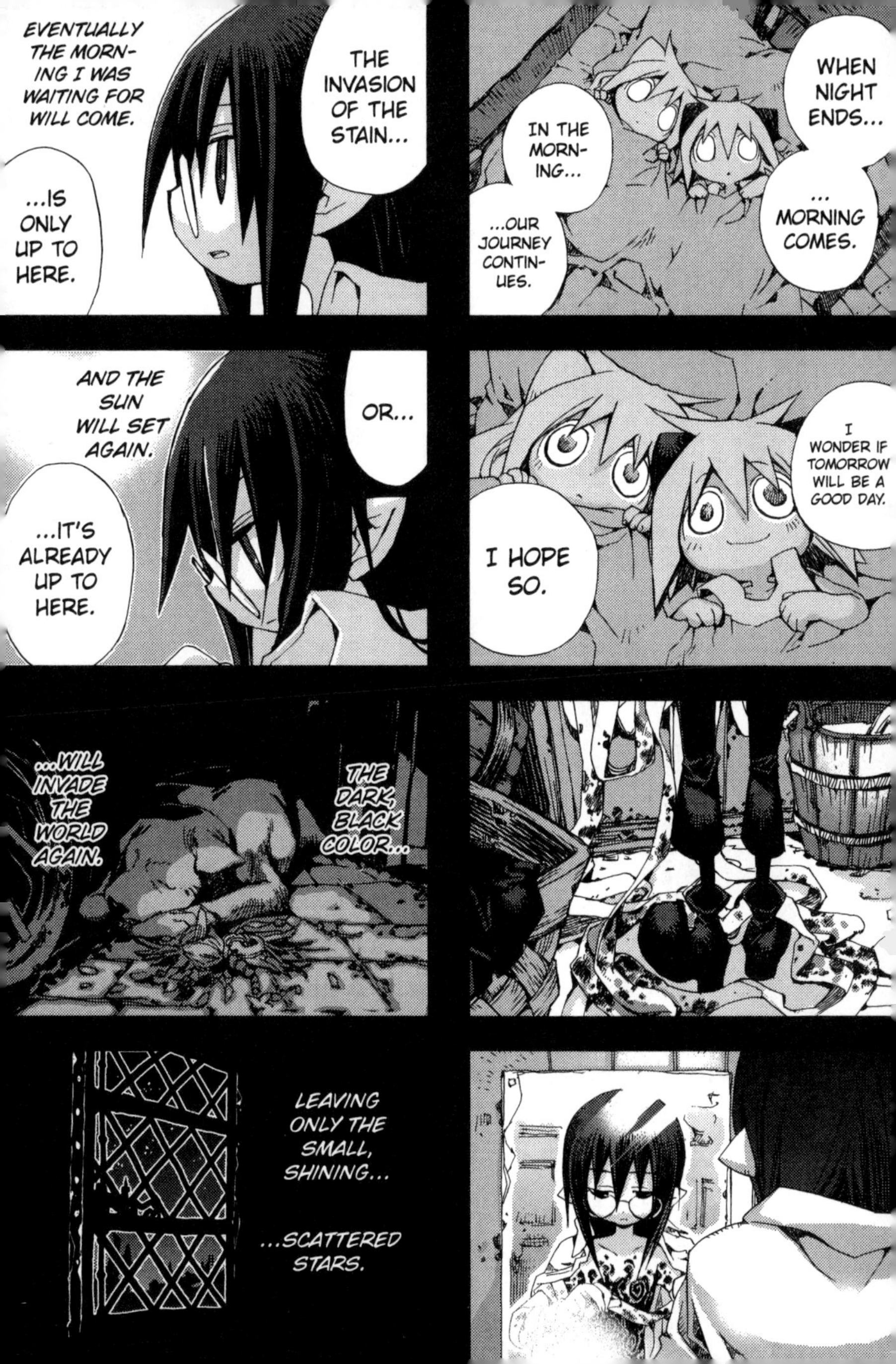
WHEN NIGHT ENDS...
... MORNING COMES.
IN THE MORNING...
...OUR JOURNEY CONTINUES.
THE INVASION OF THE STAIN...
EVENTUALLY THE MORNING I WAS WAITING FOR WILL COME.
...IS ONLY UP TO HERE.
I WONDER IF TOMORROW WILL BE A GOOD DAY.
I HOPE SO.
OR...
AND THE SUN WILL SET AGAIN.
...IT'S ALREADY UP TO HERE.
THE DARK, BLACK COLOR...
...WILL INVADE THE WORLD AGAIN.
LEAVING ONLY THE SMALL, SHINING...
...SCATTERED STARS.

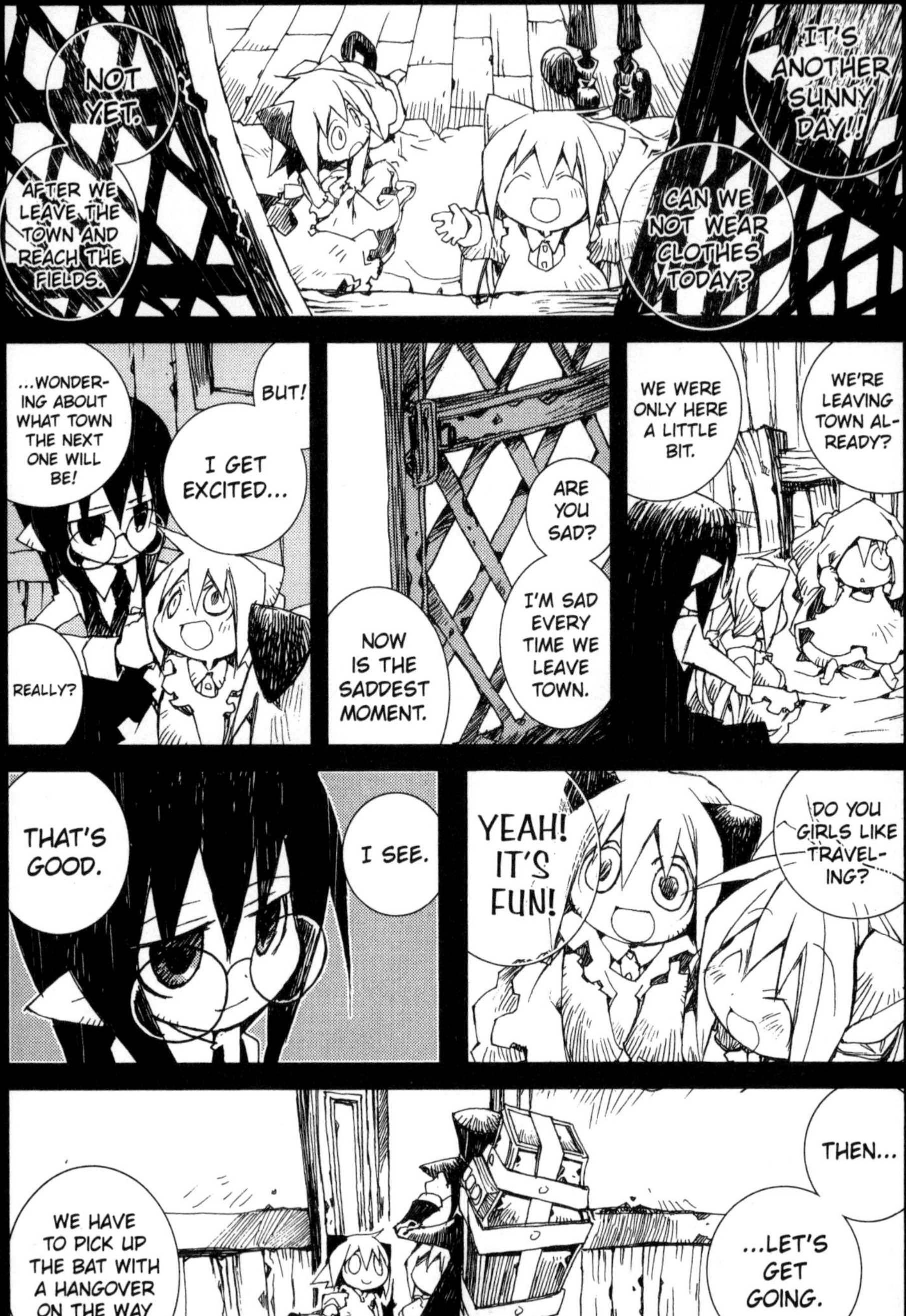
IT'S ANOTHER SUNNY DAY!!
CAN WE NOT WEAR CLOTHES TODAY?
NOT YET.
AFTER WE LEAVE THE TOWN AND REACH THE FIELDS.
WE'RE LEAVING TOWN ALREADY?
WE WERE ONLY HERE A LITTLE BIT.
ARE YOU SAD?
I'M SAD EVERY TIME WE LEAVE TOWN.
NOW IS THE SADDEST MOMENT.
BUT!
I GET EXCITED...
...WONDERING ABOUT WHAT TOWN THE NEXT ONE WILL BE!
REALLY?
DO YOU GIRLS LIKE TRAVELING?
YEAH! IT'S FUN!
I SEE.
THAT'S GOOD.
THEN...
...LET'S GET GOING.
WE HAVE TO PICK UP THE BAT WITH A HANGOVER ON THE WAY TOO.

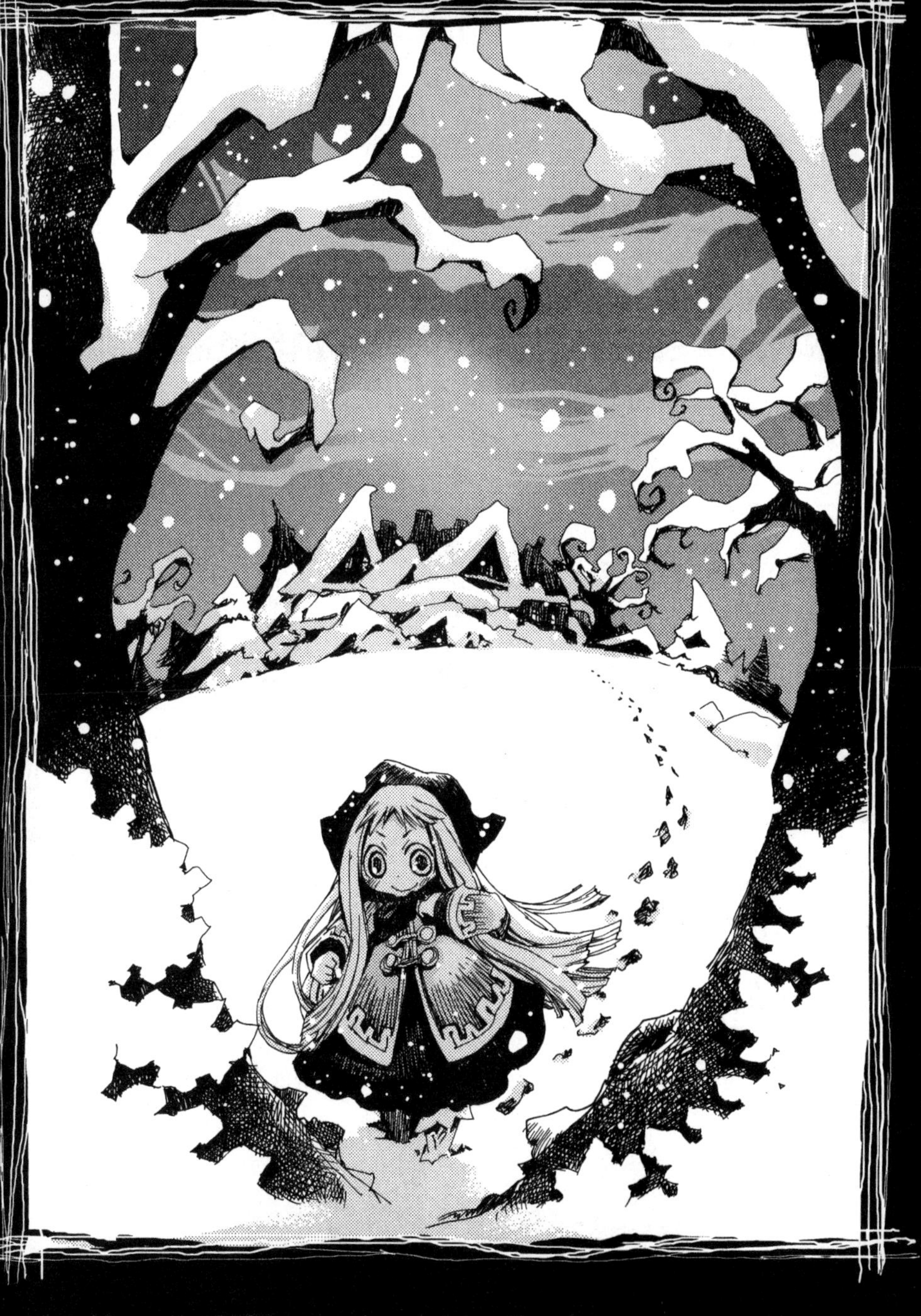

The girl snuck out of the mansion at dawn. The place was covered in snow.

She had no idea that her small bit of curiosity and her selfishness would bring such dreadful results.

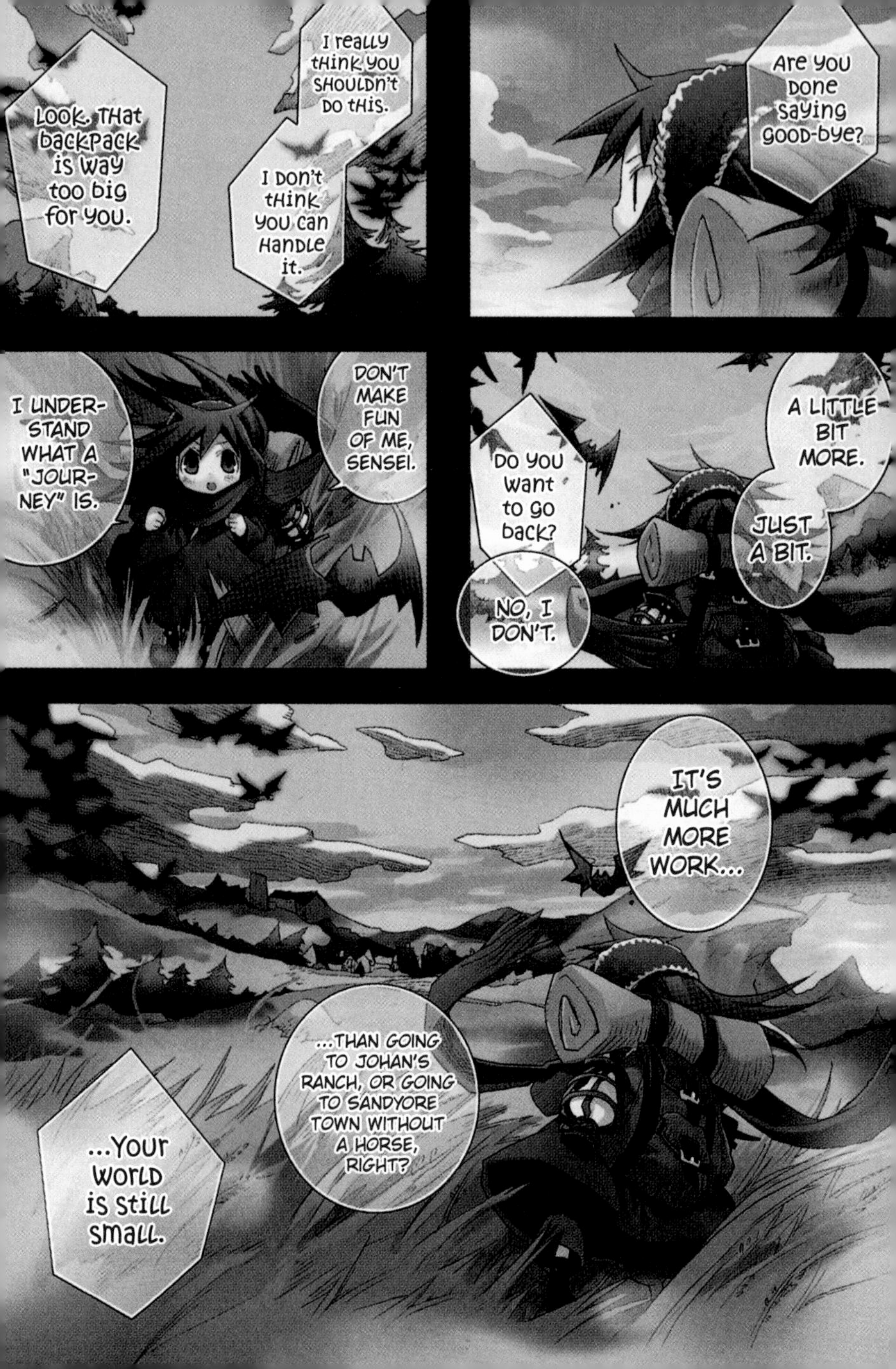
Are you done saying good-bye?
I really think you shouldn't do this.
I don't think you can handle it.
Look. That backpack is way too big for you.
A LITTLE BIT MORE.
JUST A BIT.
Do you want to go back?
NO, I DON'T.
DON'T MAKE FUN OF ME, SENSEI.
I UNDER-STAND WHAT A "JOUR-NEY" IS.
IT'S MUCH MORE WORK...
...THAN GOING TO JOHAN'S RANCH, OR GOING TO SANDYORE TOWN WITHOUT A HORSE, RIGHT?
...Your world is still small.

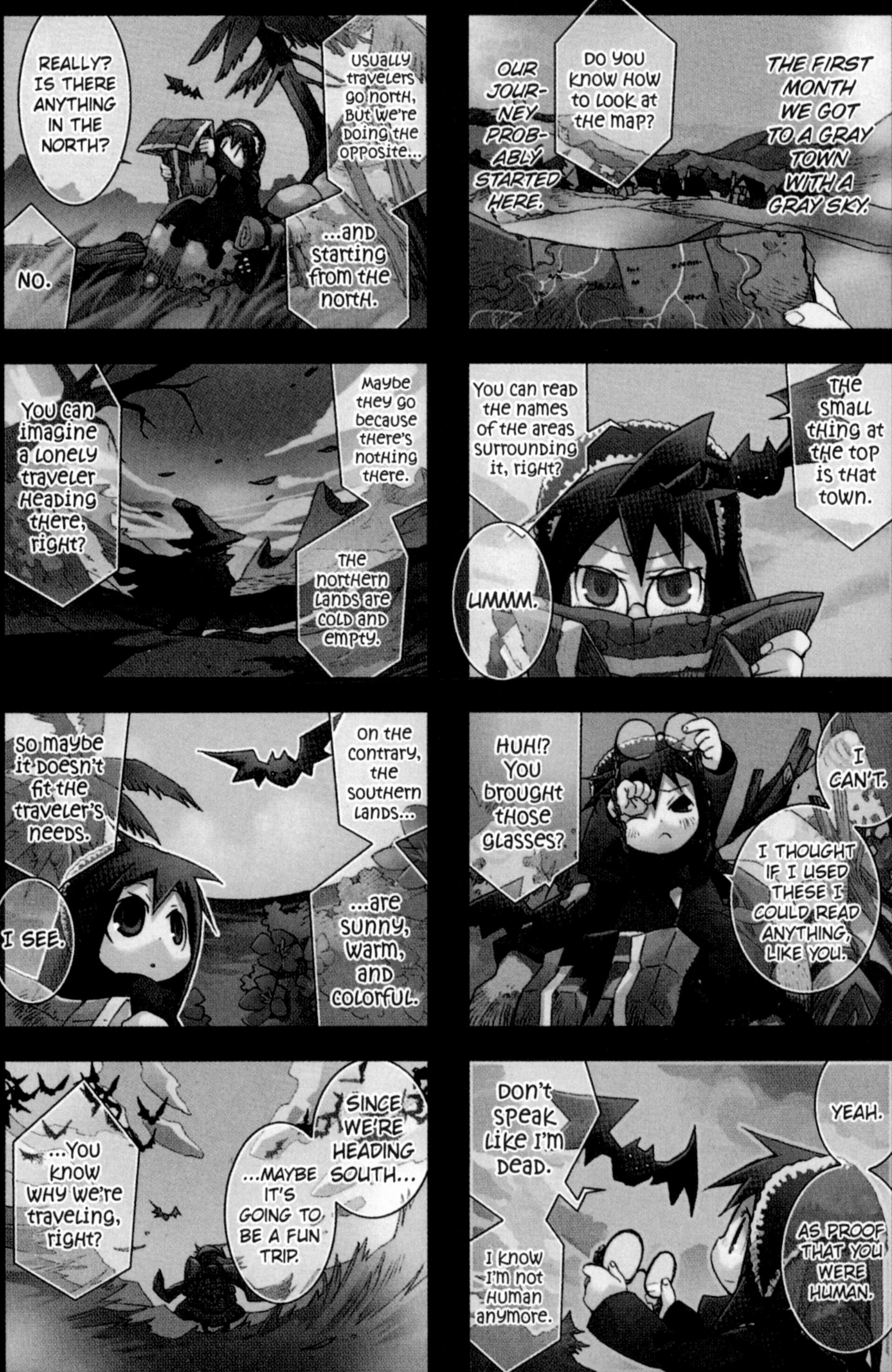
THE FIRST MONTH WE GOT TO A GRAY TOWN WITH A GRAY SKY.
DO YOU KNOW HOW TO LOOK AT THE MAP?
OUR JOURNEY PROBABLY STARTED HERE.
USUALLY TRAVELERS GO NORTH, BUT WE'RE DOING THE OPPOSITE...
REALLY? IS THERE ANYTHING IN THE NORTH?
...AND STARTING FROM THE NORTH.
NO.
THE SMALL THING AT THE TOP IS THAT TOWN.
YOU CAN READ THE NAMES OF THE AREAS SURROUNDING IT, RIGHT?
UMMM.
MAYBE THEY GO BECAUSE THERE'S NOTHING THERE.
YOU CAN IMAGINE A LONELY TRAVELER HEADING THERE, RIGHT?
THE NORTHERN LANDS ARE COLD AND EMPTY.
I CAN'T.
HUH!? YOU BROUGHT THOSE GLASSES?
I THOUGHT IF I USED THESE I COULD READ ANYTHING, LIKE YOU.
ON THE CONTRARY, THE SOUTHERN LANDS...
SO MAYBE IT DOESN'T FIT THE TRAVELER'S NEEDS.
...ARE SUNNY, WARM, AND COLORFUL.
I SEE.
YEAH.
DON'T SPEAK LIKE I'M DEAD.
AS PROOF THAT YOU WERE HUMAN.
I KNOW I'M NOT HUMAN ANYMORE.
SINCE WE'RE HEADING SOUTH...
...YOU KNOW WHY WE'RE TRAVELING, RIGHT?
...MAYBE IT'S GOING TO BE A FUN TRIP.

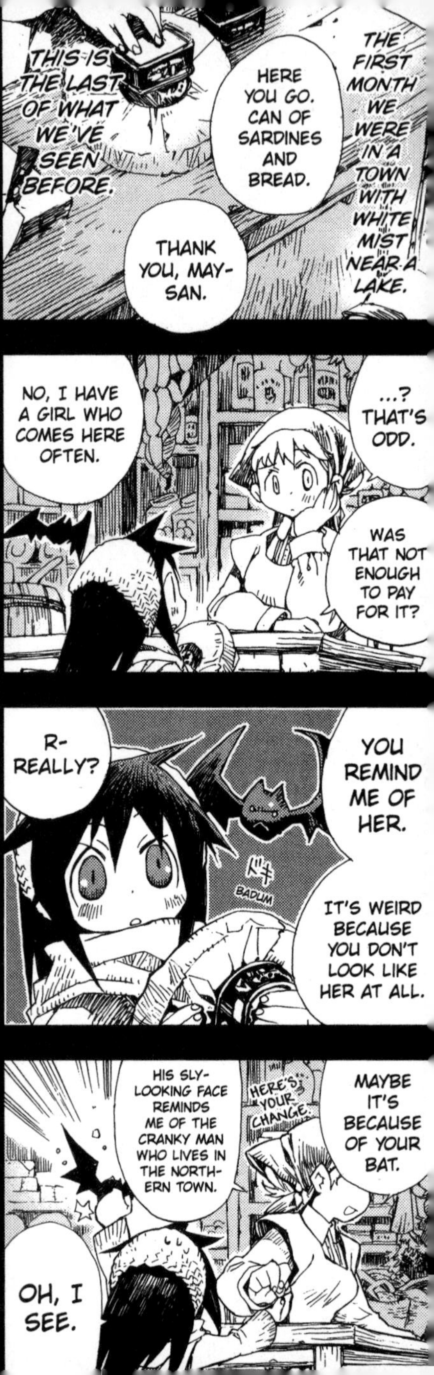
THE FIRST MONTH WE WERE IN A TOWN WITH WHITE MIST NEAR A LAKE.
HERE YOU GO. CAN OF SARDINES AND BREAD.
THIS IS THE LAST OF WHAT WE'VE SEEN BEFORE.
THANK YOU, MAY-SAN.
...? THAT'S ODD.
WAS THAT NOT ENOUGH TO PAY FOR IT?
NO, I HAVE A GIRL WHO COMES HERE OFTEN.
YOU REMIND ME OF HER.
IT'S WEIRD BECAUSE YOU DON'T LOOK LIKE HER AT ALL.
R-REALLY?
ドキ
BADUM
MAYBE IT'S BECAUSE OF YOUR BAT.
HERE'S YOUR CHANGE.
HIS SLY-LOOKING FACE REMINDS ME OF THE CRANKY MAN WHO LIVES IN THE NORTH-ERN TOWN.
OH, I SEE.

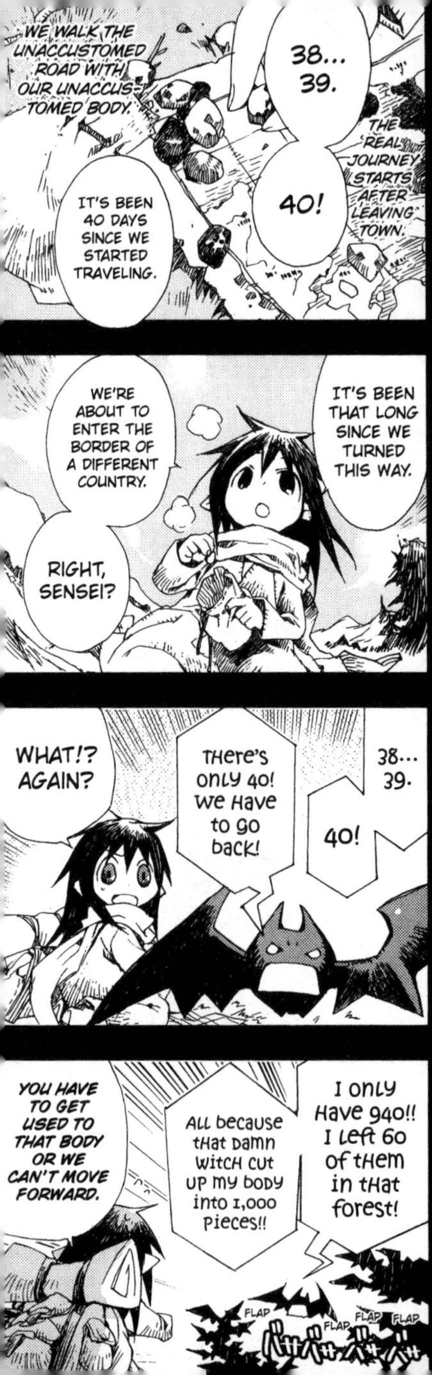
38... 39.
40!
THE REAL JOURNEY STARTS AFTER LEAVING TOWN.
WE WALK THE UNACCUSTOMED ROAD WITH OUR UNACCUS-TOMED BODY.
IT'S BEEN 40 DAYS SINCE WE STARTED TRAVELING.
IT'S BEEN THAT LONG SINCE WE TURNED THIS WAY.
WE'RE ABOUT TO ENTER THE BORDER OF A DIFFERENT COUNTRY.
RIGHT, SENSEI?
38... 39.
40!
There's only 40! We have to go back!
WHAT!? AGAIN?
I only have 940!! I left 60 of them in that forest!
All because that damn witch cut up my body into 1,000 pieces!!
YOU HAVE TO GET USED TO THAT BODY OR WE CAN'T MOVE FORWARD.
FLAP FLAP FLAP FLAP

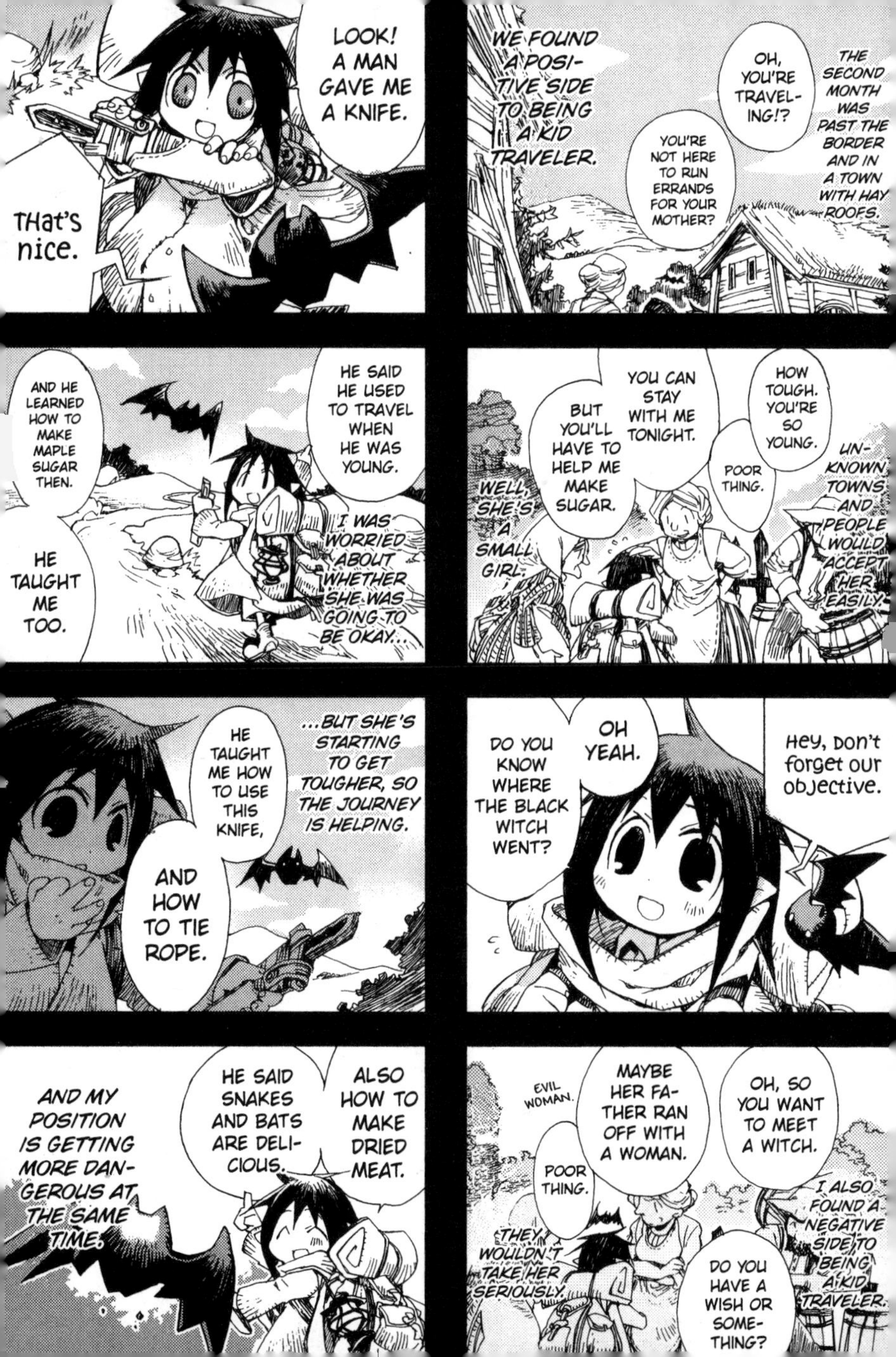
THE SECOND MONTH WAS PAST THE BORDER AND IN A TOWN WITH HAY ROOFS.
OH, YOU'RE TRAVELING!?
YOU'RE NOT HERE TO RUN ERRANDS FOR YOUR MOTHER?
WE FOUND A POSITIVE SIDE TO BEING A KID TRAVELER.
LOOK! A MAN GAVE ME A KNIFE.
THAT's nice.
HOW TOUGH. YOU'RE SO YOUNG.
UNKNOWN TOWNS AND PEOPLE WOULD ACCEPT HER EASILY.
POOR THING.
YOU CAN STAY WITH ME TONIGHT.
BUT YOU'LL HAVE TO HELP ME MAKE SUGAR.
WELL, SHE'S A SMALL GIRL.
HE SAID HE USED TO TRAVEL WHEN HE WAS YOUNG.
I WAS WORRIED ABOUT WHETHER SHE WAS GOING TO BE OKAY...
AND HE LEARNED HOW TO MAKE MAPLE SUGAR THEN.
HE TAUGHT ME TOO.
Hey, Don't forget our objective.
OH YEAH.
DO YOU KNOW WHERE THE BLACK WITCH WENT?
...BUT SHE'S STARTING TO GET TOUGHER, SO THE JOURNEY IS HELPING.
HE TAUGHT ME HOW TO USE THIS KNIFE,
AND HOW TO TIE ROPE.
OH, SO YOU WANT TO MEET A WITCH.
I ALSO FOUND A NEGATIVE SIDE TO BEING A KID TRAVELER.
MAYBE HER FATHER RAN OFF WITH A WOMAN.
EVIL WOMAN.
POOR THING.
DO YOU HAVE A WISH OR SOMETHING?
THEY WOULDN'T TAKE HER SERIOUSLY.
ALSO HOW TO MAKE DRIED MEAT.
HE SAID SNAKES AND BATS ARE DELICIOUS.
AND MY POSITION IS GETTING MORE DANGEROUS AT THE SAME TIME.

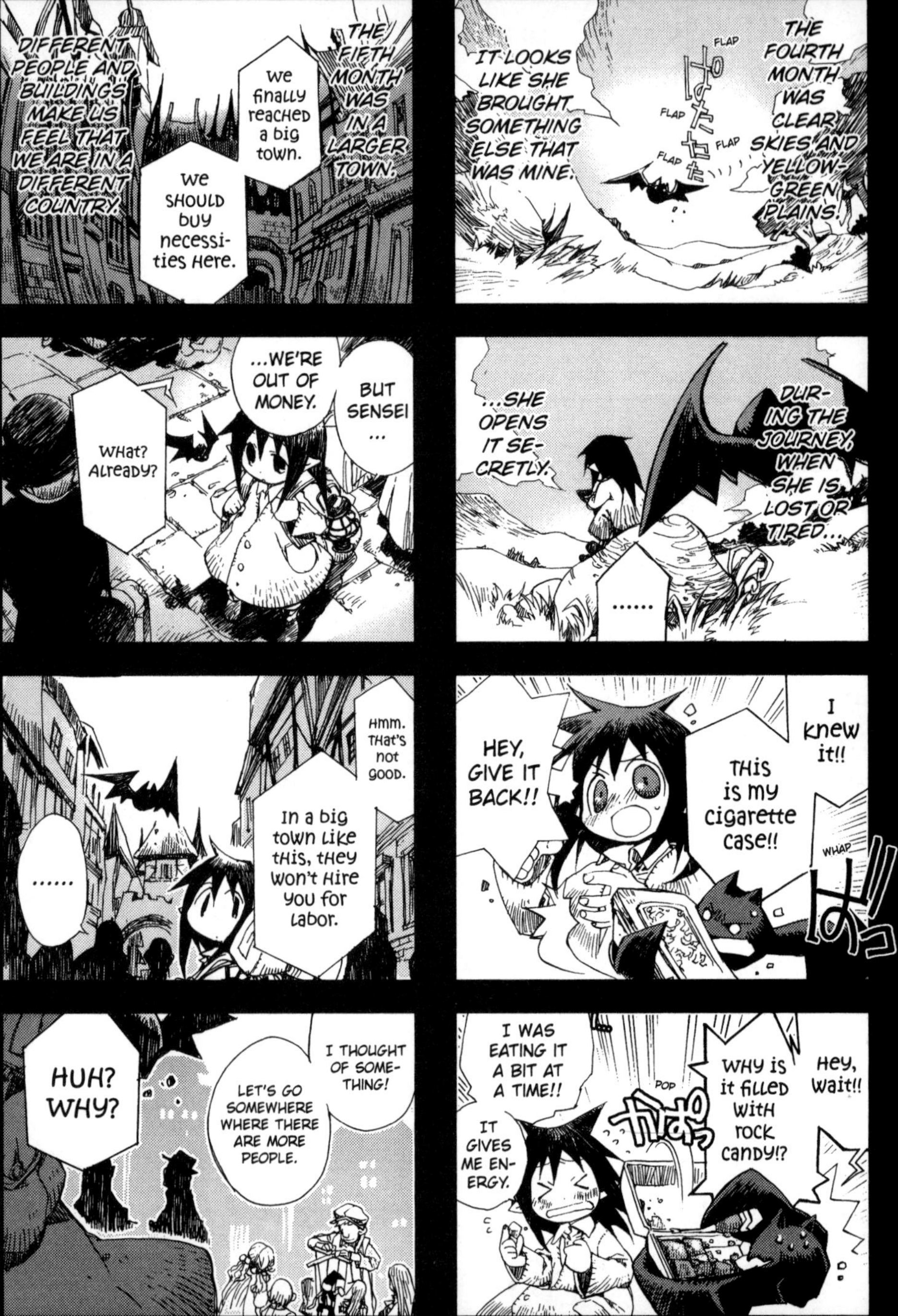
THE FOURTH MONTH WAS CLEAR SKIES AND YELLOW-GREEN PLAINS!
FLAP
ぱたたた
FLAP
FLAP
FLAP
IT LOOKS LIKE SHE BROUGHT SOMETHING ELSE THAT WAS MINE.
DURING THE JOURNEY, WHEN SHE IS LOST OR TIRED...
...SHE OPENS IT SECRETLY.
......
WHAP
はっ
I knew it!!
This is my cigarette case!!
HEY, GIVE IT BACK!!
Hey, wait!!
Why is it filled with rock candy!?
I WAS EATING IT A BIT AT A TIME!!
POP
かぽっ
IT GIVES ME ENERGY.
THE FIFTH MONTH WAS IN A LARGER TOWN.
We finally reached a big town.
DIFFERENT PEOPLE AND BUILDINGS MAKE US FEEL THAT WE ARE IN A DIFFERENT COUNTRY.
We should buy necessities here.
BUT SENSEI...
...WE'RE OUT OF MONEY.
What? Already?
Hmm. That's not good.
In a big town like this, they won't hire you for labor.
......
I THOUGHT OF SOMETHING!
LET'S GO SOMEWHERE WHERE THERE ARE MORE PEOPLE.
HUH? WHY?

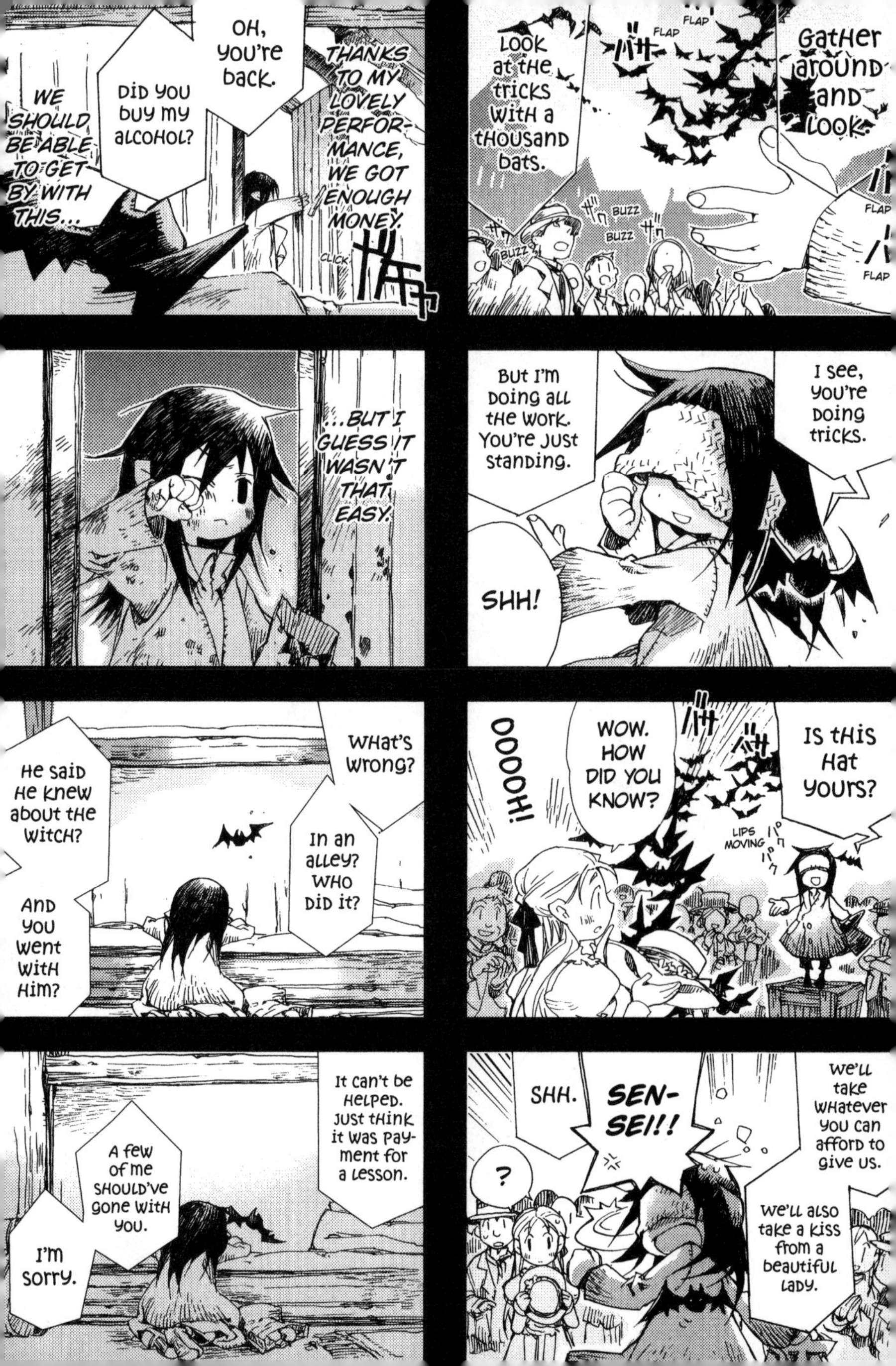
Gather around and look.
Look at the tricks with a thousand bats.
FLAP
FLAP
FLAP
FLAP
BUZZ
BUZZ
BUZZ
I see, you're doing tricks.
But I'm doing all the work. You're just standing.
SHH!
Is this hat yours?
WOW. HOW DID YOU KNOW?
OOOOOH!
LIPS MOVING
We'll take whatever you can afford to give us.
We'll also take a kiss from a beautiful lady.
SEN-SEI!!
SHH.
?
Oh, you're back.
Did you buy my alcohol?
Thanks to my lovely performance, we got enough money.
We should be able to get by with this...
CLICK
...but I guess it wasn't that easy.
What's wrong?
In an alley? Who did it?
He said he knew about the witch?
And you went with him?
It can't be helped. Just think it was payment for a lesson.
A few of me should've gone with you.
I'm sorry.

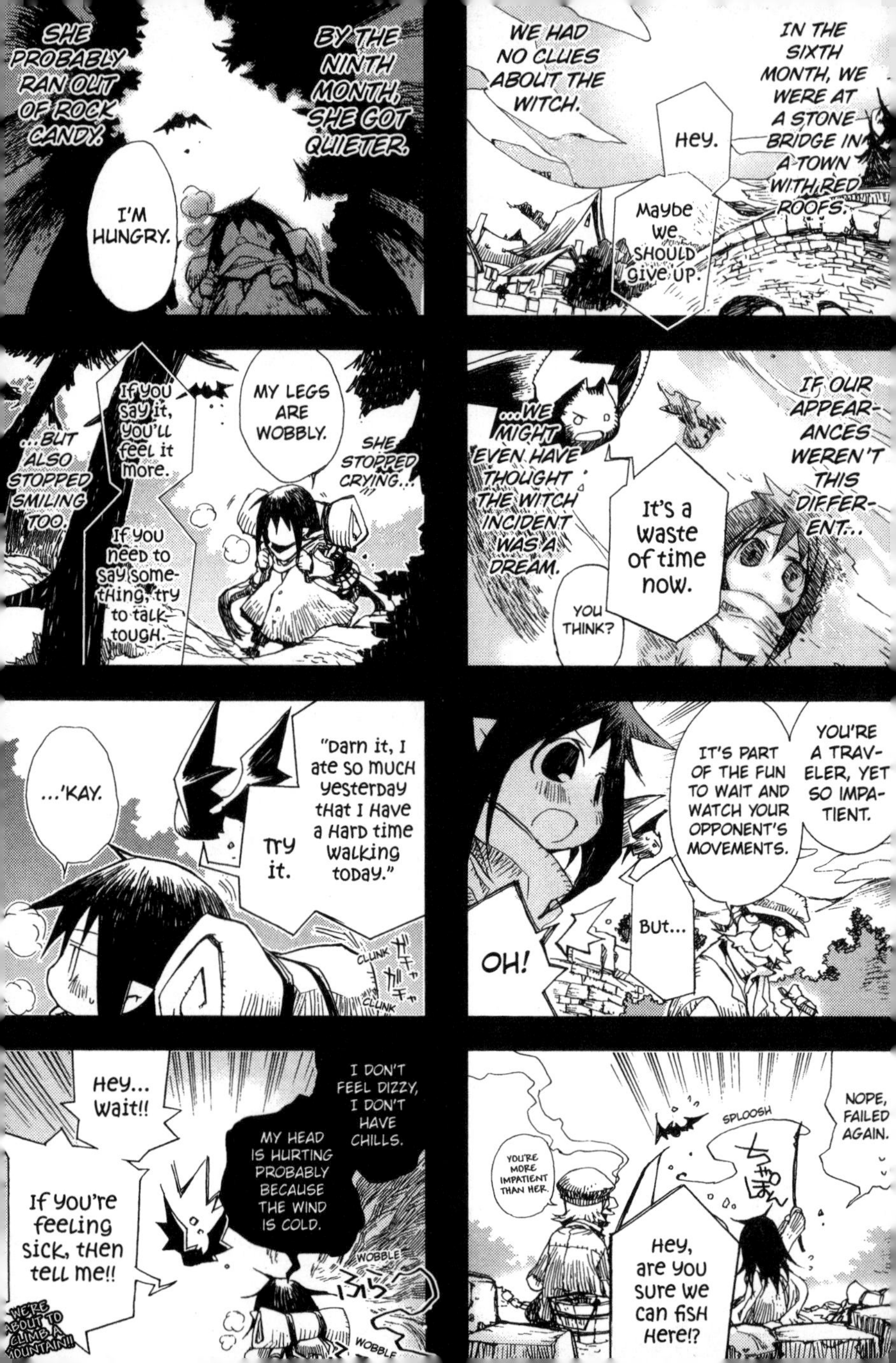
IN THE SIXTH MONTH, WE WERE AT A STONE BRIDGE IN A TOWN WITH RED ROOFS.
WE HAD NO CLUES ABOUT THE WITCH.
Hey.
Maybe we SHOULD give up.
BY THE NINTH MONTH, SHE GOT QUIETER.
SHE PROBABLY RAN OUT OF ROCK CANDY.
I'M HUNGRY.
IF OUR APPEAR-ANCES WEREN'T THIS DIFFER-ENT...
...WE MIGHT EVEN HAVE THOUGHT THE WITCH INCIDENT WAS A DREAM.
It's a waste of time now.
YOU THINK?
SHE STOPPED CRYING...
MY LEGS ARE WOBBLY.
If you say it, you'll feel it more.
...BUT ALSO STOPPED SMILING TOO.
If you need to say some-thing, try to talk tough.
YOU'RE A TRAV-ELER, YET SO IMPA-TIENT.
IT'S PART OF THE FUN TO WAIT AND WATCH YOUR OPPONENT'S MOVEMENTS.
But...
OH!
"Darn it, I ate so much yesterday that I have a hard time walking today."
Try it.
...'KAY.
CLUNK
CLUNK
NOPE, FAILED AGAIN.
SPLOOSH
YOU'RE MORE IMPATIENT THAN HER.
Hey, are you sure we can fish here!?
I DON'T FEEL DIZZY, I DON'T HAVE CHILLS.
MY HEAD IS HURTING PROBABLY BECAUSE THE WIND IS COLD.
Hey... Wait!!
If you're feeling sick, then tell me!!
WOBBLE
WOBBLE
WE'RE ABOUT TO CLIMB A MOUNTAIN!!

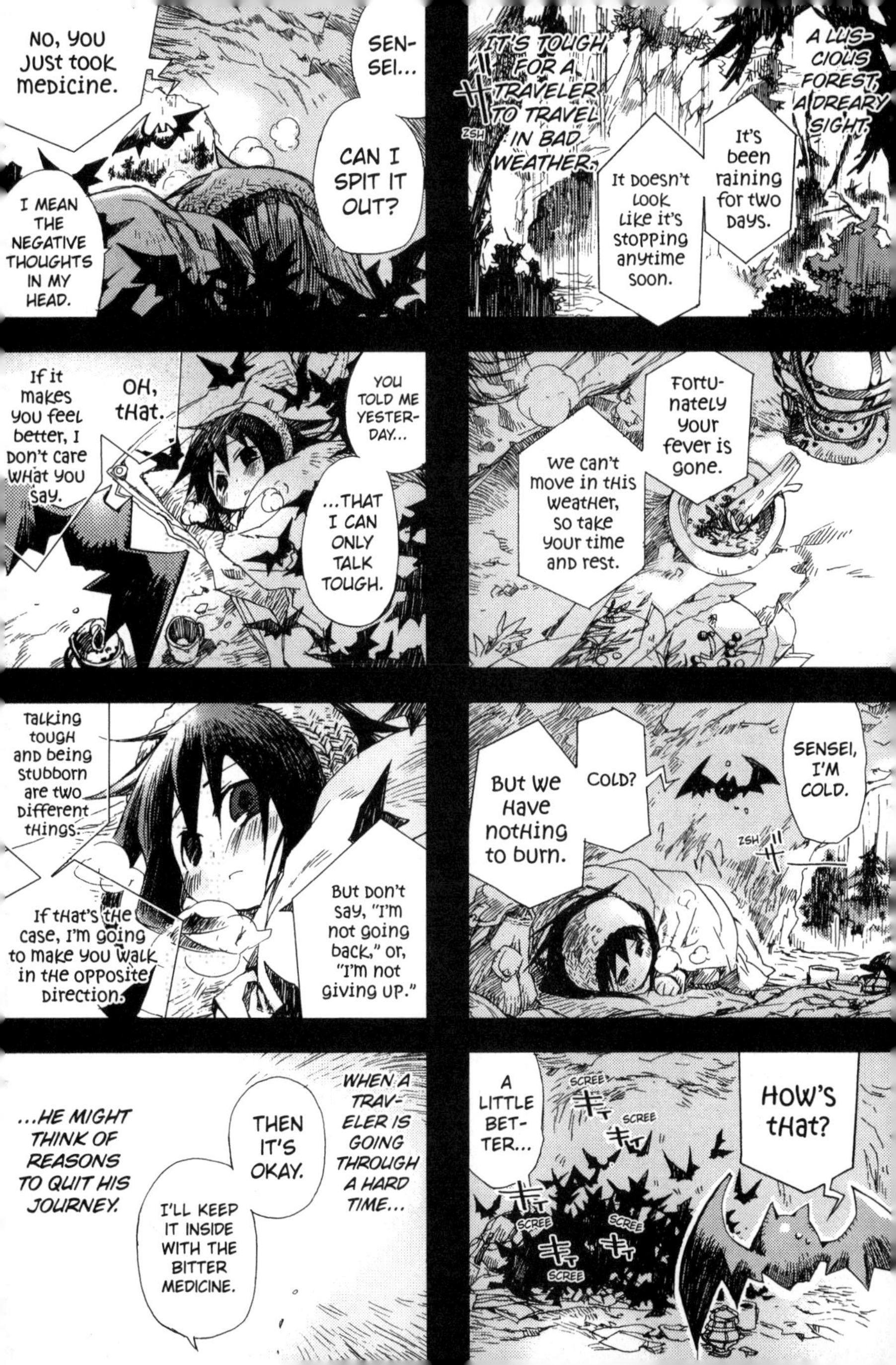
A LUSCIOUS FOREST, A DREARY SIGHT.
IT'S TOUGH FOR A TRAVELER TO TRAVEL IN BAD WEATHER.
ZSH
It's been raining for two days.
It doesn't look like it's stopping anytime soon.
SENSEI...
CAN I SPIT IT OUT?
NO, YOU JUST TOOK MEDICINE.
I MEAN THE NEGATIVE THOUGHTS IN MY HEAD.
Fortunately your fever is gone.
We can't move in this weather, so take your time and rest.
YOU TOLD ME YESTERDAY...
...THAT I CAN ONLY TALK TOUGH.
OH, THAT.
If it makes you feel better, I don't care what you say.
SENSEI, I'M COLD.
ZSH
COLD?
But we have nothing to burn.
Talking tough and being stubborn are two different things.
But don't say, "I'm not going back," or, "I'm not giving up."
If that's the case, I'm going to make you walk in the opposite direction.
HOW'S THAT?
SCREE
SCREE
A LITTLE BETTER...
SCREE
SCREE
SCREE
WHEN A TRAVELER IS GOING THROUGH A HARD TIME...
...HE MIGHT THINK OF REASONS TO QUIT HIS JOURNEY.
THEN IT'S OKAY.
I'LL KEEP IT INSIDE WITH THE BITTER MEDICINE.

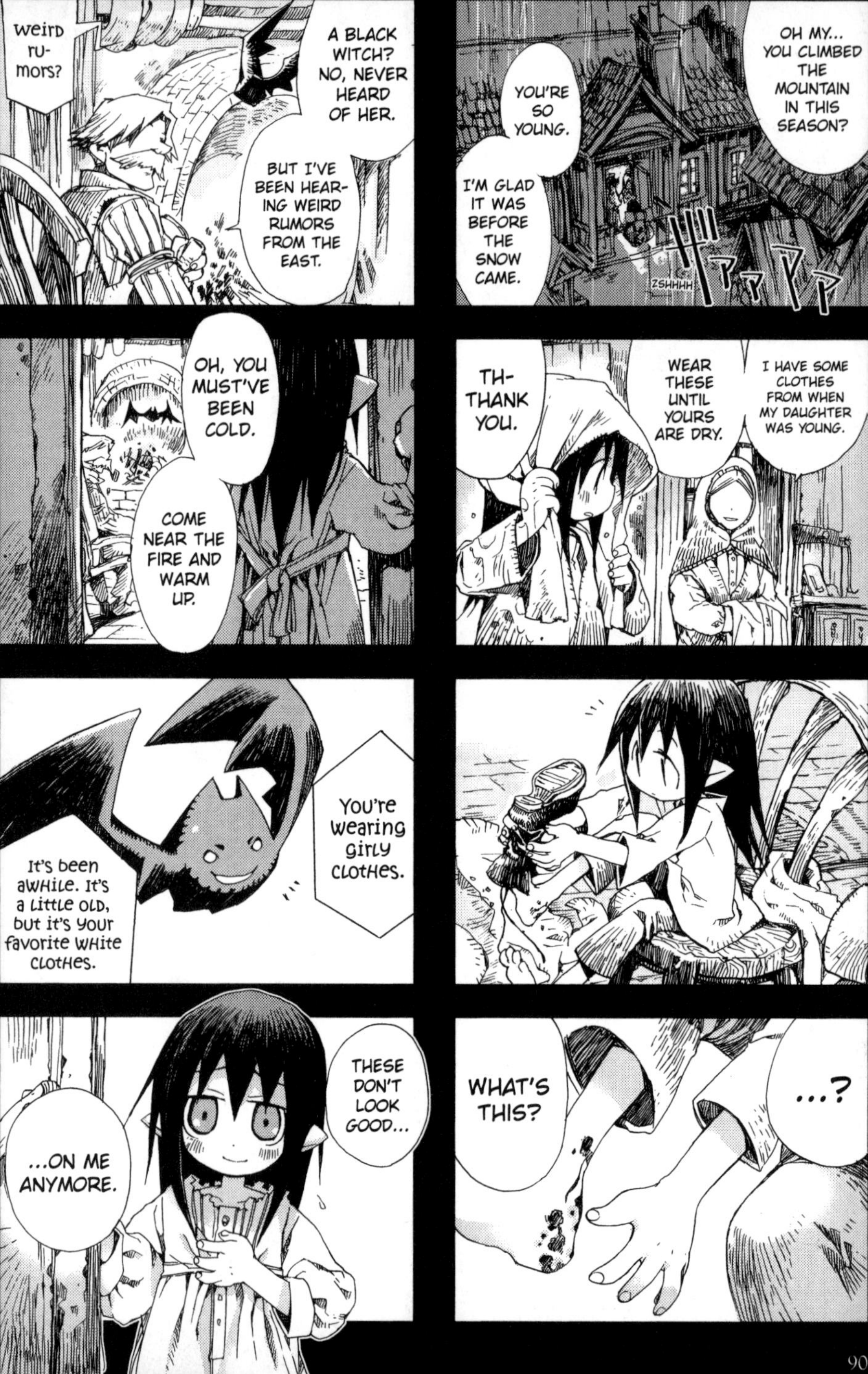
OH MY... YOU CLIMBED THE MOUNTAIN IN THIS SEASON?
YOU'RE SO YOUNG.
I'M GLAD IT WAS BEFORE THE SNOW CAME.
ZSHHHH
A BLACK WITCH? NO, NEVER HEARD OF HER.
BUT I'VE BEEN HEARING WEIRD RUMORS FROM THE EAST.
weird rumors?
I HAVE SOME CLOTHES FROM WHEN MY DAUGHTER WAS YOUNG.
WEAR THESE UNTIL YOURS ARE DRY.
TH- THANK YOU.
OH, YOU MUST'VE BEEN COLD.
COME NEAR THE FIRE AND WARM UP.
You're wearing girly clothes.
It's been awhile. It's a little old, but it's your favorite white clothes.
...?
WHAT'S THIS?
THESE DON'T LOOK GOOD...
...ON ME ANYMORE.

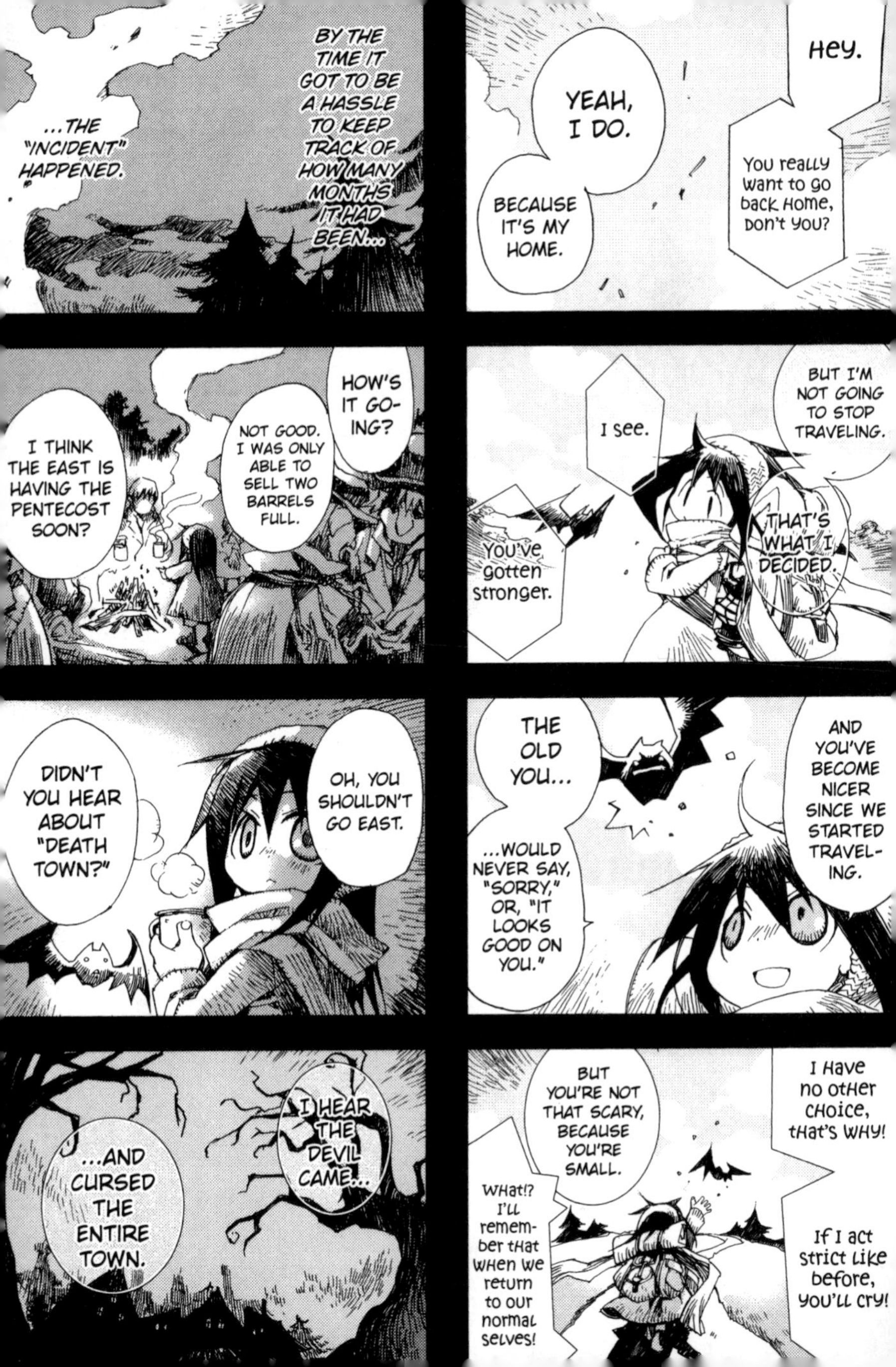
Hey.
You really want to go back home, don't you?
YEAH, I DO.
BECAUSE IT'S MY HOME.
BUT I'M NOT GOING TO STOP TRAVELING.
I see.
THAT'S WHAT I DECIDED.
You've gotten stronger.
AND YOU'VE BECOME NICER SINCE WE STARTED TRAVEL-ING.
THE OLD YOU...
...WOULD NEVER SAY, "SORRY," OR, "IT LOOKS GOOD ON YOU."
I Have no other choice, that's WHY!
BUT YOU'RE NOT THAT SCARY, BECAUSE YOU'RE SMALL.
If I act strict like before, you'll cry!
WHAT!? I'll remem-ber that when we return to our normal selves!
BY THE TIME IT GOT TO BE A HASSLE TO KEEP TRACK OF HOW MANY MONTHS IT HAD BEEN...
..."THE "INCIDENT" HAPPENED.
HOW'S IT GO-ING?
NOT GOOD. I WAS ONLY ABLE TO SELL TWO BARRELS FULL.
I THINK THE EAST IS HAVING THE PENTECOST SOON?
OH, YOU SHOULDN'T GO EAST.
DIDN'T YOU HEAR ABOUT "DEATH TOWN?"
I HEAR THE DEVIL CAME...
...AND CURSED THE ENTIRE TOWN.

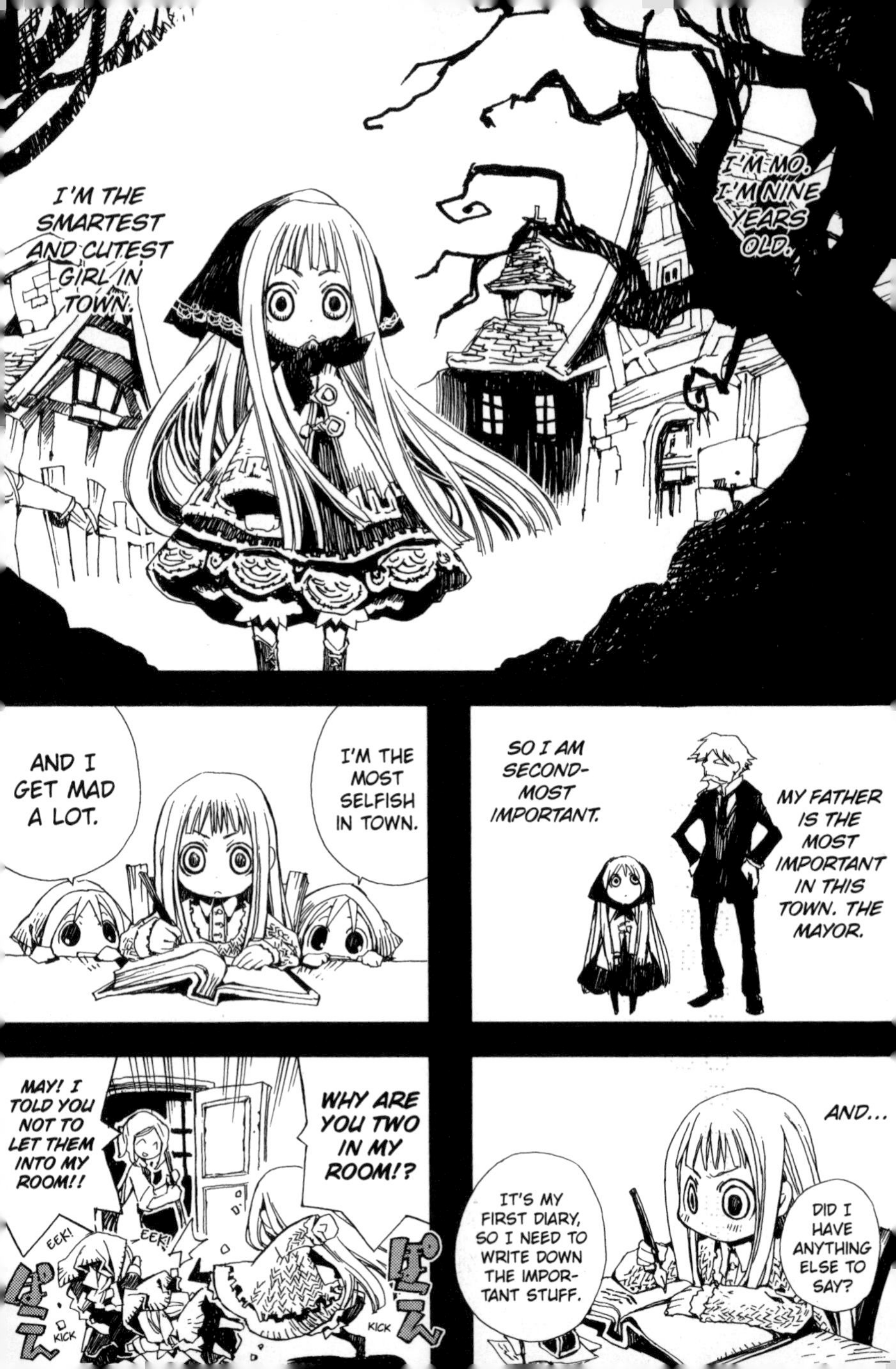
I'M MO. I'M NINE YEARS OLD.
I'M THE SMARTEST AND CUTEST GIRL IN TOWN.
MY FATHER IS THE MOST IMPORTANT IN THIS TOWN. THE MAYOR.
SO I AM SECOND-MOST IMPORTANT.
I'M THE MOST SELFISH IN TOWN.
AND I GET MAD A LOT.
AND...
DID I HAVE ANYTHING ELSE TO SAY?
IT'S MY FIRST DIARY, SO I NEED TO WRITE DOWN THE IMPOR-TANT STUFF.
WHY ARE YOU TWO IN MY ROOM!?
ぽん
KICK
MAY! I TOLD YOU NOT TO LET THEM INTO MY ROOM!!
EEK!
EEK!
ぱん
KICK

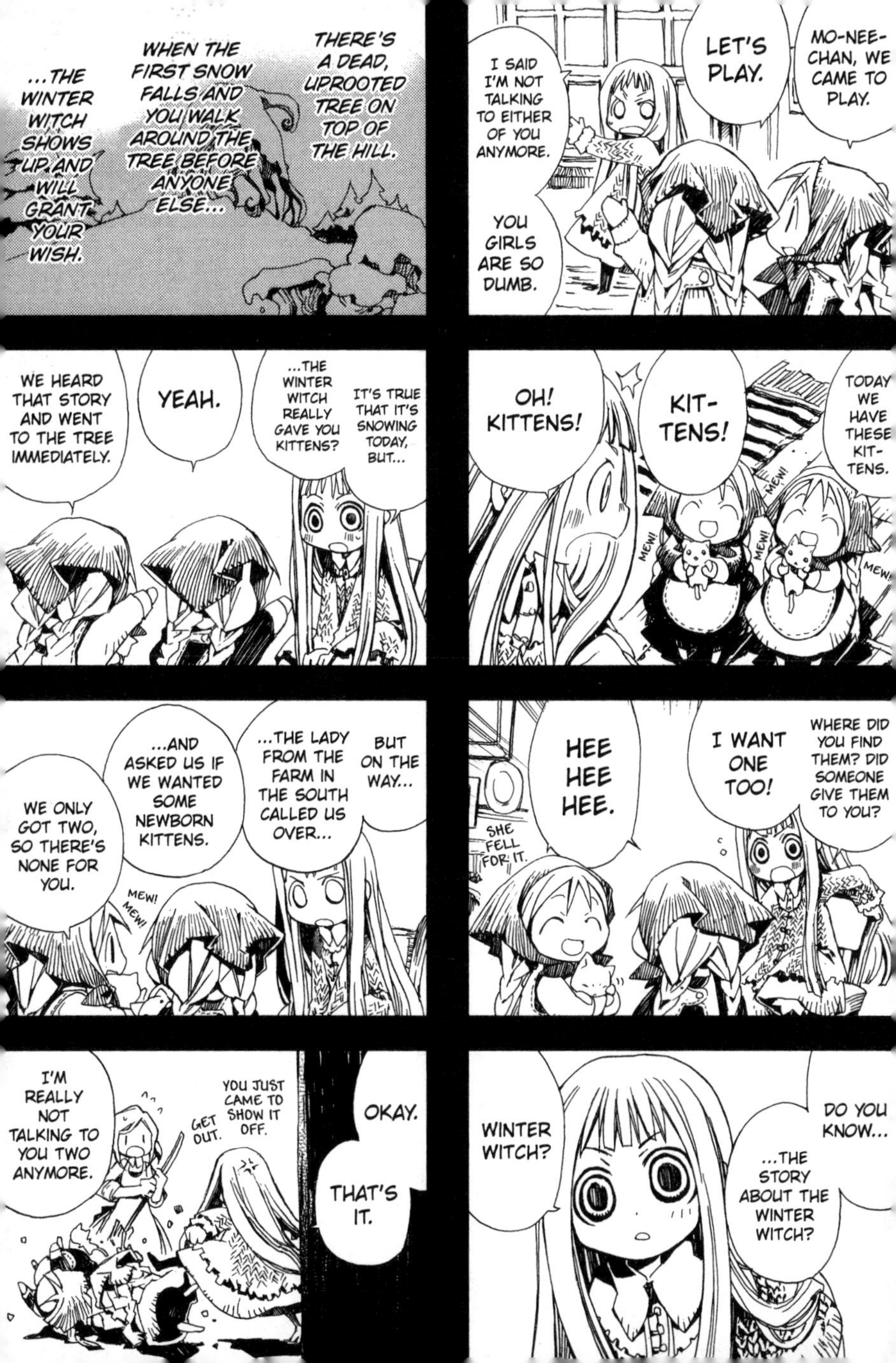
MO-NEE-CHAN, WE CAME TO PLAY.
LET'S PLAY.
I SAID I'M NOT TALKING TO EITHER OF YOU ANYMORE.
YOU GIRLS ARE SO DUMB.
THERE'S A DEAD, UPROOTED TREE ON TOP OF THE HILL.
WHEN THE FIRST SNOW FALLS AND YOU WALK AROUND THE TREE BEFORE ANYONE ELSE...
...THE WINTER WITCH SHOWS UP AND WILL GRANT YOUR WISH.
TODAY WE HAVE THESE KIT-TENS.
MEW!
MEW!
MEW!
KIT-TENS!
MEW!
OH! KITTENS!
IT'S TRUE THAT IT'S SNOWING TODAY, BUT...
...THE WINTER WITCH REALLY GAVE YOU KITTENS?
YEAH.
WE HEARD THAT STORY AND WENT TO THE TREE IMMEDIATELY.
WHERE DID YOU FIND THEM? DID SOMEONE GIVE THEM TO YOU?
I WANT ONE TOO!
HEE HEE HEE.
SHE FELL FOR IT.
BUT ON THE WAY...
...THE LADY FROM THE FARM IN THE SOUTH CALLED US OVER...
...AND ASKED US IF WE WANTED SOME NEWBORN KITTENS.
WE ONLY GOT TWO, SO THERE'S NONE FOR YOU.
MEW! MEW!
DO YOU KNOW...
...THE STORY ABOUT THE WINTER WITCH?
WINTER WITCH?
OKAY.
THAT'S IT.
YOU JUST CAME TO SHOW IT OFF.
GET OUT.
I'M REALLY NOT TALKING TO YOU TWO ANYMORE.

I DIDN'T WANT THE TWO TO FIND ME.

I LEFT EARLY THAT MORNING.

I STARTED TO THINK WHAT TO ASK FOR WHEN I SAW THE WITCH.

THE 12TH MONTH IS THE MONTH WHEN THE SUN DIES.

I WONDER IF SOMEONE BEAT ME TO IT.

SOMEONE'S THERE.

OH.

ALL THE CANDY IN TOWN.

BUT IF I EAT IT ALL, IT WILL BE GONE.

NEW CLOTHES FOR MY DOLL.

NO, I DON'T WANT TO WASTE MY WISH ON THAT.

A BIG DOLLHOUSE IN RED AND GREEN.

I WANT TO BE AN ADULT NOW.

THREE KITTENS.

THAT'S NO ONE FROM THE TOWN.

I WAS SMART, SO I REALIZED IT SOON.

MAYBE I COULD ASK FOR A HUNDRED WISHES.

AND THAT WOULD BE MY WISH.

....
....

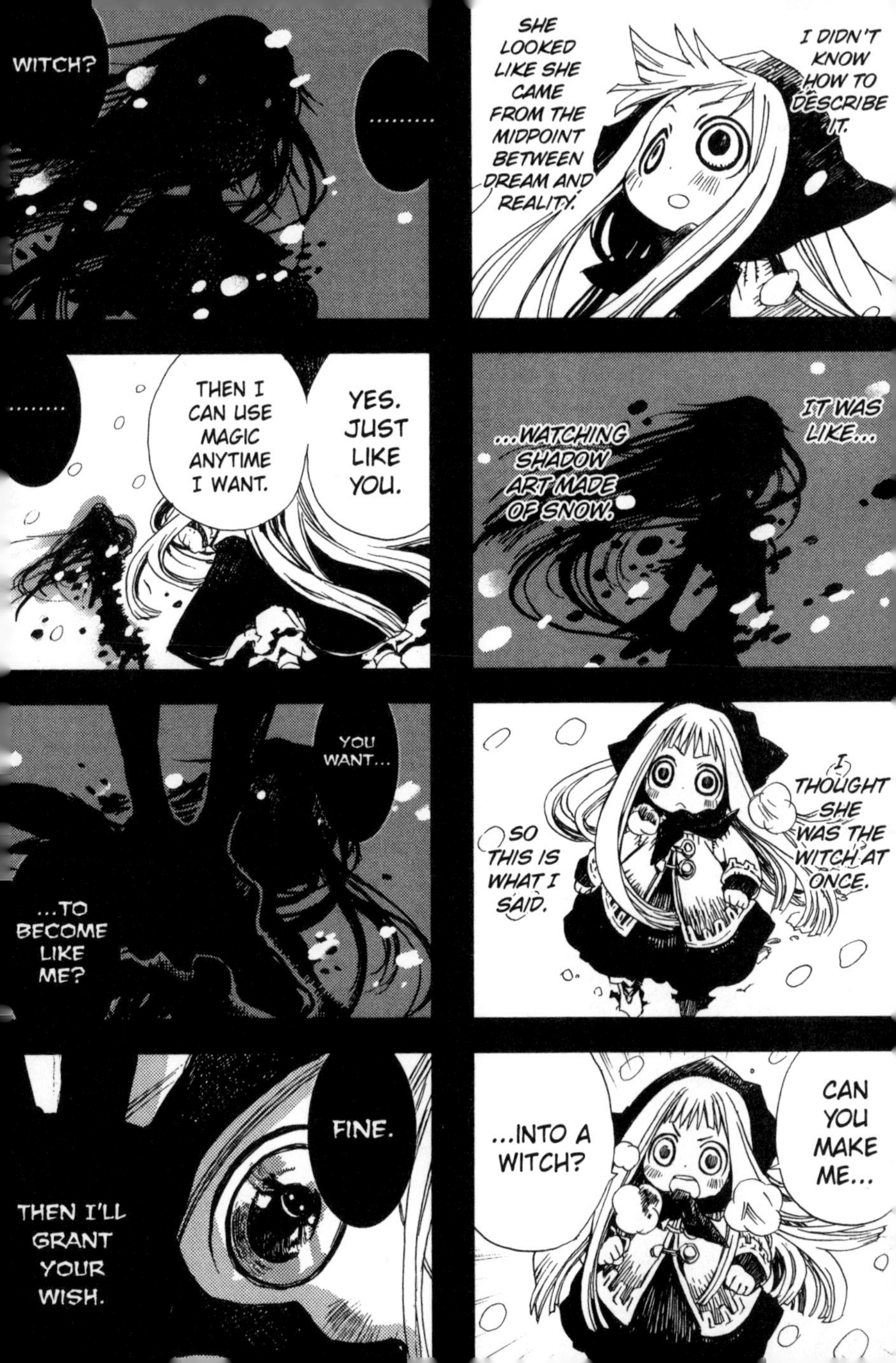
I DIDN'T KNOW HOW TO DESCRIBE IT.
SHE LOOKED LIKE SHE CAME FROM THE MIDPOINT BETWEEN DREAM AND REALITY.
WITCH?
....
IT WAS LIKE...
...WATCHING SHADOW ART MADE OF SNOW.
YES. JUST LIKE YOU.
THEN I CAN USE MAGIC ANYTIME I WANT.
....
I THOUGHT SHE WAS THE WITCH AT ONCE.
SO THIS IS WHAT I SAID.
YOU WANT...
...TO BECOME LIKE ME?
CAN YOU MAKE ME...
...INTO A WITCH?
FINE.
THEN I'LL GRANT YOUR WISH.

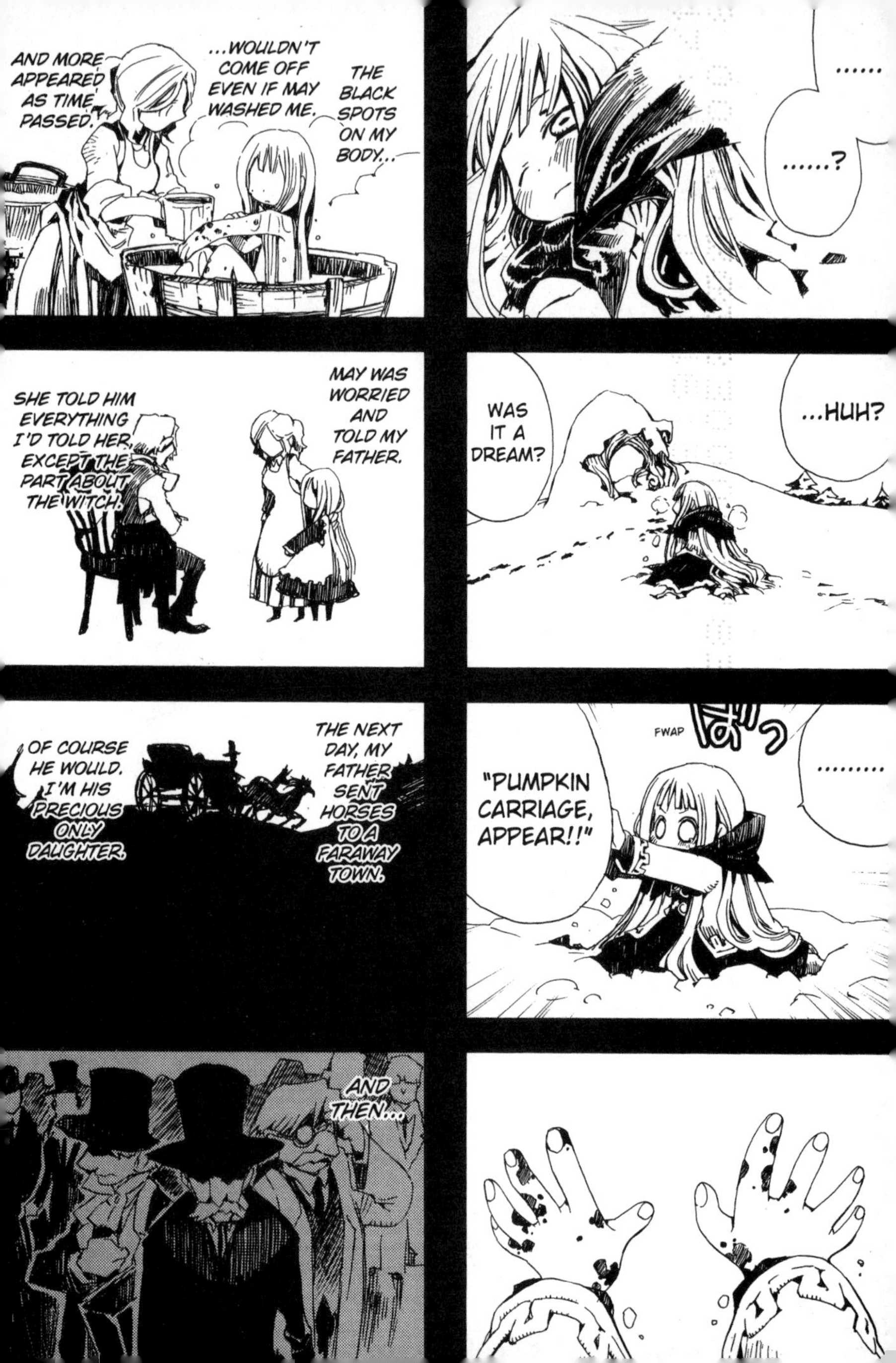
......
......?
THE BLACK SPOTS ON MY BODY...
...WOULDN'T COME OFF EVEN IF MAY WASHED ME.
AND MORE APPEARED AS TIME PASSED.
...HUH?
WAS IT A DREAM?
MAY WAS WORRIED AND TOLD MY FATHER.
SHE TOLD HIM EVERYTHING I'D TOLD HER, EXCEPT THE PART ABOUT THE WITCH.
ぱっ
FWAP
....
"PUMPKIN CARRIAGE, APPEAR!!"
THE NEXT DAY, MY FATHER SENT HORSES TO A FARAWAY TOWN.
OF COURSE HE WOULD. I'M HIS PRECIOUS ONLY DAUGHTER.
AND THEN...

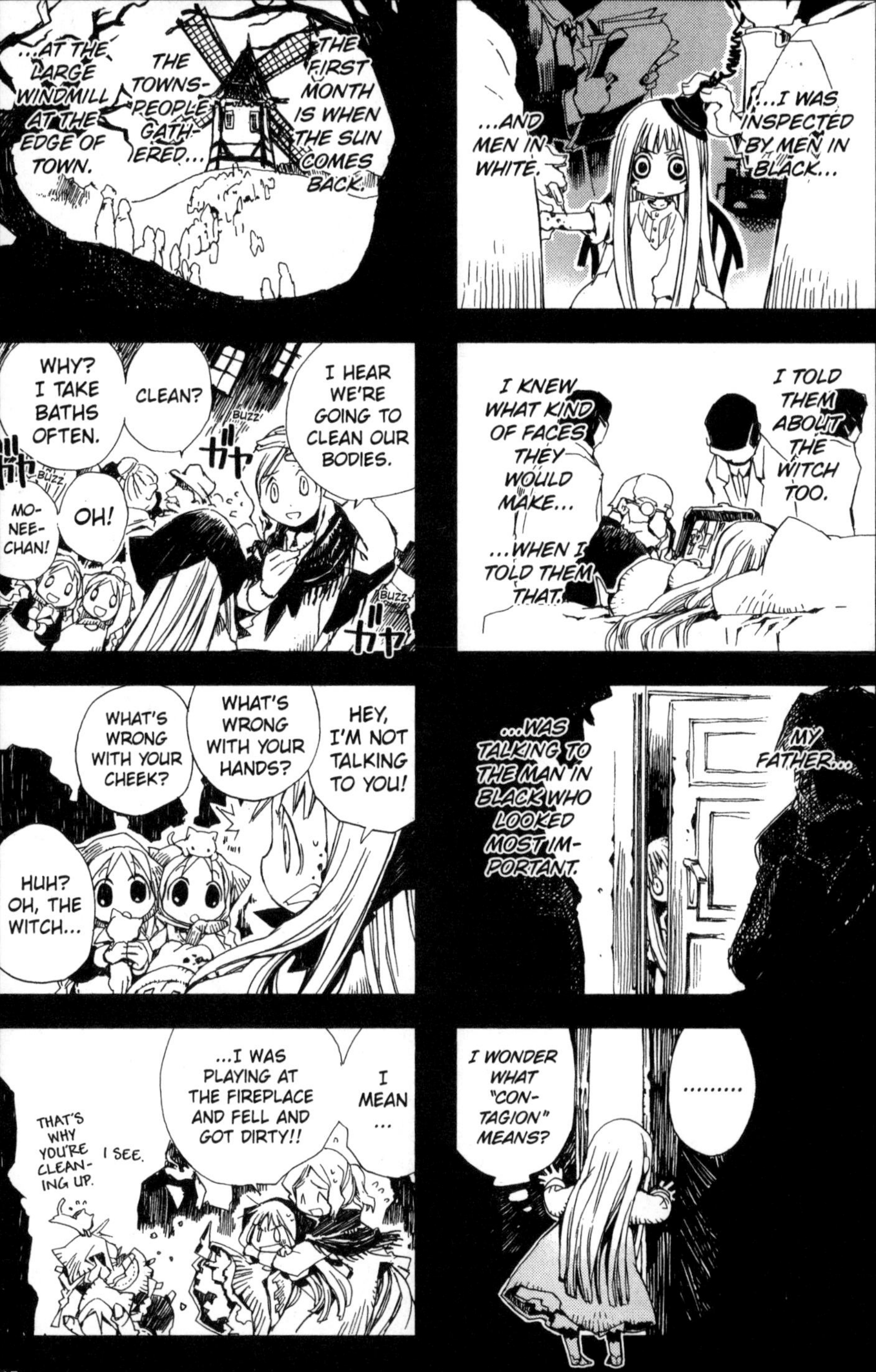
...I WAS INSPECTED BY MEN IN BLACK...
...AND MEN IN WHITE.
THE FIRST MONTH IS WHEN THE SUN COMES BACK.
THE TOWNSPEOPLE GATHERED...
...AT THE LARGE WINDMILL AT THE EDGE OF TOWN.
I TOLD THEM ABOUT THE WITCH TOO.
I KNEW WHAT KIND OF FACES THEY WOULD MAKE...
...WHEN I TOLD THEM THAT.
I HEAR WE'RE GOING TO CLEAN OUR BODIES.
BUZZ
ガヤ
CLEAN?
WHY? I TAKE BATHS OFTEN.
ガヤ
BUZZ
OH!
MO-NEE-CHAN!
BUZZ
ガヤ
MY FATHER...
...WAS TALKING TO THE MAN IN BLACK WHO LOOKED MOST IMPORTANT.
HEY, I'M NOT TALKING TO YOU!
WHAT'S WRONG WITH YOUR HANDS?
WHAT'S WRONG WITH YOUR CHEEK?
HUH? OH, THE WITCH...
....
I WONDER WHAT "CONTAGION" MEANS?
I MEAN...
...I WAS PLAYING AT THE FIREPLACE AND FELL AND GOT DIRTY!!
I SEE.
THAT'S WHY YOU'RE CLEANING UP.

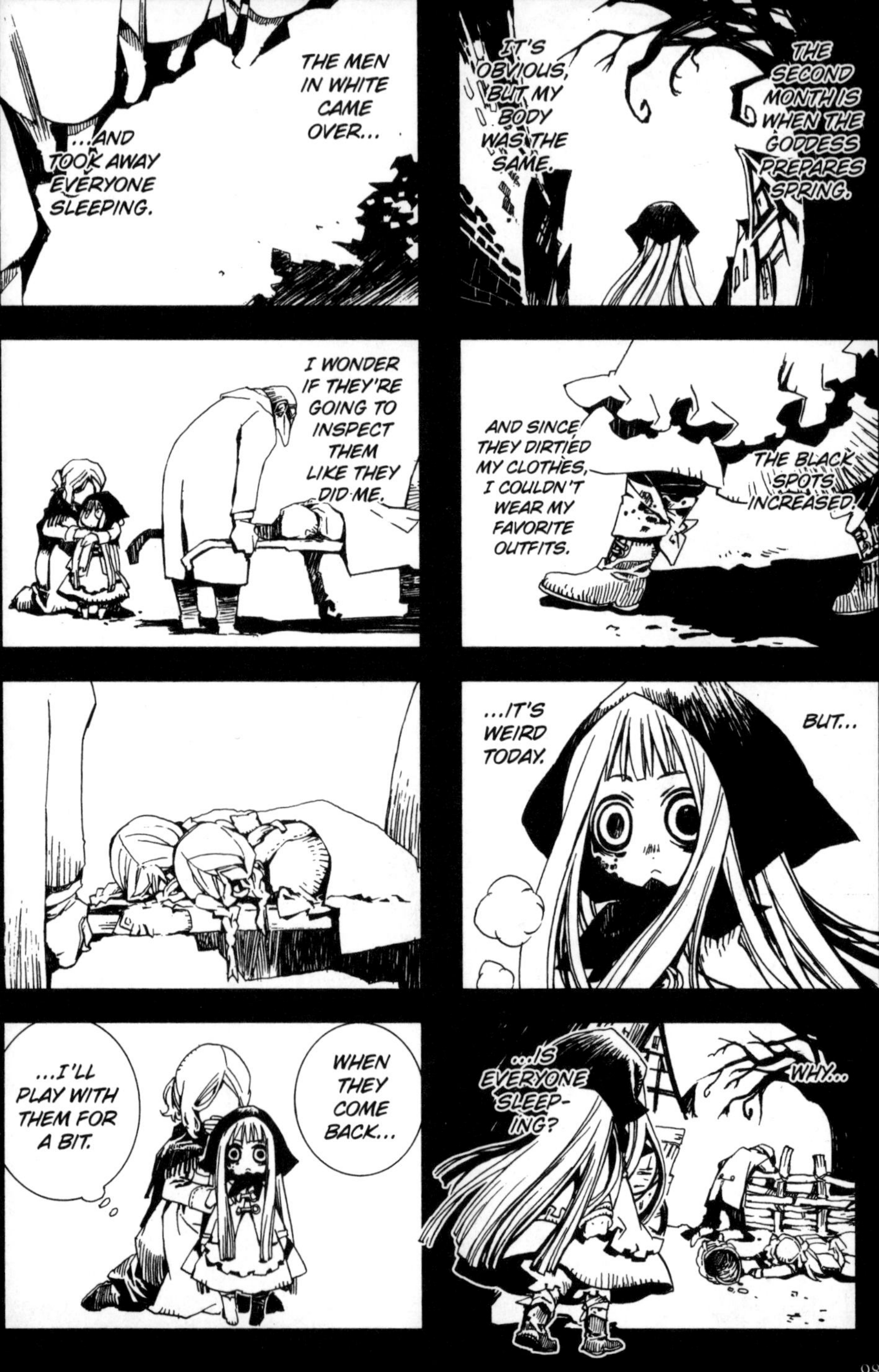
THE SECOND MONTH IS WHEN THE GODDESS PREPARES SPRING.
IT'S OBVIOUS, BUT MY BODY WAS THE SAME.
THE MEN IN WHITE CAME OVER...
...AND TOOK AWAY EVERYONE SLEEPING.
THE BLACK SPOTS INCREASED.
AND SINCE THEY DIRTIED MY CLOTHES, I COULDN'T WEAR MY FAVORITE OUTFITS.
I WONDER IF THEY'RE GOING TO INSPECT THEM LIKE THEY DID ME.
BUT...
...IT'S WEIRD TODAY.
WHY...
...IS EVERYONE SLEEPING?
WHEN THEY COME BACK...
...I'LL PLAY WITH THEM FOR A BIT.

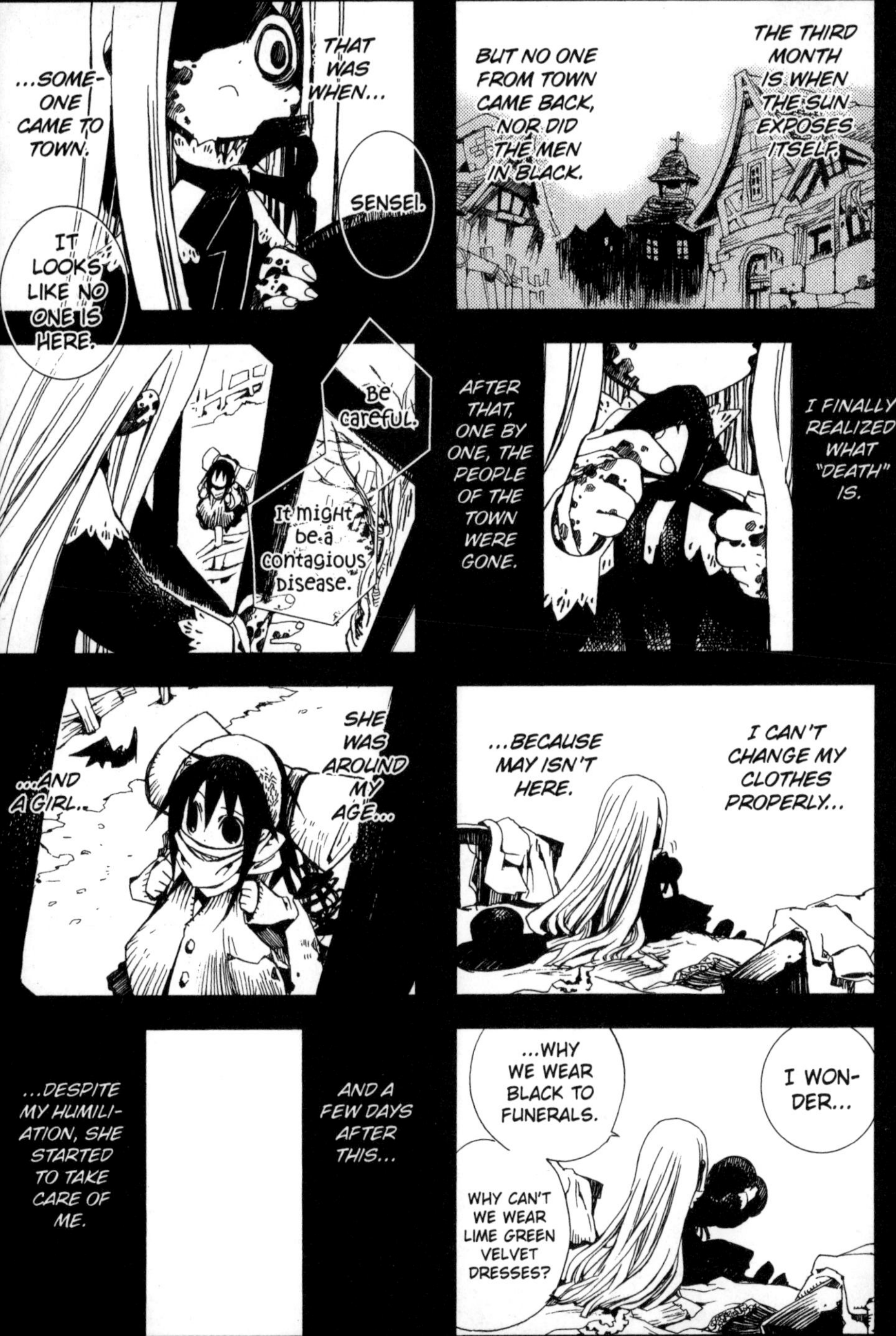
THE THIRD MONTH IS WHEN THE SUN EXPOSES ITSELF.
BUT NO ONE FROM TOWN CAME BACK, NOR DID THE MEN IN BLACK.
THAT WAS WHEN...
...SOME-ONE CAME TO TOWN.
SENSEI.
IT LOOKS LIKE NO ONE IS HERE.
I FINALLY REALIZED WHAT "DEATH" IS.
AFTER THAT, ONE BY ONE, THE PEOPLE OF THE TOWN WERE GONE.
Be careful.
It might be a contagious disease.
I CAN'T CHANGE MY CLOTHES PROPERLY...
...BECAUSE MAY ISN'T HERE.
SHE WAS AROUND MY AGE...
...AND A GIRL..
I WON-DER...
...WHY WE WEAR BLACK TO FUNERALS.
WHY CAN'T WE WEAR LIME GREEN VELVET DRESSES?
AND A FEW DAYS AFTER THIS...
...DESPITE MY HUMILI-ATION, SHE STARTED TO TAKE CARE OF ME.

"...WAS WHAT A WEIRD TOWN."

...THE FIRST THING I THOUGHT WHEN I ENTERED THE TOWN...

THE FIRST DAY...

IT'S LIKE A CEMETERY.

...A MYSTERIOUS GIRL SHOWED UP...

THAT'S WHEN...

I SEE. IT'S A DEAD TOWN INDEED.

THERE ARE MANY COFFINS HERE.

AND ASKED US TO HELP HER WITH HER WEIRD CEREMONY.

IF YOU'RE BORED, CAN YOU HELP?

I'M HOLDING A FUNERAL.

WE'RE LOOKING FOR A WITCH, THOUGH.

GHOSTS WON'T SHOW UP, RIGHT?

HEY.

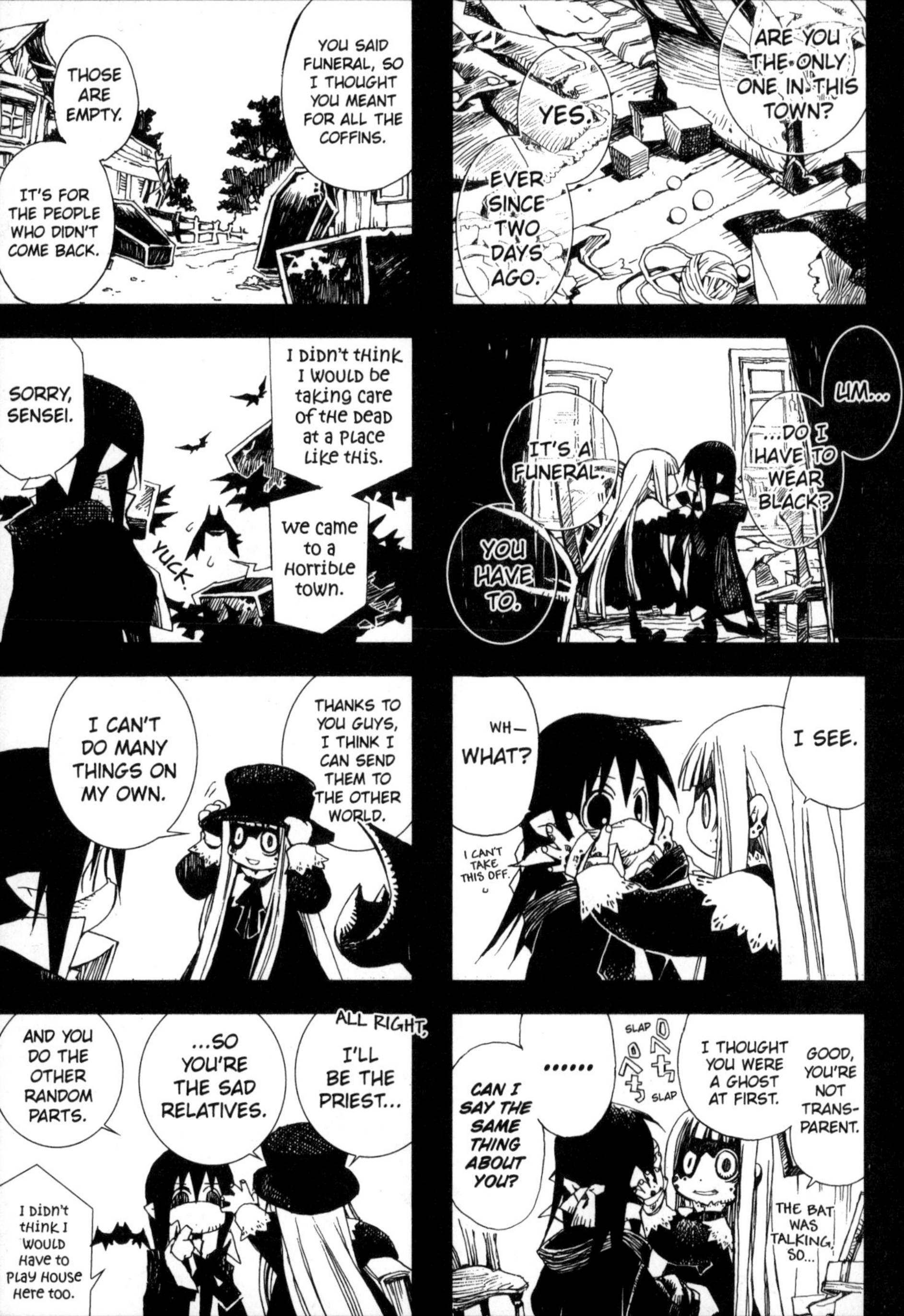
ARE YOU THE ONLY ONE IN THIS TOWN?
YES.
EVER SINCE TWO DAYS AGO.
YOU SAID FUNERAL, SO I THOUGHT YOU MEANT FOR ALL THE COFFINS.
THOSE ARE EMPTY.
IT'S FOR THE PEOPLE WHO DIDN'T COME BACK.
UM...
...DO I HAVE TO WEAR BLACK?
IT'S A FUNERAL.
YOU HAVE TO.
I didn't think I would be taking care of the dead at a place like this.
We came to a horrible town.
SORRY, SENSEI.
YUCK.
I SEE.
WH— WHAT?
I CAN'T TAKE THIS OFF.
THANKS TO YOU GUYS, I THINK I CAN SEND THEM TO THE OTHER WORLD.
I CAN'T DO MANY THINGS ON MY OWN.
GOOD, YOU'RE NOT TRANS-PARENT.
I THOUGHT YOU WERE A GHOST AT FIRST.
SLAP
SLAP
......
CAN I SAY THE SAME THING ABOUT YOU?
THE BAT WAS TALKING, SO...
ALL RIGHT, I'LL BE THE PRIEST...
...SO YOU'RE THE SAD RELATIVES.
AND YOU DO THE OTHER RANDOM PARTS.
I didn't think I would have to play house here too.

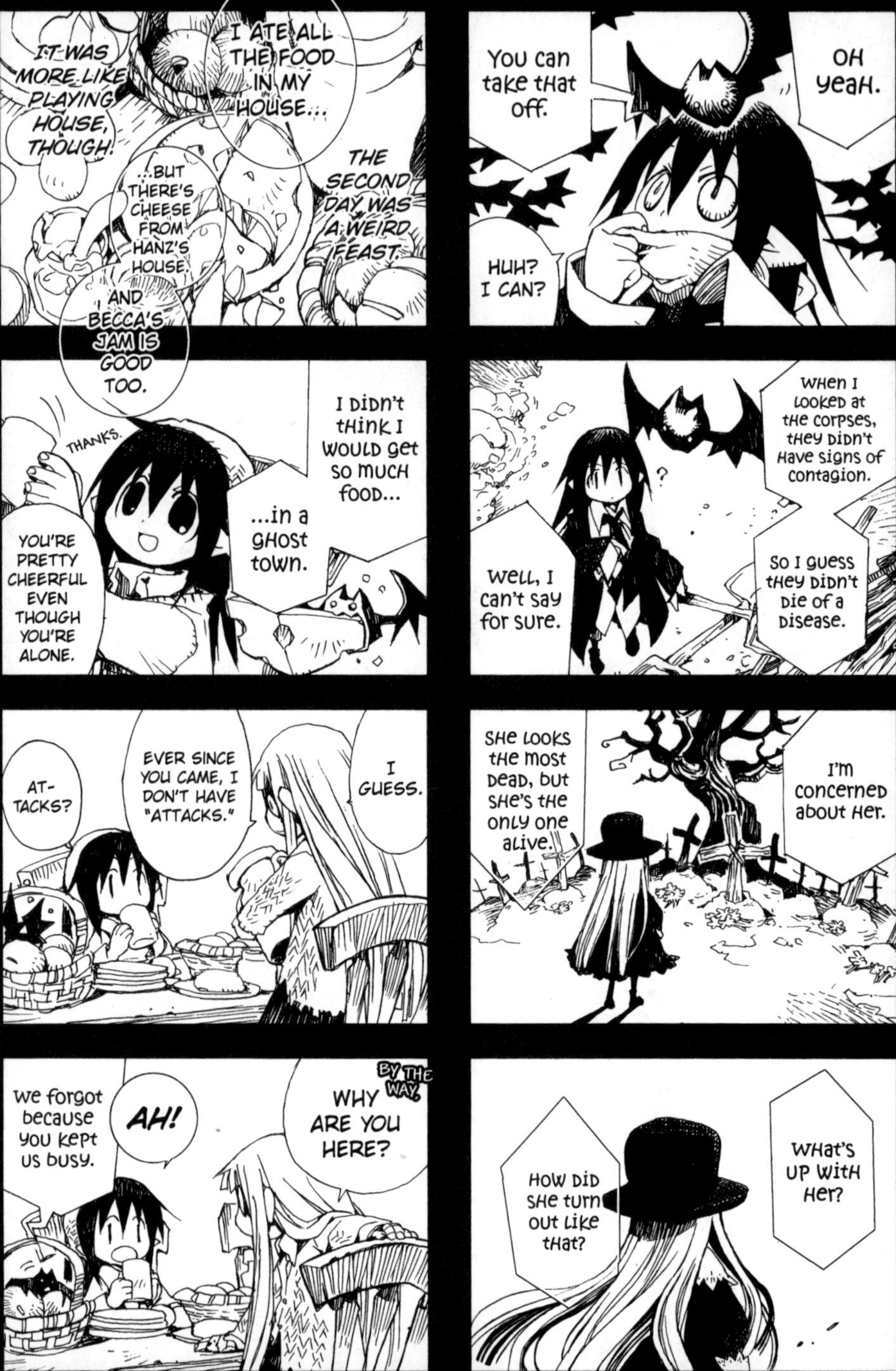
OH YEAH.
You can take that off.
HUH? I CAN?
THE SECOND DAY WAS A WEIRD FEAST.
I ATE ALL THE FOOD IN MY HOUSE...
IT WAS MORE LIKE PLAYING HOUSE, THOUGH!
...BUT THERE'S CHEESE FROM HANZ'S HOUSE.
AND BECCA'S JAM IS GOOD TOO.
When I looked at the corpses, they didn't have signs of contagion.
So I guess they didn't die of a disease.
Well, I can't say for sure.
I didn't think I would get so much food...
...in a ghost town.
THANKS.
YOU'RE PRETTY CHEERFUL EVEN THOUGH YOU'RE ALONE.
I'm concerned about her.
She looks the most dead, but she's the only one alive.
I GUESS.
EVER SINCE YOU CAME, I DON'T HAVE "ATTACKS."
AT-TACKS?
What's up with her?
How did she turn out like that?
BY THE WAY.
WHY ARE YOU HERE?
AH!
We forgot because you kept us busy.

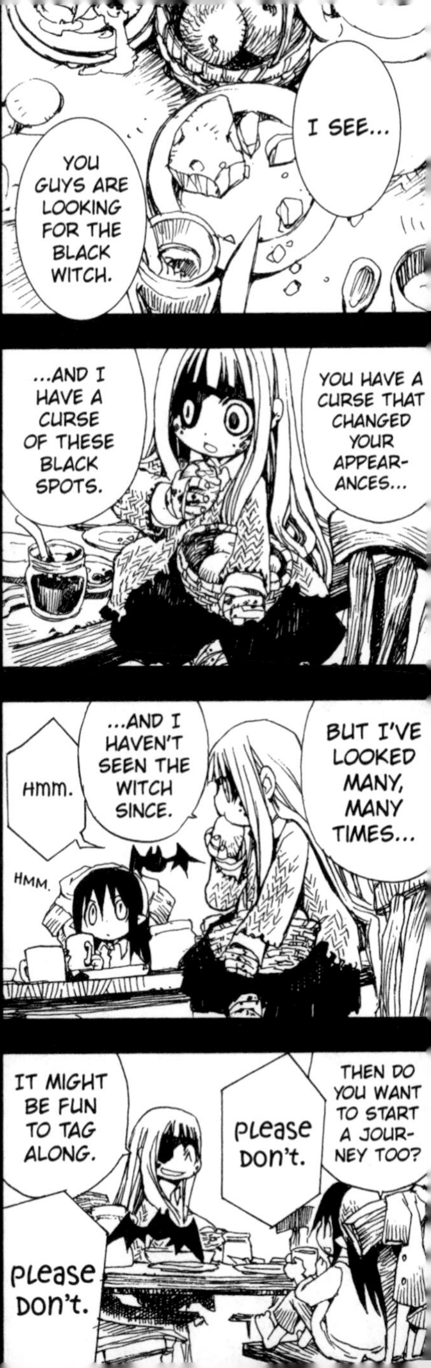
I SEE...
YOU GUYS ARE LOOKING FOR THE BLACK WITCH.
YOU HAVE A CURSE THAT CHANGED YOUR APPEARANCES...
...AND I HAVE A CURSE OF THESE BLACK SPOTS.
BUT I'VE LOOKED MANY, MANY TIMES...
...AND I HAVEN'T SEEN THE WITCH SINCE.
Hmm.
HMM.
THEN DO YOU WANT TO START A JOURNEY TOO?
Please Don't.
IT MIGHT BE FUN TO TAG ALONG.
Please Don't.
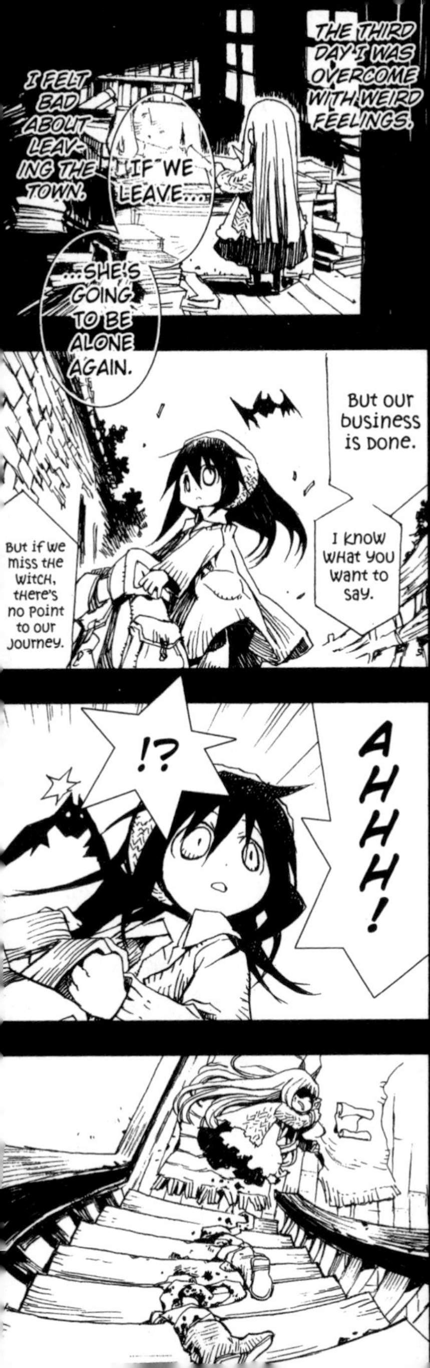
THE THIRD DAY I WAS OVERCOME WITH WEIRD FEELINGS.
I FELT BAD ABOUT LEAVING THE TOWN.
IF WE LEAVE...
...SHE'S GOING TO BE ALONE AGAIN.
But our business is Done.
I know what you want to say.
But if we miss the witch, there's no point to our journey.
AHHHH!
!?

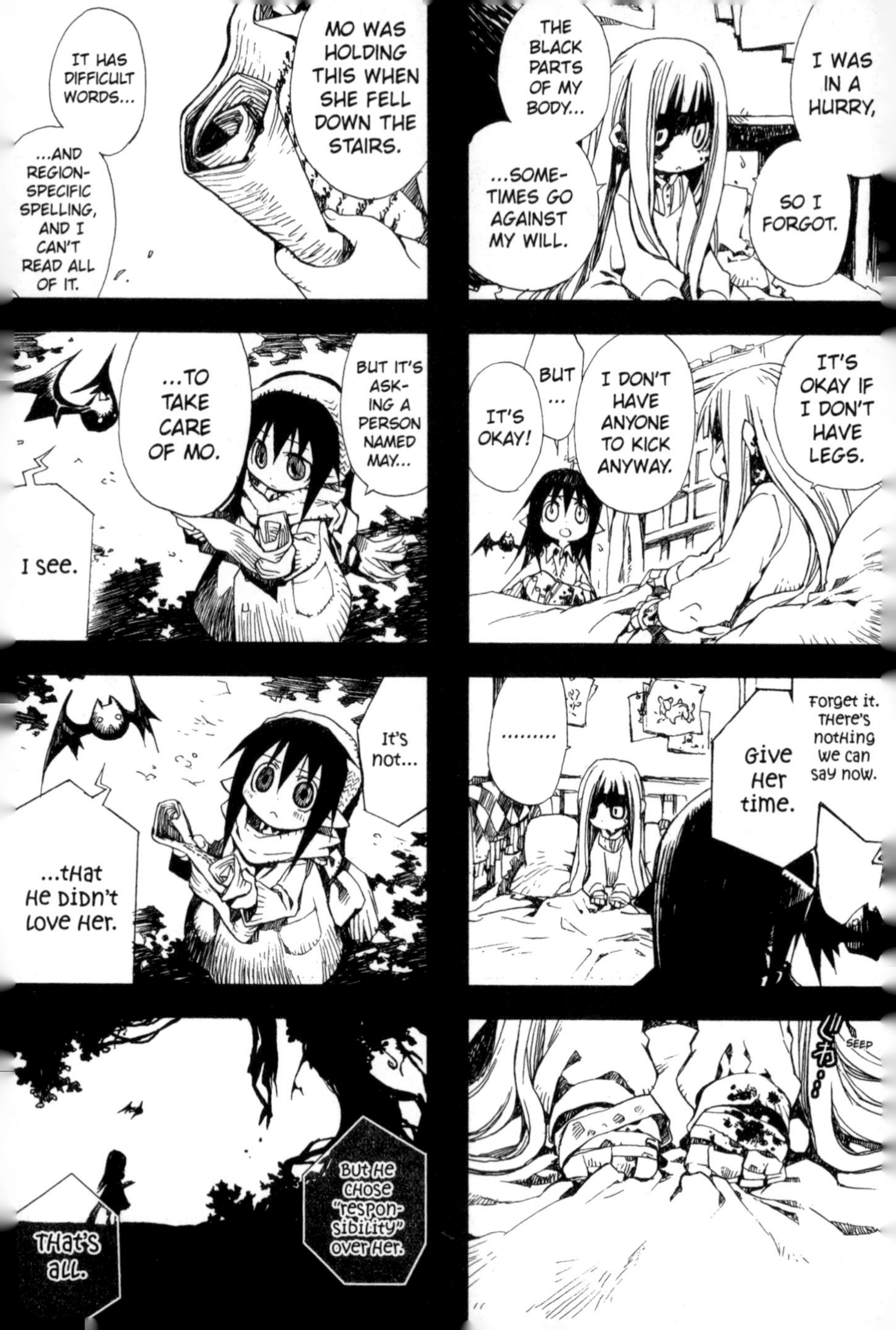
I WAS IN A HURRY,
SO I FORGOT.
THE BLACK PARTS OF MY BODY...
...SOMETIMES GO AGAINST MY WILL.
MO WAS HOLDING THIS WHEN SHE FELL DOWN THE STAIRS.
IT HAS DIFFICULT WORDS...
...AND REGION-SPECIFIC SPELLING, AND I CAN'T READ ALL OF IT.
IT'S OKAY IF I DON'T HAVE LEGS.
I DON'T HAVE ANYONE TO KICK ANYWAY.
BUT ...
IT'S OKAY!
BUT IT'S ASKING A PERSON NAMED MAY...
...TO TAKE CARE OF MO.
I see.
....
Forget it. There's nothing we can say now.
Give Her time.
It's not...
...tHat He DIDn't Love Her.
SEEP
But He chose "responsibility" over Her.
THat's all.

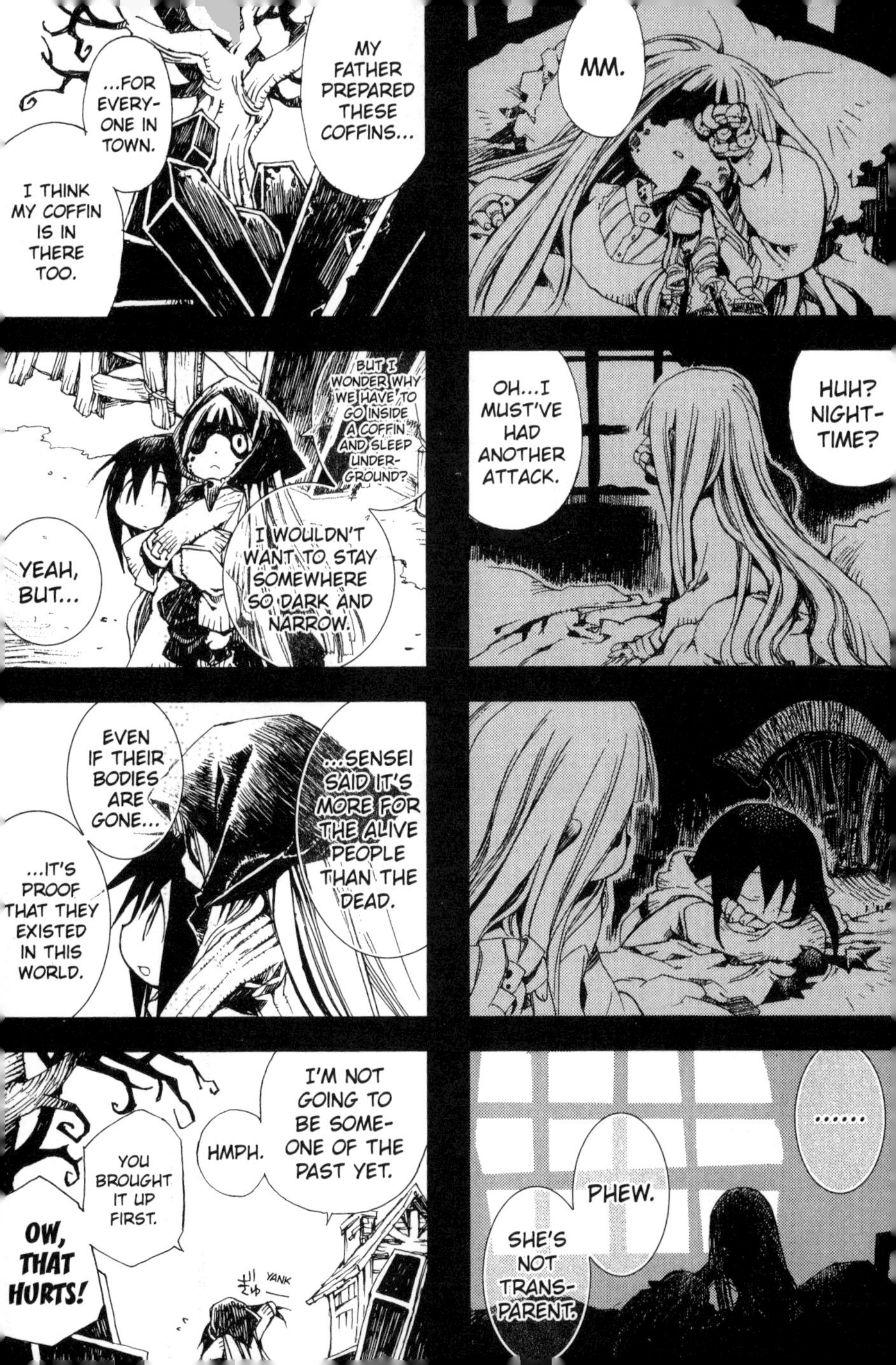
MM.
MY FATHER PREPARED THESE COFFINS...
...FOR EVERY-ONE IN TOWN.
I THINK MY COFFIN IS IN THERE TOO.
HUH? NIGHT-TIME?
OH...I MUST'VE HAD ANOTHER ATTACK.
BUT I WONDER WHY WE HAVE TO GO INSIDE A COFFIN AND SLEEP UNDER-GROUND?
I WOULDN'T WANT TO STAY SOMEWHERE SO DARK AND NARROW.
YEAH, BUT...
...SENSEI SAID IT'S MORE FOR THE ALIVE PEOPLE THAN THE DEAD.
EVEN IF THEIR BODIES ARE GONE...
...IT'S PROOF THAT THEY EXISTED IN THIS WORLD.
......
PHEW.
SHE'S NOT TRANS-PARENT.
I'M NOT GOING TO BE SOME-ONE OF THE PAST YET.
HMPH.
YOU BROUGHT IT UP FIRST.
YANK
OW, THAT HURTS!

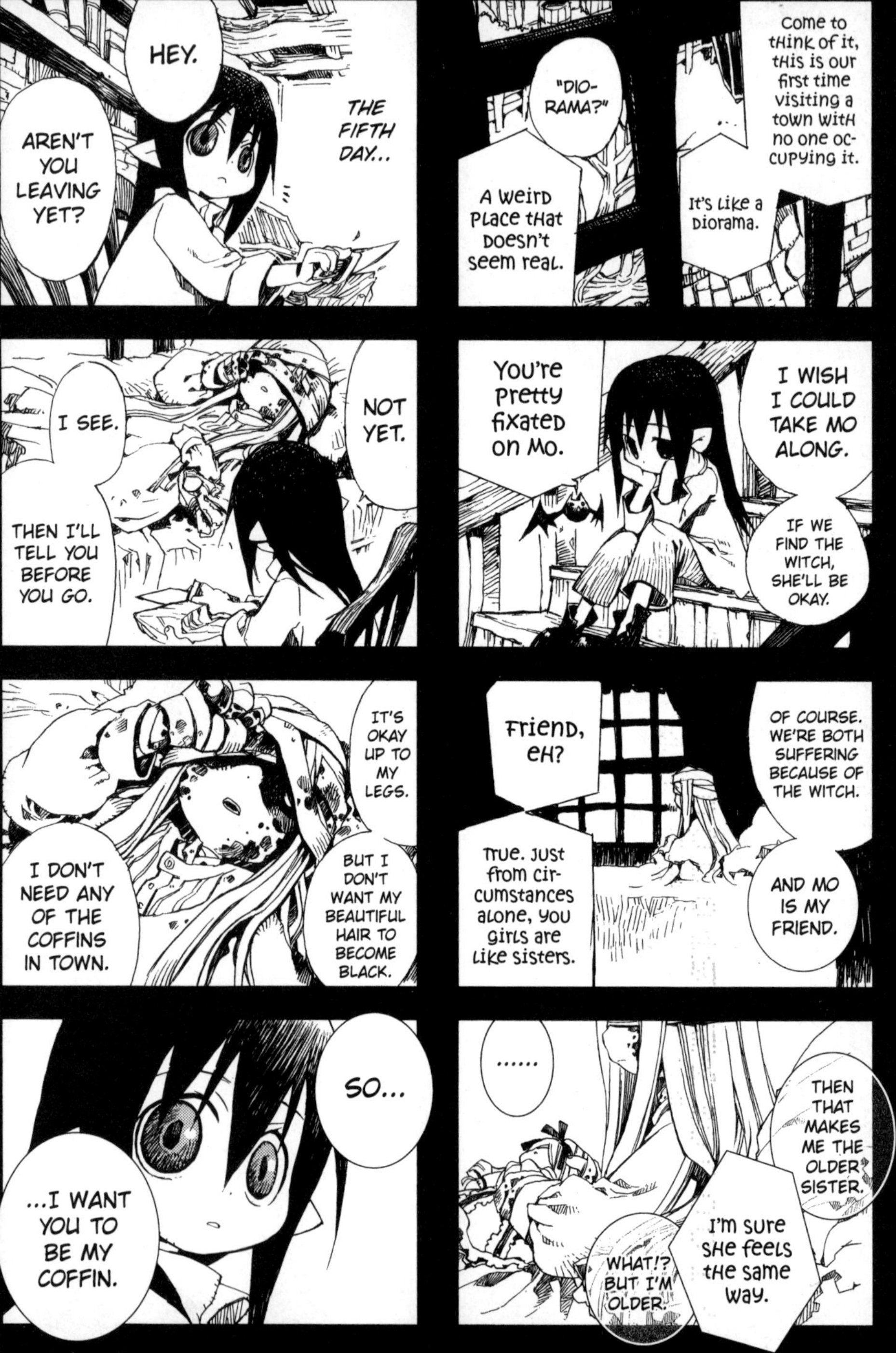
Come to think of it, this is our first time visiting a town with no one oc-cupying it.
It's like a Diorama.
"DIO-RAMA?"
A weird place that Doesn't seem real.
THE FIFTH DAY...
HEY.
AREN'T YOU LEAVING YET?
I WISH I COULD TAKE MO ALONG.
You're pretty fixated on Mo.
IF WE FIND THE WITCH, SHE'LL BE OKAY.
NOT YET.
I SEE.
THEN I'LL TELL YOU BEFORE YOU GO.
OF COURSE. WE'RE BOTH SUFFERING BECAUSE OF THE WITCH.
AND MO IS MY FRIEND.
Friend, eH?
True. Just from cir-cumstances alone, you girls are like sisters.
IT'S OKAY UP TO MY LEGS.
BUT I DON'T WANT MY BEAUTIFUL HAIR TO BECOME BLACK.
I DON'T NEED ANY OF THE COFFINS IN TOWN.
......
THEN THAT MAKES ME THE OLDER SISTER.
I'm sure she feels the same way.
WHAT!? BUT I'M OLDER.
SO...
...I WANT YOU TO BE MY COFFIN.

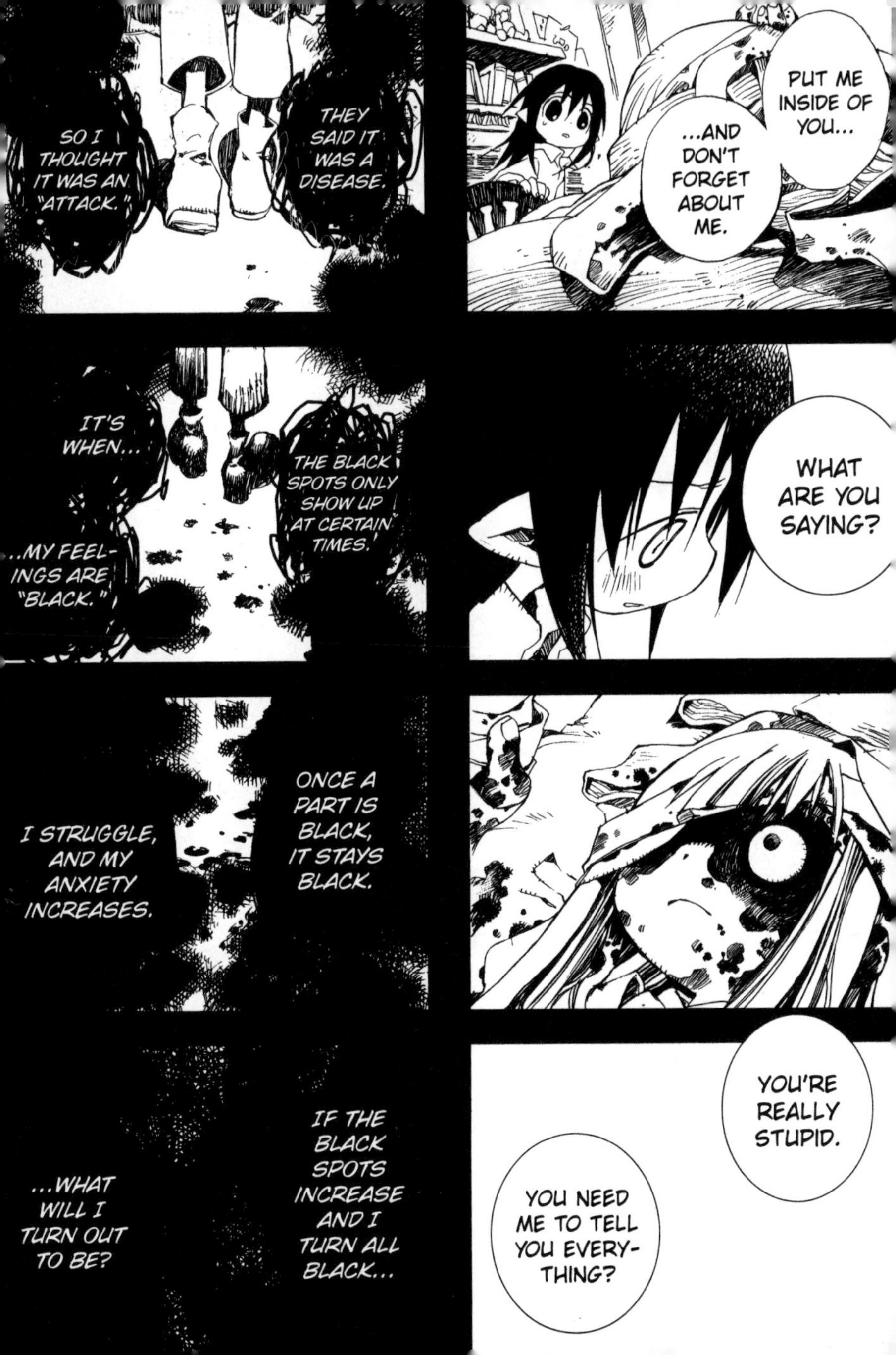
PUT ME INSIDE OF YOU...
...AND DON'T FORGET ABOUT ME.
THEY SAID IT WAS A DISEASE.
SO I THOUGHT IT WAS AN "ATTACK."
WHAT ARE YOU SAYING?
THE BLACK SPOTS ONLY SHOW UP AT CERTAIN TIMES.
IT'S WHEN...
...MY FEEL-INGS ARE "BLACK."
ONCE A PART IS BLACK, IT STAYS BLACK.
I STRUGGLE, AND MY ANXIETY INCREASES.
YOU'RE REALLY STUPID.
YOU NEED ME TO TELL YOU EVERY-THING?
IF THE BLACK SPOTS INCREASE AND I TURN ALL BLACK...
...WHAT WILL I TURN OUT TO BE?

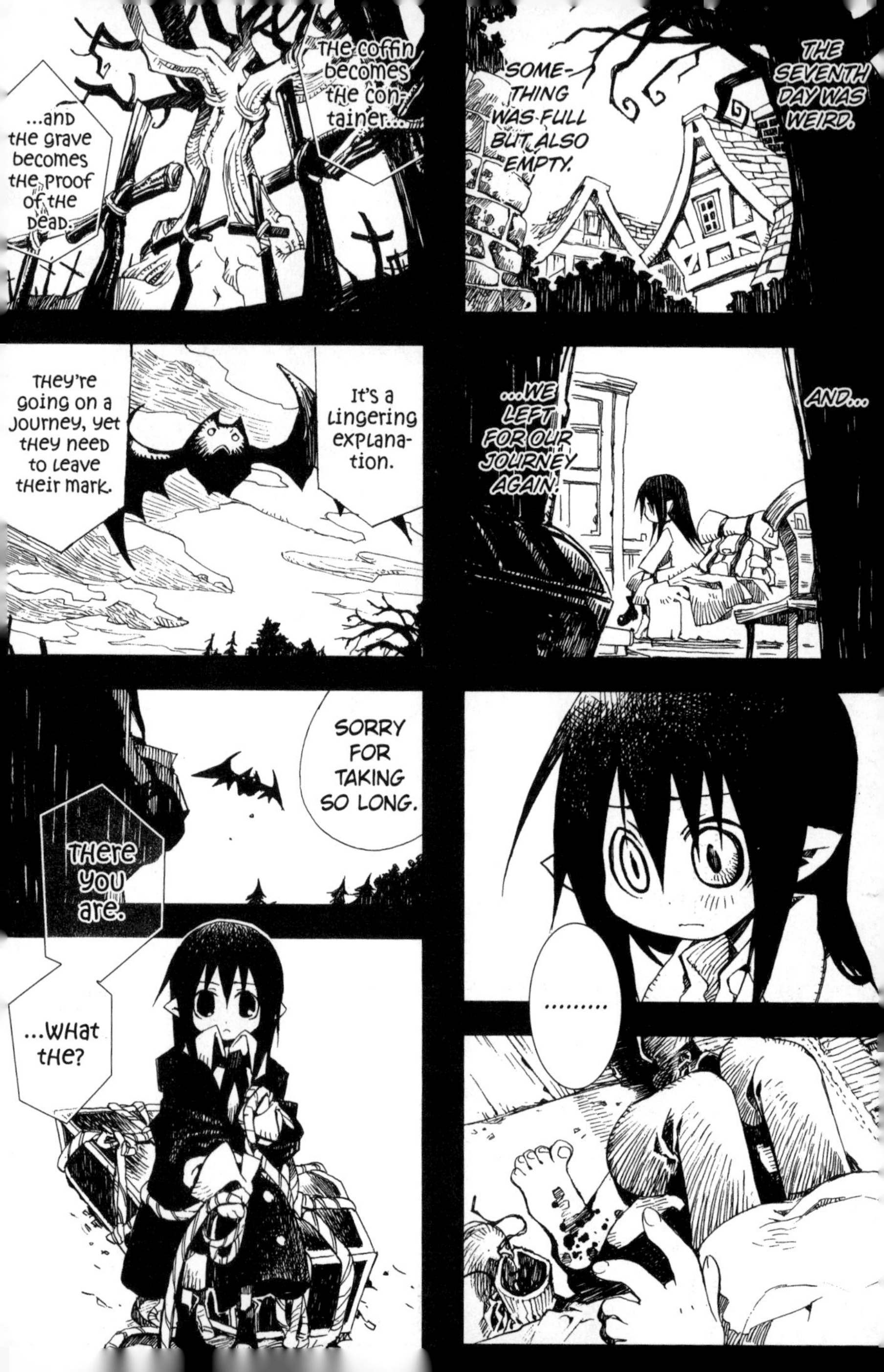
THE SEVENTH DAY WAS WEIRD.
SOME-THING WAS FULL BUT ALSO EMPTY.
THE coffin becomes the con-tainer...
...and the grave becomes the proof of the dead.
AND...
...WE LEFT FOR OUR JOURNEY AGAIN.
It's a lingering explana-tion.
They're going on a journey, yet they need to leave their mark.
....
SORRY FOR TAKING SO LONG.
There you are.
...What the?

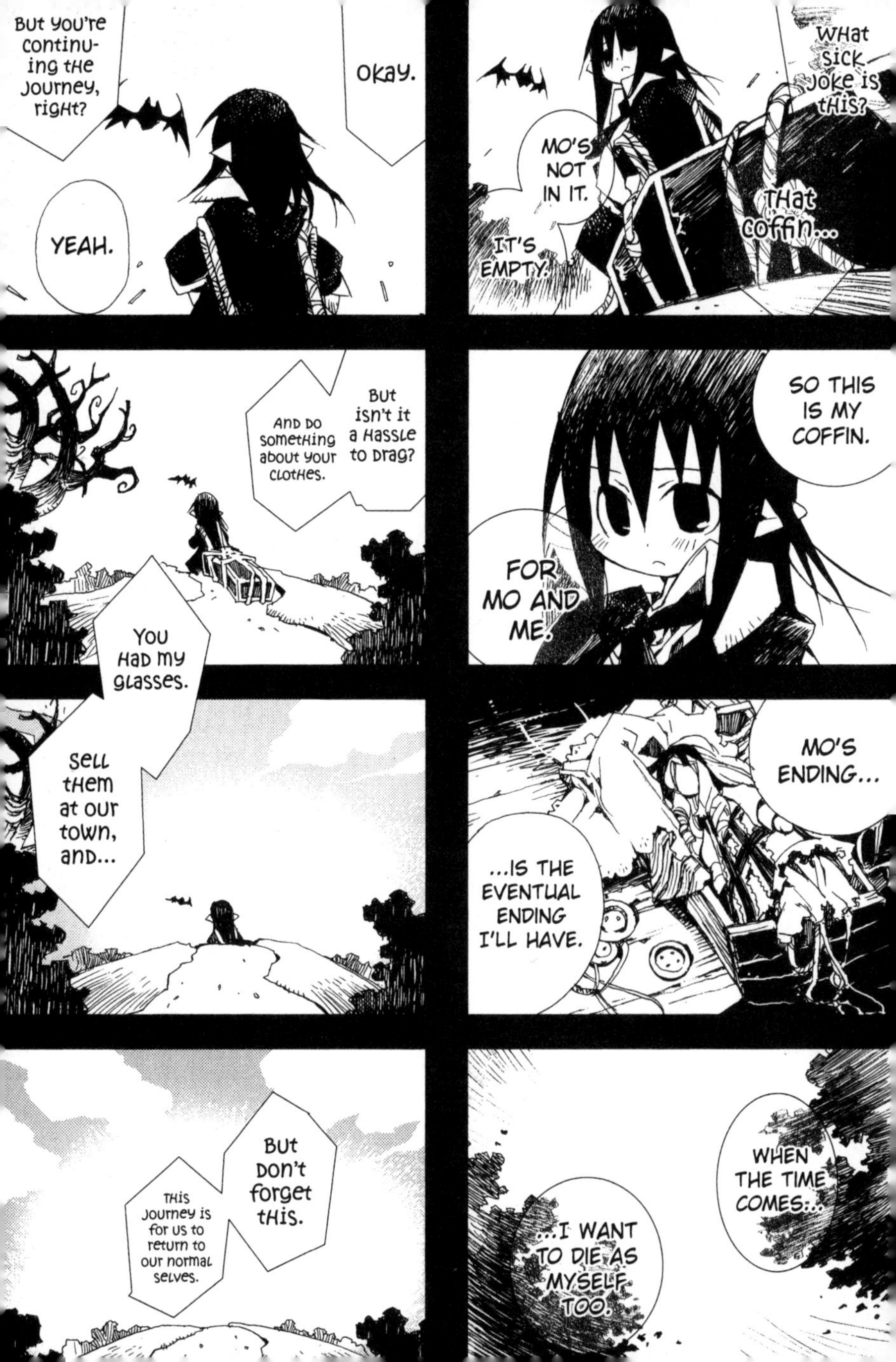
WHAT SICK JOKE IS THIS?
THAT COFFIN...
MO'S NOT IN IT.
IT'S EMPTY.
OKAY.
But you're continuing the journey, right?
YEAH.
SO THIS IS MY COFFIN.
FOR MO AND ME.
But isn't it a hassle to drag?
And do something about your clothes.
You had my glasses.
Sell them at our town, and...
MO'S ENDING...
...IS THE EVENTUAL ENDING I'LL HAVE.
WHEN THE TIME COMES...
...I WANT TO DIE AS MYSELF TOO.
But don't forget this.
This journey is for us to return to our normal selves.

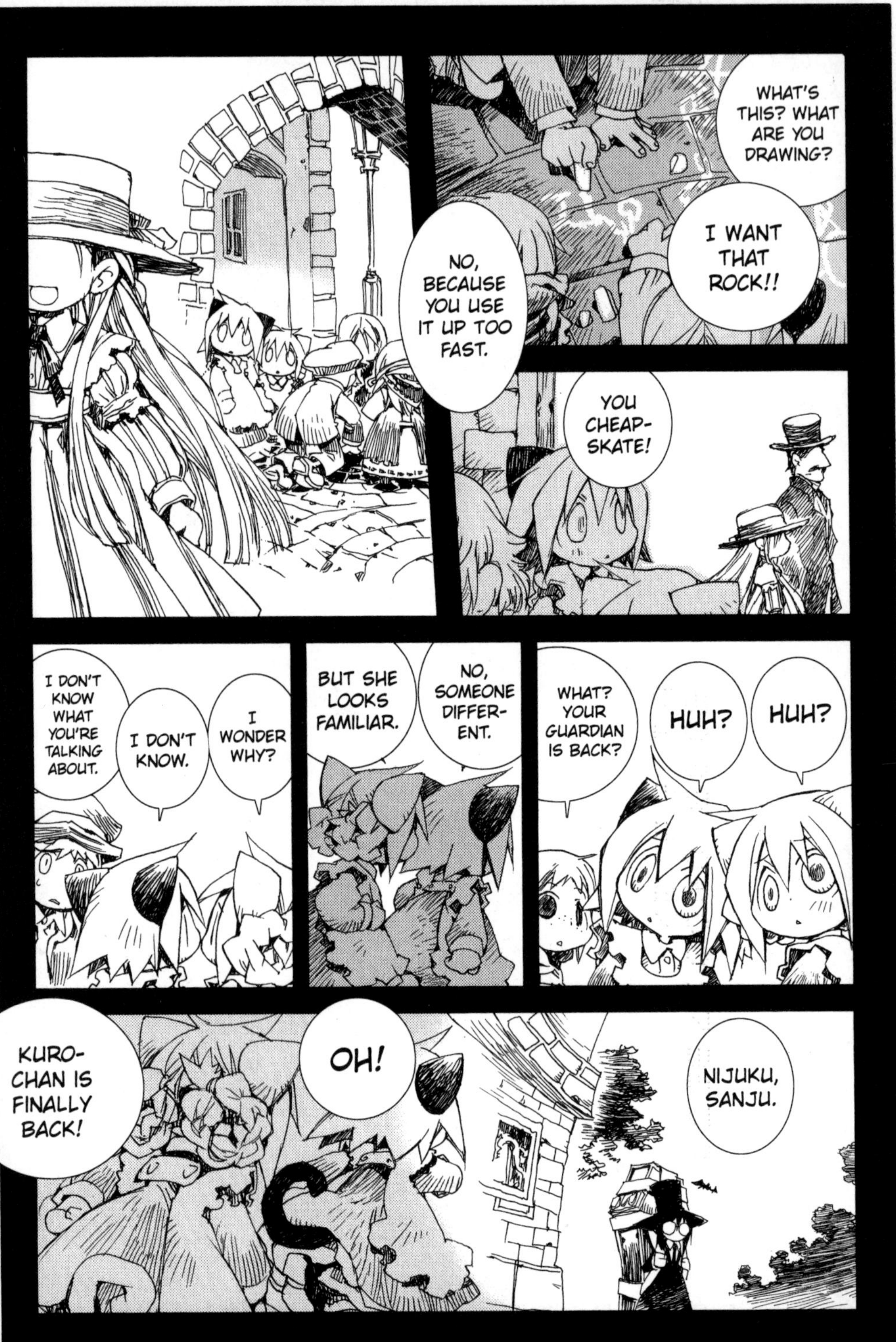
WHAT'S THIS? WHAT ARE YOU DRAWING?
I WANT THAT ROCK!!
NO, BECAUSE YOU USE IT UP TOO FAST.
YOU CHEAP-SKATE!
HUH?
HUH?
WHAT? YOUR GUARDIAN IS BACK?
NO, SOMEONE DIFFER-ENT.
BUT SHE LOOKS FAMILIAR.
I WONDER WHY?
I DON'T KNOW.
I DON'T KNOW WHAT YOU'RE TALKING ABOUT.
NIJUKU, SANJU.
OH!
KURO-CHAN IS FINALLY BACK!

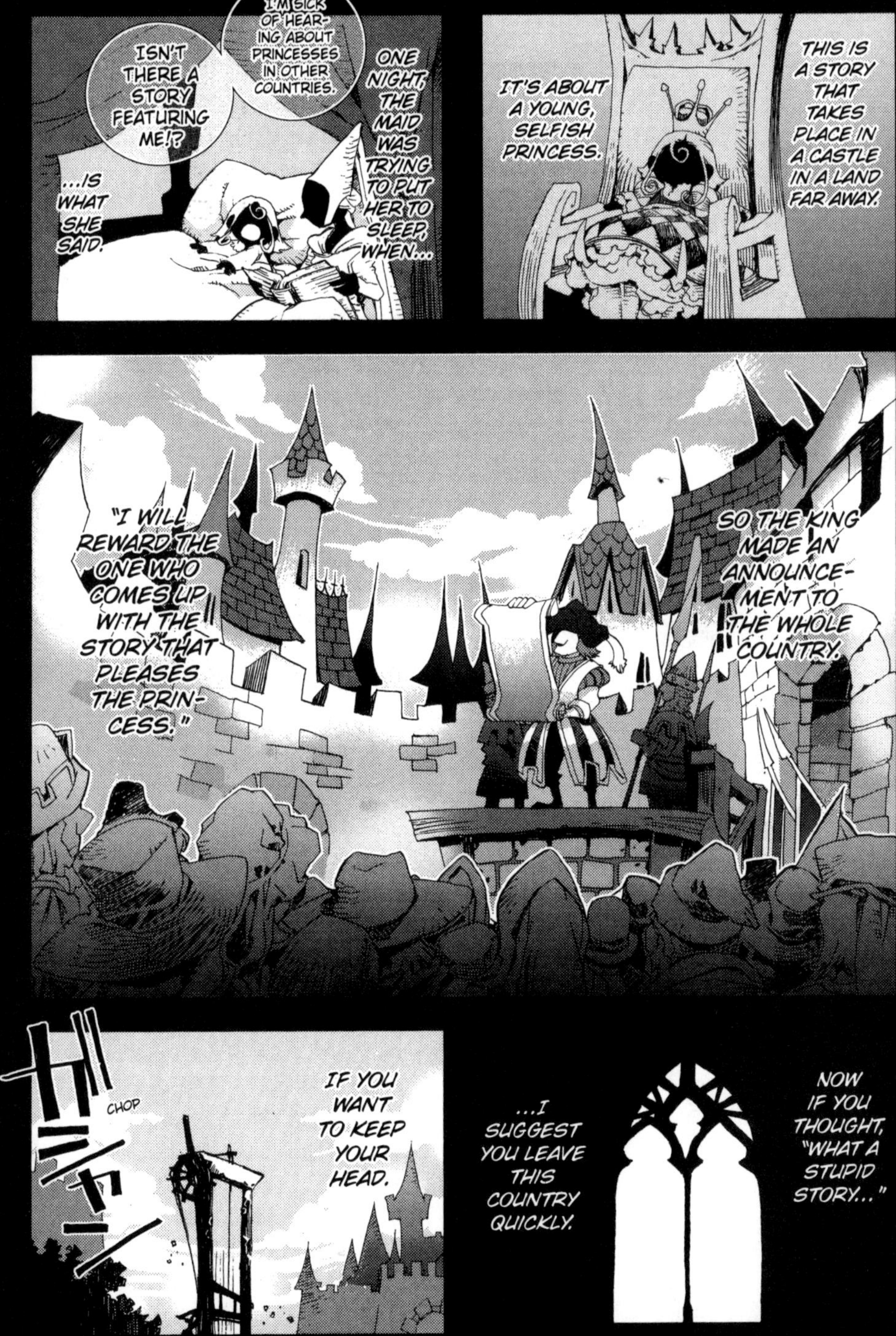
THIS IS A STORY THAT TAKES PLACE IN A CASTLE IN A LAND FAR AWAY.
IT'S ABOUT A YOUNG, SELFISH PRINCESS.
ONE NIGHT, THE MAID WAS TRYING TO PUT HER TO SLEEP, WHEN...
I'M SICK OF HEAR-ING ABOUT PRINCESSES IN OTHER COUNTRIES.
ISN'T THERE A STORY FEATURING ME!?
...IS WHAT SHE SAID.
SO THE KING MADE AN ANNOUNCE-MENT TO THE WHOLE COUNTRY.
"I WILL REWARD THE ONE WHO COMES UP WITH THE STORY THAT PLEASES THE PRIN-CESS."
NOW IF YOU THOUGHT, "WHAT A STUPID STORY..."
...I SUGGEST YOU LEAVE THIS COUNTRY QUICKLY.
IF YOU WANT TO KEEP YOUR HEAD.
CHOP

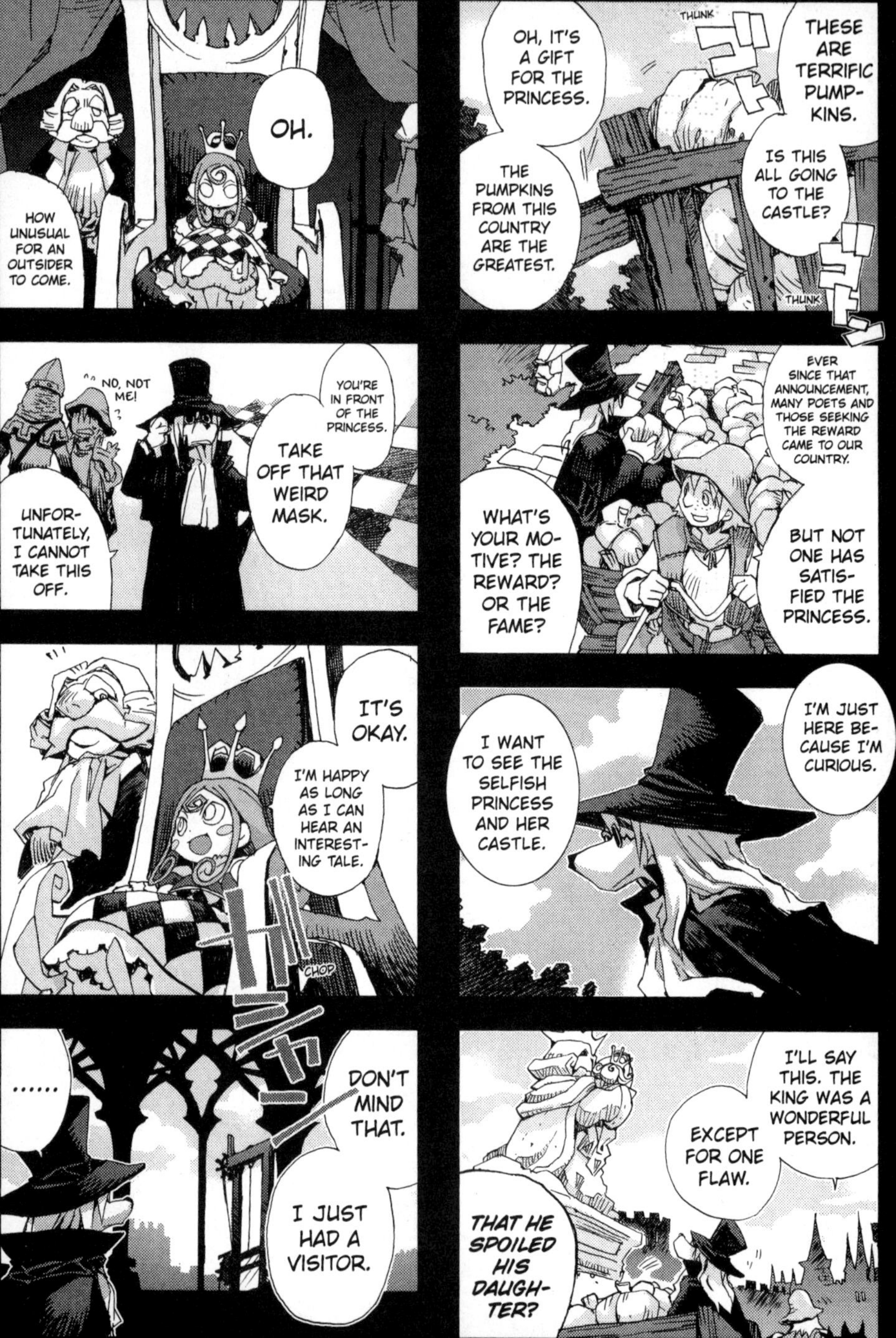
THESE ARE TERRIFIC PUMPKINS.
THUNK
OH, IT'S A GIFT FOR THE PRINCESS.
IS THIS ALL GOING TO THE CASTLE?
THE PUMPKINS FROM THIS COUNTRY ARE THE GREATEST.
THUNK
OH.
HOW UNUSUAL FOR AN OUTSIDER TO COME.
EVER SINCE THAT ANNOUNCEMENT, MANY POETS AND THOSE SEEKING THE REWARD CAME TO OUR COUNTRY.
BUT NOT ONE HAS SATISFIED THE PRINCESS.
WHAT'S YOUR MOTIVE? THE REWARD? OR THE FAME?
YOU'RE IN FRONT OF THE PRINCESS.
TAKE OFF THAT WEIRD MASK.
NO, NOT ME!
UNFORTUNATELY, I CANNOT TAKE THIS OFF.
I'M JUST HERE BECAUSE I'M CURIOUS.
I WANT TO SEE THE SELFISH PRINCESS AND HER CASTLE.
IT'S OKAY.
I'M HAPPY AS LONG AS I CAN HEAR AN INTERESTING TALE.
CHOP
I'LL SAY THIS. THE KING WAS A WONDERFUL PERSON.
EXCEPT FOR ONE FLAW.
THAT HE SPOILED HIS DAUGHTER?
DON'T MIND THAT.
I JUST HAD A VISITOR.
......

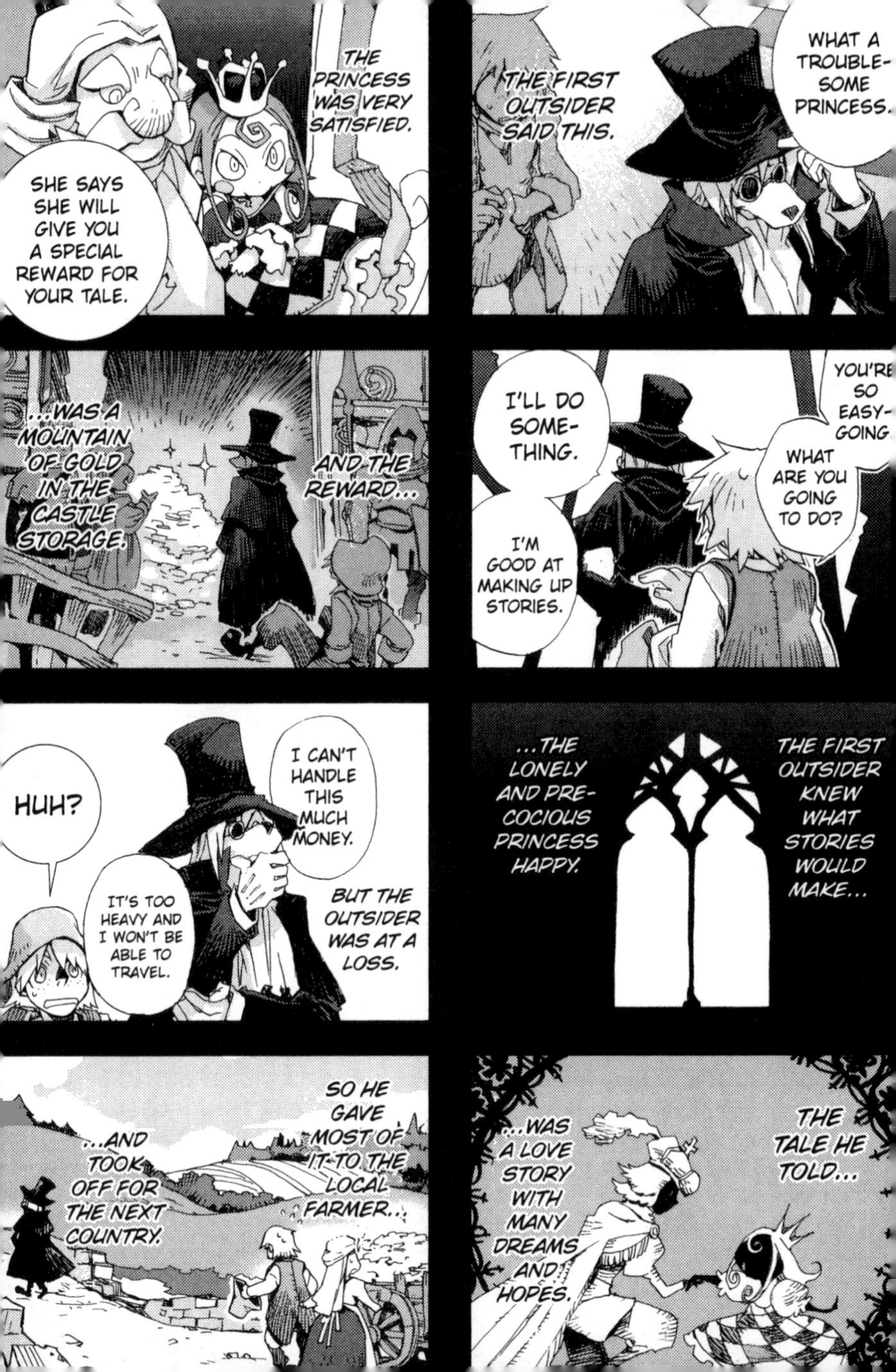
WHAT A TROUBLESOME PRINCESS.
THE FIRST OUTSIDER SAID THIS.
THE PRINCESS WAS VERY SATISFIED.
SHE SAYS SHE WILL GIVE YOU A SPECIAL REWARD FOR YOUR TALE.
YOU'RE SO EASY-GOING
WHAT ARE YOU GOING TO DO?
I'LL DO SOMETHING.
I'M GOOD AT MAKING UP STORIES.
AND THE REWARD...
...WAS A MOUNTAIN OF GOLD IN THE CASTLE STORAGE.
THE FIRST OUTSIDER KNEW WHAT STORIES WOULD MAKE...
...THE LONELY AND PRECOCIOUS PRINCESS HAPPY.
I CAN'T HANDLE THIS MUCH MONEY.
HUH?
IT'S TOO HEAVY AND I WON'T BE ABLE TO TRAVEL.
BUT THE OUTSIDER WAS AT A LOSS.
THE TALE HE TOLD...
...WAS A LOVE STORY WITH MANY DREAMS AND HOPES.
SO HE GAVE MOST OF IT TO THE LOCAL FARMER...
...AND TOOK OFF FOR THE NEXT COUNTRY.

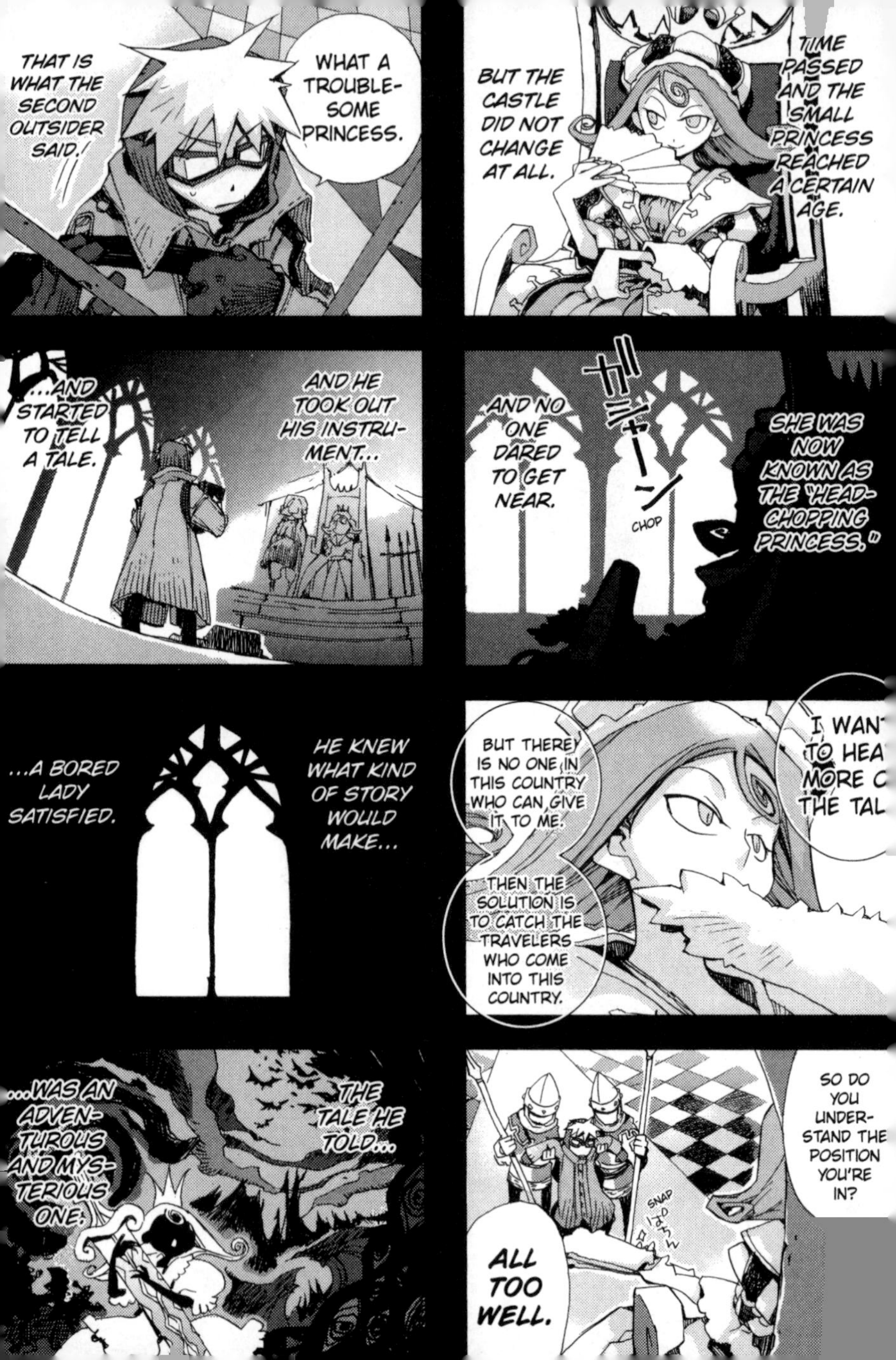
TIME PASSED AND THE SMALL PRINCESS REACHED A CERTAIN AGE.
BUT THE CASTLE DID NOT CHANGE AT ALL.
WHAT A TROUBLE-SOME PRINCESS.
THAT IS WHAT THE SECOND OUTSIDER SAID.
SHE WAS NOW KNOWN AS THE "HEAD-CHOPPING PRINCESS."
ガシャーン
CHOP
AND NO ONE DARED TO GET NEAR.
AND HE TOOK OUT HIS INSTRU-MENT...
...AND STARTED TO TELL A TALE.
I WAN TO HEA MORE O THE TAL
BUT THERE IS NO ONE IN THIS COUNTRY WHO CAN GIVE IT TO ME.
THEN THE SOLUTION IS TO CATCH THE TRAVELERS WHO COME INTO THIS COUNTRY.
HE KNEW WHAT KIND OF STORY WOULD MAKE...
...A BORED LADY SATISFIED.
SO DO YOU UNDER-STAND THE POSITION YOU'RE IN?
SNAP
ALL TOO WELL.
THE TALE HE TOLD...
...WAS AN ADVEN-TUROUS AND MYS-TERIOUS ONE.

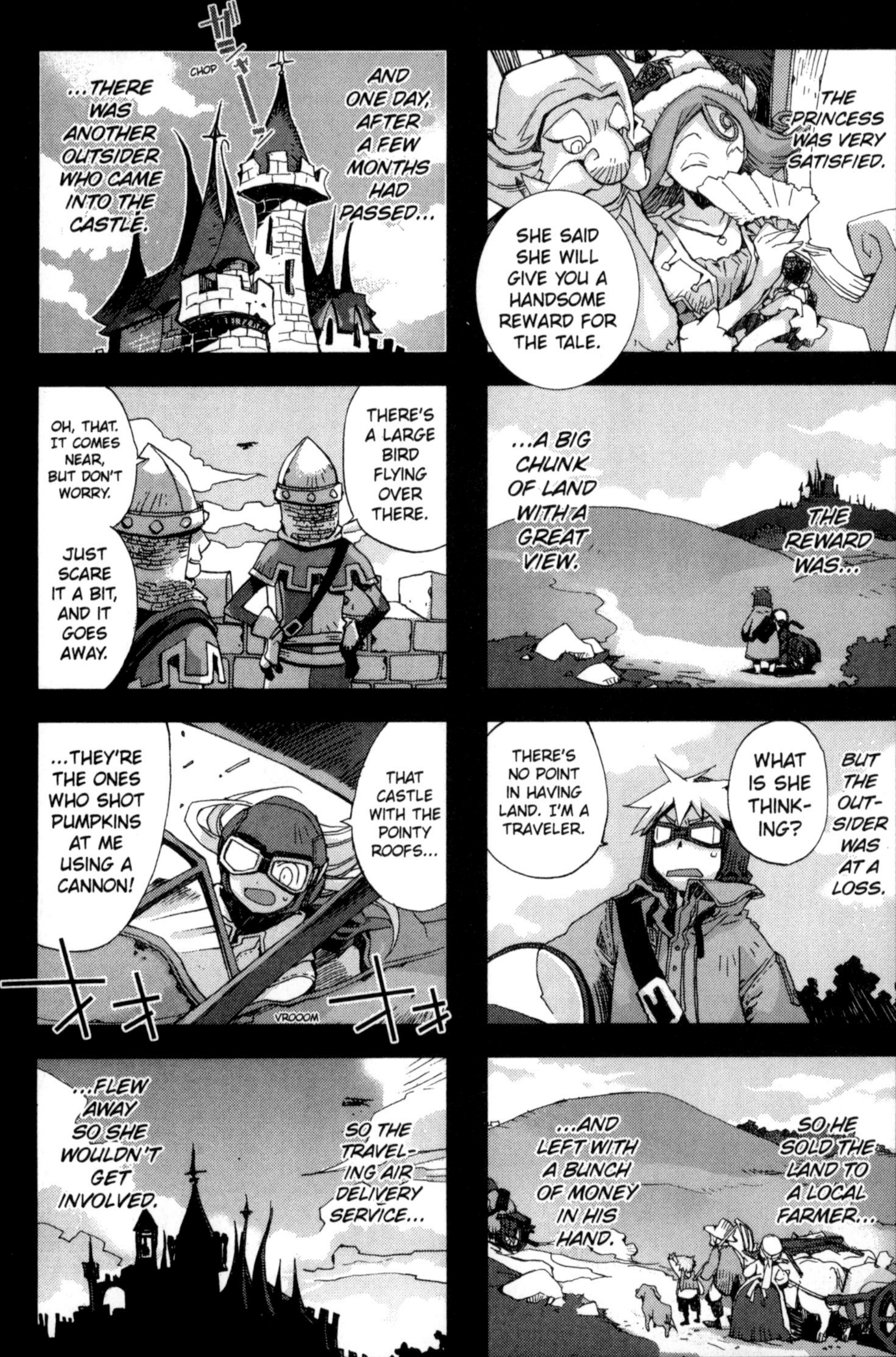
THE PRINCESS WAS VERY SATISFIED.
SHE SAID SHE WILL GIVE YOU A HANDSOME REWARD FOR THE TALE.
THE REWARD WAS...
...A BIG CHUNK OF LAND WITH A GREAT VIEW.
BUT THE OUTSIDER WAS AT A LOSS.
WHAT IS SHE THINKING?
THERE'S NO POINT IN HAVING LAND. I'M A TRAVELER.
SO HE SOLD THE LAND TO A LOCAL FARMER...
...AND LEFT WITH A BUNCH OF MONEY IN HIS HAND.
CHOP
AND ONE DAY, AFTER A FEW MONTHS HAD PASSED...
...THERE WAS ANOTHER OUTSIDER WHO CAME INTO THE CASTLE.
THERE'S A LARGE BIRD FLYING OVER THERE.
OH, THAT. IT COMES NEAR, BUT DON'T WORRY.
JUST SCARE IT A BIT, AND IT GOES AWAY.
THAT CASTLE WITH THE POINTY ROOFS...
...THEY'RE THE ONES WHO SHOT PUMPKINS AT ME USING A CANNON!
VROOOM
SO THE TRAVELING AIR DELIVERY SERVICE...
...FLEW AWAY SO SHE WOULDN'T GET INVOLVED.

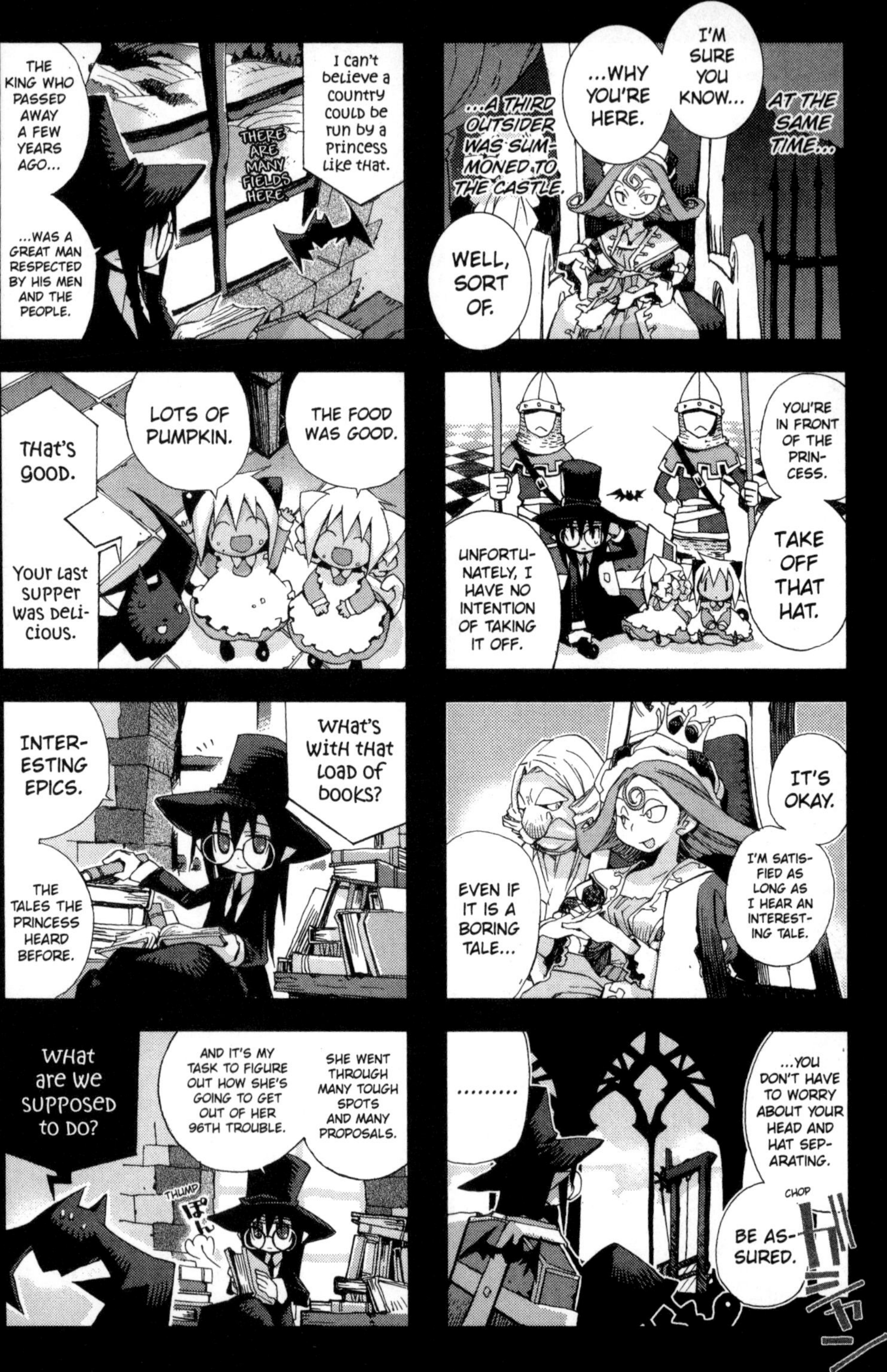
AT THE SAME TIME...
...A THIRD OUTSIDER WAS SUMMONED TO THE CASTLE.
I'M SURE YOU KNOW...
...WHY YOU'RE HERE.
WELL, SORT OF.
YOU'RE IN FRONT OF THE PRINCESS.
TAKE OFF THAT HAT.
UNFORTUNATELY, I HAVE NO INTENTION OF TAKING IT OFF.
IT'S OKAY.
I'M SATISFIED AS LONG AS I HEAR AN INTERESTING TALE.
EVEN IF IT IS A BORING TALE...
...YOU DON'T HAVE TO WORRY ABOUT YOUR HEAD AND HAT SEPARATING.
CHOP
BE ASSURED.
....
I can't believe a country could be run by a princess like that.
THERE ARE MANY FIELDS HERE.
THE KING WHO PASSED AWAY A FEW YEARS AGO...
...WAS A GREAT MAN RESPECTED BY HIS MEN AND THE PEOPLE.
THE FOOD WAS GOOD.
LOTS OF PUMPKIN.
That's good.
Your last supper was delicious.
What's with that load of books?
INTERESTING EPICS.
THE TALES THE PRINCESS HEARD BEFORE.
SHE WENT THROUGH MANY TOUGH SPOTS AND MANY PROPOSALS.
AND IT'S MY TASK TO FIGURE OUT HOW SHE'S GOING TO GET OUT OF HER 96TH TROUBLE.
THUMP
ぽん
What are we supposed to do?

THAT IS WHAT HER PRINCE SAID BEFORE RIDING OFF ON HIS WHITE HORSE.

"WAIT FOR ME. I'LL COME BACK AND GET YOU."

MOST OF THE SCENARIOS HAVE BEEN PROVIDED. THERE'S NOTHING ELSE.

DAMN IT...

I DON'T KNOW WHO IT WAS, BUT HE PUT US IN A TOUGH SPOT.

FLIP

A WITCH WHO ENVIED HER BEAUTY PLOTTED WITH THE DARK KING AND PUT A CURSE ON THE PRINCESS.

WHILE THE PRINCESS WAITED, SHE WENT THROUGH MANY ADVENTURES.

WHAT'S THE STORY?

WHAT KIND OF STORY?

"WATCH OUT!" THE PRINCESS WAS ATTACKED IN THE DARKNESS WHEN...

AND EVEN THE PRINCE SHE FINALLY REUNITED WITH WAS A PAWN OF THE WITCH.

I WANT TO HEAR.

CAN YOU READ TO US?

...AND STARTED TO EAT IT.

...SHE BROKE THE MONSTER'S BODY INTO PIECES...

......

THAT'S TRUE.

THEN HERE'S THE ABRIDGED VERSION.

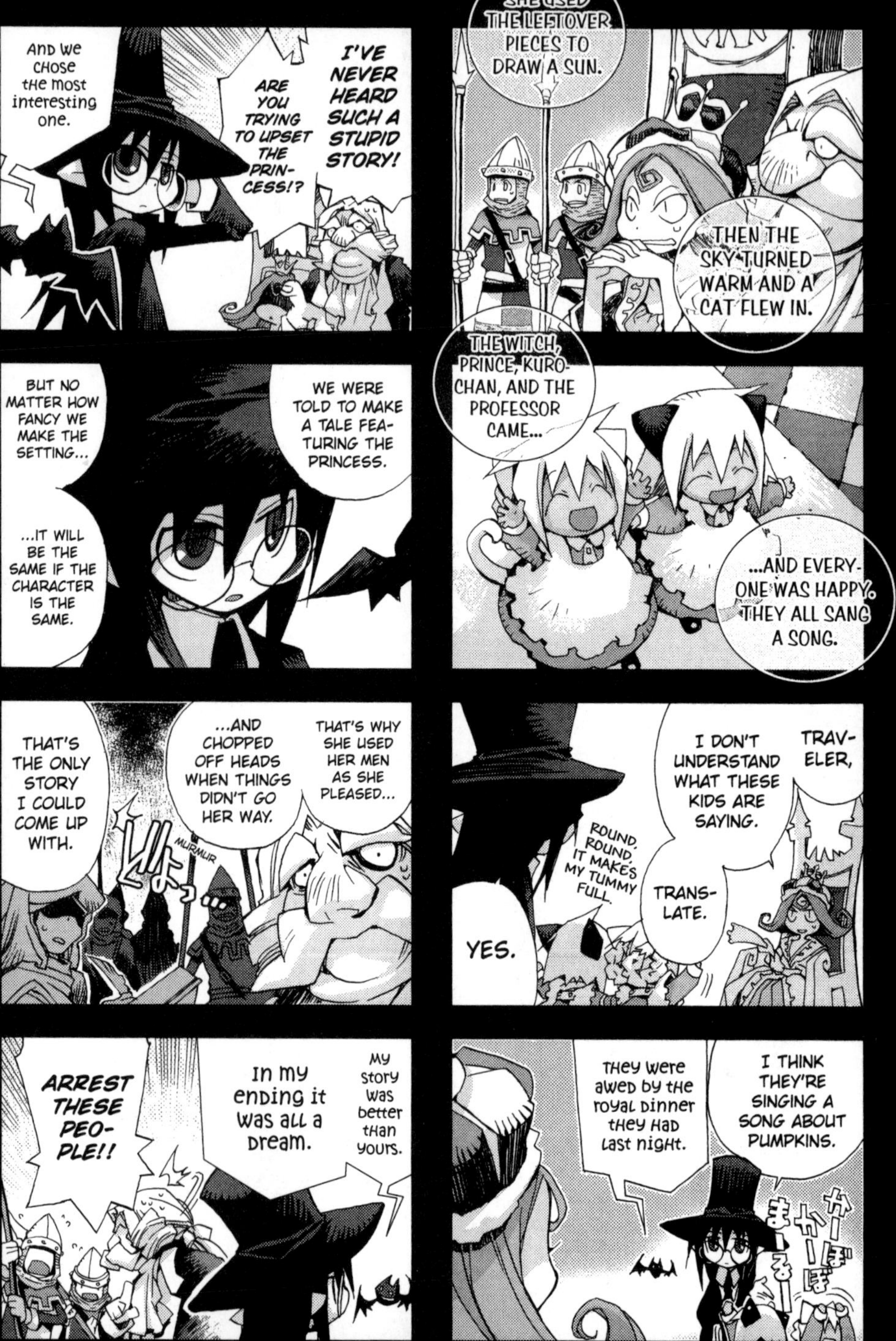
SHE USED THE LEFTOVER PIECES TO DRAW A SUN.
THEN THE SKY TURNED WARM AND A CAT FLEW IN.
I'VE NEVER HEARD SUCH A STUPID STORY!
ARE YOU TRYING TO UPSET THE PRINCESS!?
AND WE CHOSE THE MOST INTERESTING ONE.
THE WITCH, PRINCE, KURO-CHAN, AND THE PROFESSOR CAME...
...AND EVERYONE WAS HAPPY. THEY ALL SANG A SONG.
WE WERE TOLD TO MAKE A TALE FEATURING THE PRINCESS.
BUT NO MATTER HOW FANCY WE MAKE THE SETTING...
...IT WILL BE THE SAME IF THE CHARACTER IS THE SAME.
TRAVELER,
I DON'T UNDERSTAND WHAT THESE KIDS ARE SAYING.
ROUND, ROUND, IT MAKES MY TUMMY FULL.
TRANSLATE.
YES.
THAT'S WHY SHE USED HER MEN AS SHE PLEASED...
...AND CHOPPED OFF HEADS WHEN THINGS DIDN'T GO HER WAY.
MURMUR
THAT'S THE ONLY STORY I COULD COME UP WITH.
I THINK THEY'RE SINGING A SONG ABOUT PUMPKINS.
They were awed by the royal dinner they had last night.
My story was better than yours.
In my ending it was all a dream.
ARREST THESE PEOPLE!!

SFX: PUMPKINS, ROUND PUMPKINS.

...TO MAKE ME REALIZE THAT WITH YOUR STUPID STORY, RIGHT?

TRAV- ELER.

IT WAS YOUR PLAN...

STUPID?

PAT PAT

NO WAY.

...A VOICE WAS HEARD.

STOP.

THAT'S WHEN...

...AND THEY ASKED FOR MORE.

THE TWO REALLY LIKED YOUR TALE...

SO I TOLD THEM...

...WITH THE REST AS THEY PLEASED.

...THAT THEY COULD COME UP...

YOUR REAC- TION IS PROOF...

...THAT YOU GUYS FELT THE SAME WAY.

IT'S OKAY.

PRIN- CESS...

THAT'S TRUE.

THAT'S WHAT I...

...SHOULD HAVE DONE IN THE BEGINNING.

YOU GUESSED WELL, SEN.

GOOD.

I AM NOW AWAKE FROM MY BLIND- NESS.

I THINK THE BAT WAS THE MOST TRUTH- FUL.

I GUESS.

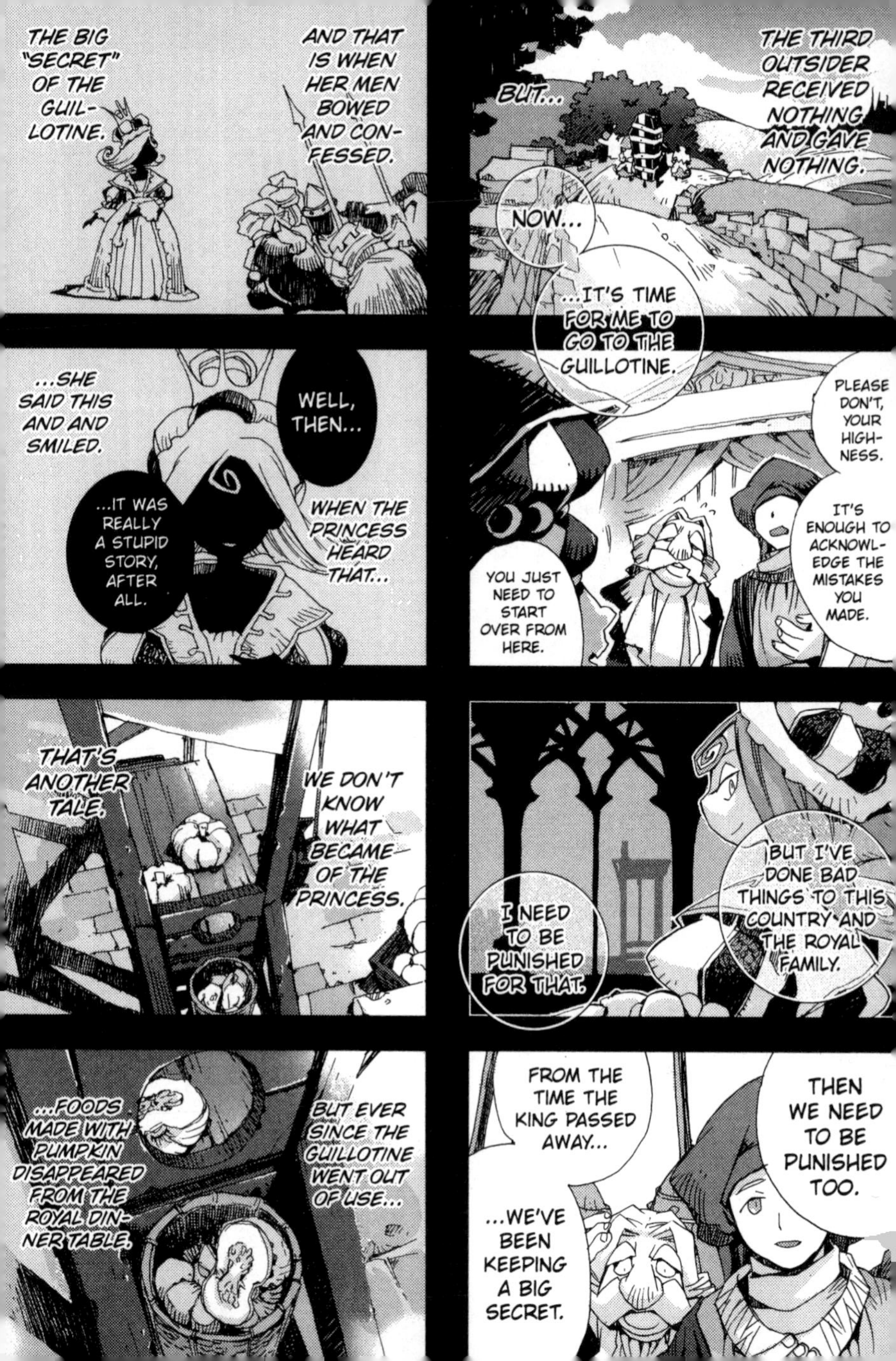
THE THIRD OUTSIDER RECEIVED NOTHING AND GAVE NOTHING.
BUT...
NOW...
...IT'S TIME FOR ME TO GO TO THE GUILLOTINE.
AND THAT IS WHEN HER MEN BOWED AND CONFESSED.
THE BIG "SECRET" OF THE GUILLOTINE.
PLEASE DON'T, YOUR HIGHNESS.
IT'S ENOUGH TO ACKNOWLEDGE THE MISTAKES YOU MADE.
YOU JUST NEED TO START OVER FROM HERE.
WELL, THEN...
...SHE SAID THIS AND AND SMILED.
WHEN THE PRINCESS HEARD THAT...
...IT WAS REALLY A STUPID STORY, AFTER ALL.
BUT I'VE DONE BAD THINGS TO THIS COUNTRY AND THE ROYAL FAMILY.
I NEED TO BE PUNISHED FOR THAT.
WE DON'T KNOW WHAT BECAME OF THE PRINCESS.
THAT'S ANOTHER TALE.
THEN WE NEED TO BE PUNISHED TOO.
FROM THE TIME THE KING PASSED AWAY...
...WE'VE BEEN KEEPING A BIG SECRET.
BUT EVER SINCE THE GUILLOTINE WENT OUT OF USE...
...FOODS MADE WITH PUMPKIN DISAPPEARED FROM THE ROYAL DINNER TABLE.

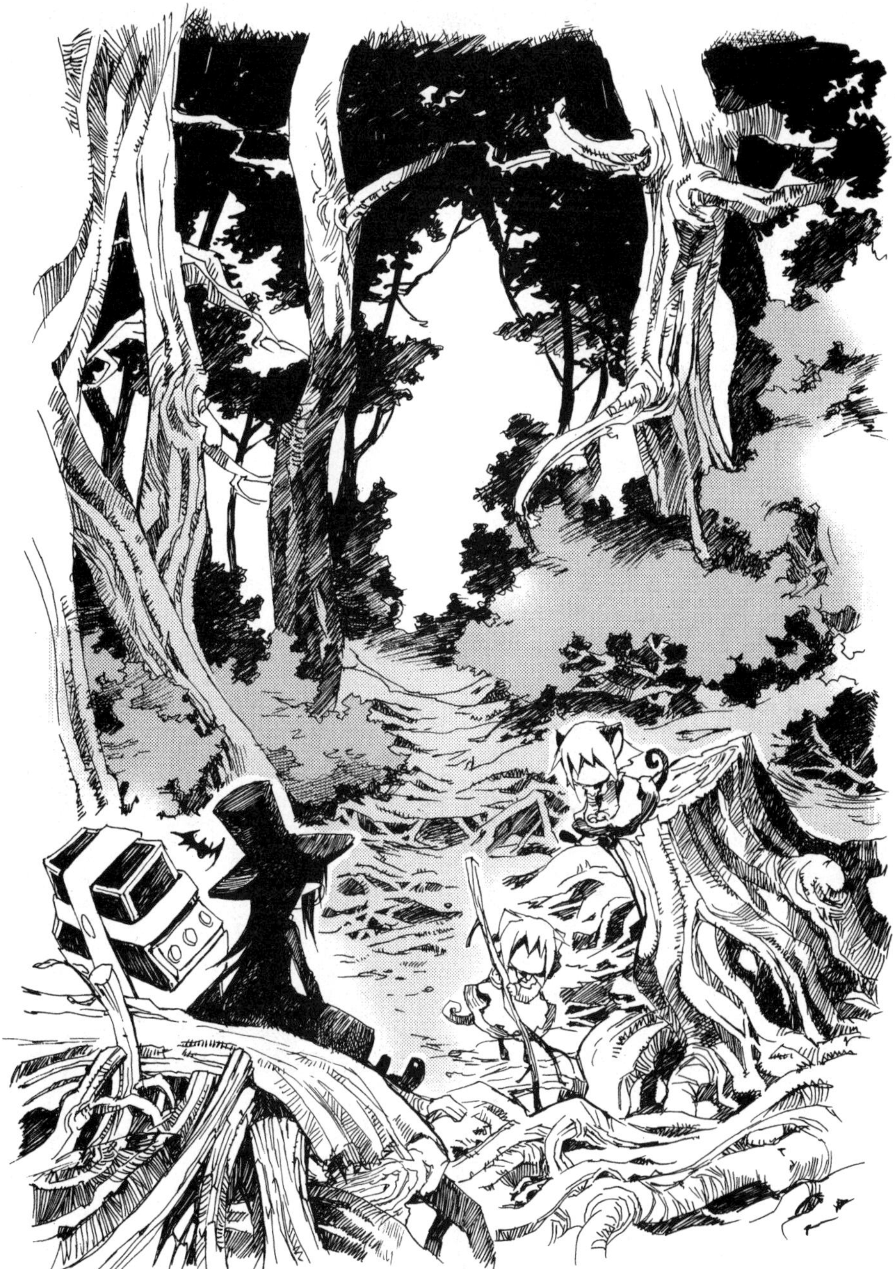

THANK YOU FOR READING *SHOULDER-A-COFFIN KURO* VOLUME 2.
I'LL BE HAPPY IF I CAN SEE YOU IN THE NEXT VOLUME TOO.

SATOKO KIYUDUKI

TRANSLATION NOTES

Page 56
Nijuku and Sanju
Nijuku and *Sanju* are shortened terms for the numbers "twenty-nine" (*nijuuku*) and "thirty" (*sanjuu*) in Japanese. In drawings, the number "3" looks like an ear.

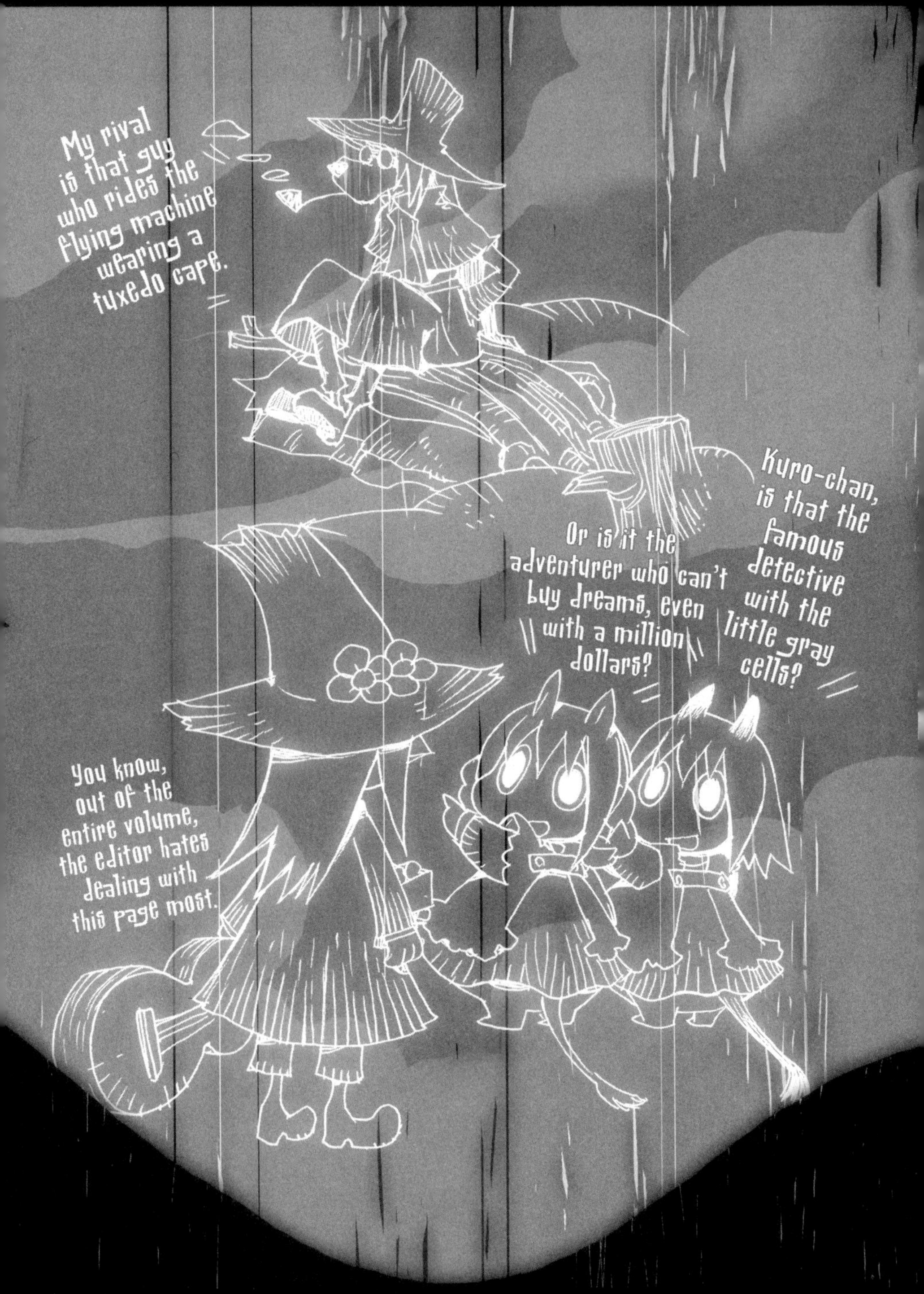

My rival is that guy who rides the flying machine wearing a tuxedo cape.
Kuro-chan, is that the famous detective with the little gray cells?
Or is it the adventurer who can't buy dreams, even with a million dollars?
You know, out of the entire volume, the editor hates dealing with this page most.

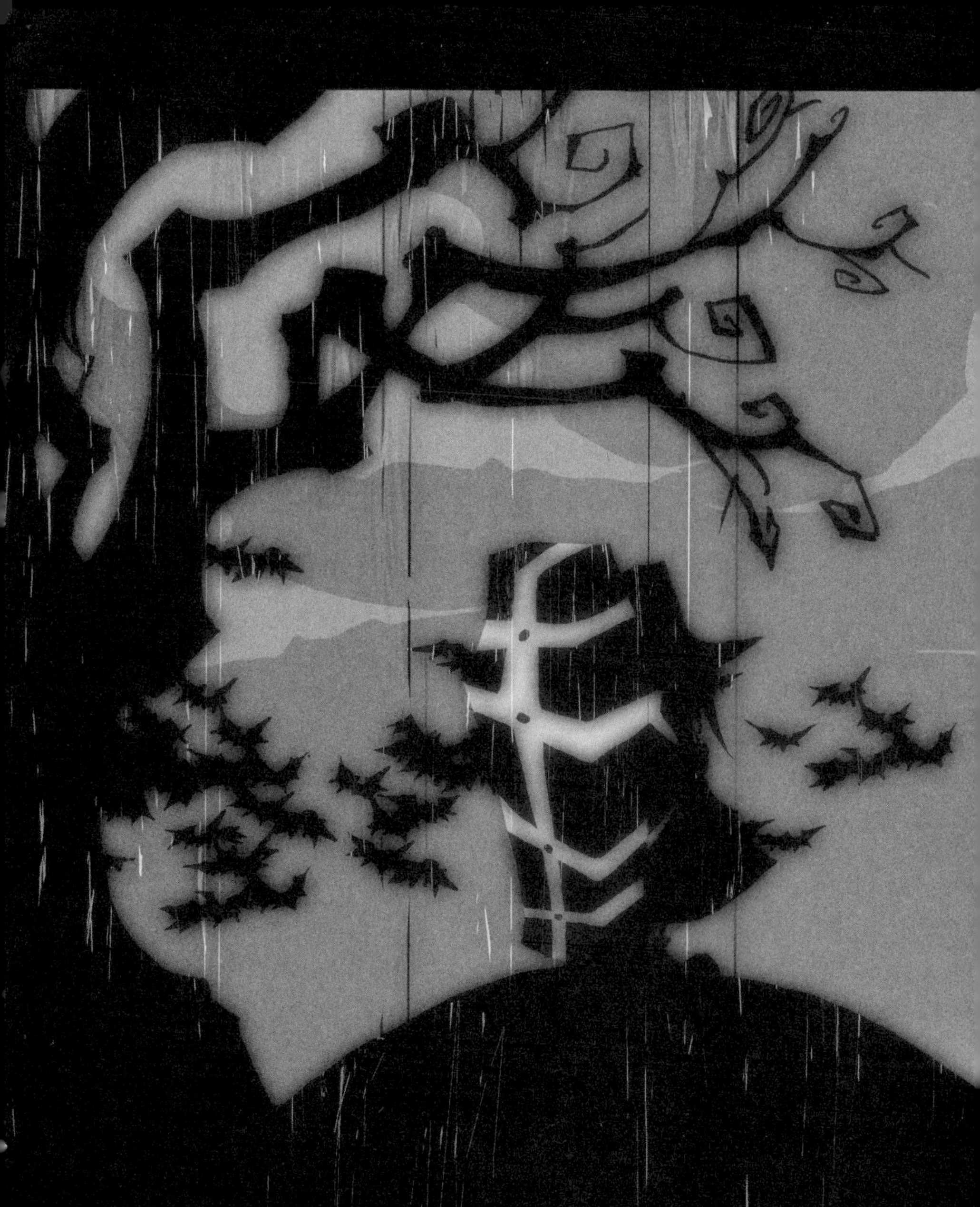

Shoulder-a-Coffin Kuro, Satoko Kiyuduki

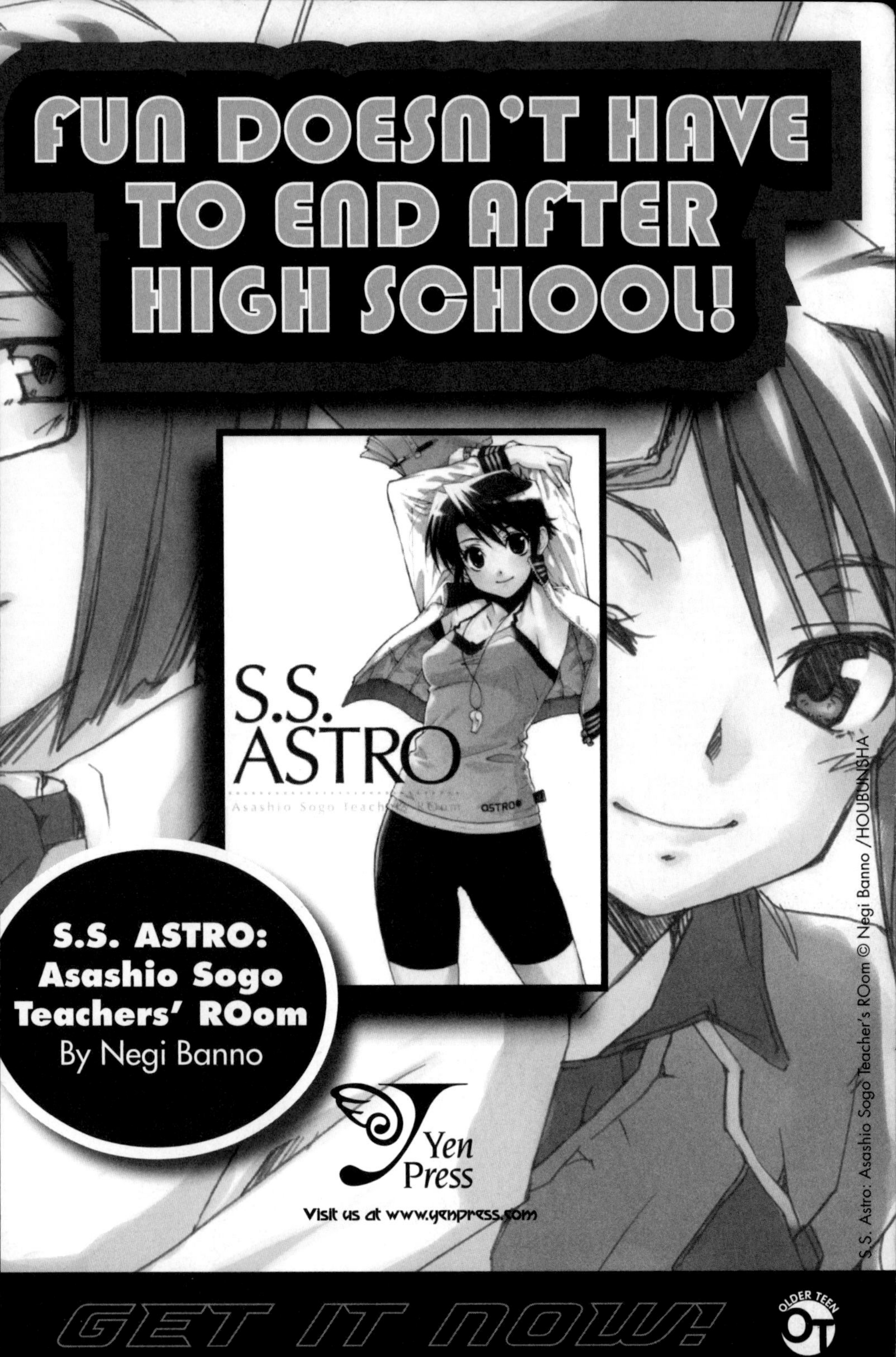
FUN DOESN'T HAVE TO END AFTER HIGH SCHOOL!
S.S. ASTRO
S.S. ASTRO: Asashio Sogo Teachers' ROom
By Negi Banno
Yen Press
Visit us at www.yenpress.com
S.S. Astro: Asashio Sogo Teacher's ROom © Negi Banno /HOUBUNSHA
GET IT NOW!
OLDER TEEN
OT

SHOULDER-A-COFFIN KURO ②

SATOKO KIYUDUKI

Translation: Satsuki Yamashita   Lettering: Alexis Eckerman

HITSUGI KATSUGI NO KURO ~KAICHU TABINOWA~ Vol. 2 © 2007
Satoko Kiyuduki. All rights reserved. First published in Japan in 2007 by
HOUBUNSHA CO., LTD, Tokyo. English translation rights in the United
States, Canada, and the United Kingdom arranged with HOUBUNSHA CO.,
LTD. through Tuttle-Mori Agency, Inc., Tokyo.

English translation © 2008 by Hachette Book Group USA, Inc.

Yen Press
Hachette Book Group USA
237 Park Avenue, New York, NY 10017

Visit our Web sites at www.HachetteBookGroupUSA.com and
www.YenPress.com.

Yen Press is an imprint of Hachette Book Group USA, Inc. The Yen Press
name and logo are trademarks of Hachette Book Group USA, Inc.

First Yen Press Edition: October 2008

ISBN-10: 0-7595-2901-9
ISBN-13: 978-0-7595-2901-4

10 9 8 7 6 5 4 3 2 1

WOR

Printed in the United States of America